Se ode

Laying down some basics

I continue to be in complete awe at how the Internet brings people together. And I don't even like people.

—Office watercooler conversation

A Visual Glossary

1

In this book we use a lot of design and web jargon. Rather than define a term every time we use it *or* assume you know everything already, we've defined items in this chapter that you should already know. Please refer to this chapter when you come across an unfamiliar word.

We've also included at the end of this chapter references to books where you can get detailed information about topics you may want to learn more about.

This chapter does *not* include jargon that we don't expect you to know, such as XML, PHP, ASP, cascading style sheets, and other technical terms that we explain elsewhere. Look in the index for a word or acronym if you don't find it in this chapter.

Things you should know

alias, anti-alias

You'll see this term frequently. If a graphic or text is **aliased,** it typically means it has the "jaggies," or rough edges. These rough edges appear because the text or graphic has a curved or angled edge that has to be displayed using "square" pixels. It's like trying to make a curve with square blocks.

If text or a graphic is **anti-aliased,** that means the edges have been blended in with the color of the background so that *on the screen* our eyes see the edge as smoother instead of jaggy.

Type on a printed page, like what you're reading now, is never anti-aliased (unless it's part of a graphic image). That's because on a high-quality printed page the resolution is about 2540 dots per inch so the edges can be rendered (drawn) smoothly. On a monitor, there are only about 72 to 125 dots to create the smooth edges, and it's not enough to fool your eyes into seeing the edges as smooth.

This text is anti-aliased; you can see how the edges are trying to blend into the background on the screen.

This text graphic is aliased; you can see the jaggies. Alias

Anti-Alias

This type is designed to be aliased and fits directly into the pixels on the screen. This kind of face is incredibly readable at very small sizes on the screen. alias

CMYK

CMYK stands for the four process (transparent) inks that are used in professional printing on a printing press: **c**yan, **m**agenta, **y**ellow, and a **k**ey color, which is usually black. Many color inkjet printers also use CMYK. If you look through a magnifying glass at any printed color piece, you can see the rosette shape formed from the over-lapping dots of the four process colors. CMYK is never used in web design; the color model for monitors is RGB (red, green blue).

These are the four process colors used in print. Almost everything you see in color on paper is made of these four colors (occasionally printers add fifth or sixth colors, such as deep red or metallics). This book is printed with CMYK.

dither

Not all monitors can display every color that a web designer can build. When a monitor comes across a color it can't display, it attempts to simulate that color by combining two or more other colors in the little pixels (dots) of the screen and hopes your eyes will blend the two colors together. So instead of seeing one smooth color, you see speckles, which is **dithering.**

The more colors a monitor can display, the less likely it will have to dither.

You will also see dithering in GIF files if the image attempts to display a blend of colors, such as a sunset or shadow. Depending on how the GIF was made, you may see the dithering no matter how many colors your monitor displays. Also see *flat color* and *GIF.*

On the left is an illustration that uses a lot of graduated shading from one color to the next. On the right is what happens if this graphic appears on a monitor that cannot display all those colors that are used in the transition from one color to the next. That's DitherMan.

dpi

The acronym **dpi** stands for **d**ots **p**er **i**nch, which is really an output term referring to how many dots of toner or silver are used to create, or resolve, printed images on the paper or film. People often use the term dpi when they really mean *ppi,* or *pixels per inch.*

> On a **monitor,** an image resolution is in **ppi.**
>
> When **output,** the resolution is in **dpi.**

You might have a 72 ppi image on your web page; when you print it to your laser printer, those 72 ppi are printed onto the paper at a resolution of 600 dots per inch (which doesn't make it look any better on paper because the image is still created with only 72 pixels per inch of color). Also see *resolution.*

feather-edged

Some images have a hard, smooth edge, and some have a **feather edge,** which is fuzzy. The feather edge is where the outer edges of the image just fade away to transparent. See also *hard-edged.*

flat color

If **color** is **flat,** that means it is one smooth expanse of *one* color with no blends or interruptions.

If you choose a flat color that is not *web-safe,* the color may dither on the screen (see *web-safe color* and *dither).*

This image is composed of two flat colors, black and yellow.

The color inside this image blends from yellow to mustard with lots of subtle variations in-between, which means it is not flat.

FTP

FTP stands for **f**ile **t**ransfer **p**rotocol. You can upload files to another computer in the world or download files from another computer in the world using FTP. With free software, or software included with your email client or web authoring program, you "ftp" your web site to the *server* (host computer) of your choice where your web site will be stored to be "served" to the Internet. If you're reading this book, you've surely used FTP by now. If not, there are step-by-step directions in *The Non-Designer's Web Book* for where to get the software and how to use it.

GIF

GIF stands for **g**raphic **i**nterchange **f**ormat, which is a compressed file format specifically designed for cross-platform use. It has a limited color palette of 256 colors (technically, 8-bit color, indexed), but rarely does a GIF need that many colors. Because you can limit the number of colors, you can get GIFs down to very small file sizes.

GIFs are typically used for graphics that have *flat color,* such as type, logos, or some illustrations. Also see *JPEG.*

If you are not familiar with GIFs, how to create them, how to make them as small as possible, please see *The Non-Designer's Web Book.* They are a critical component of web graphics.

hard-edged

A graphic with a **hard edge** has smooth lines, as opposed to a *feather edge* where the edges gradually blur out to nothing. Unless the edges are perfectly straight, it's easier to get a hard edge in print; hard edges on the web usually need extra work (like *anti-aliasing* or manually cleaning up the messy pixels around the edge) to look good.

This illustration is composed of hard, clean edges.

You can clearly see in this illustration how the colors are flat and smooth, as opposed to the photograph on page 6 or the graduated airbrush colors in DitherMan on page 3.

HTML

If you don't know what HTML is, you definitely need to read *The Non-Designer's Web Book* before you read this book. HTML stands for **h**ypertext **m**arkup **l**anguage and is the "code" that tells a browser what to display in the browser window.

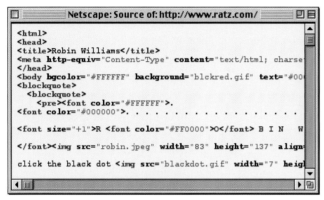

This is what the hypertext markup language (HTML) looks like on the page.

HTML text

When we talk about HTML text, we are referring to any text displayed in a browser window that has been typed directly into the HTML code, as opposed to text that has been placed on the browser page as a graphic. Unless the web page calls on cascading style sheets (see Chapter 19), the HTML text will constantly change its look as visitors change their browser default font settings.

The text in black is written directly into the HTML code. Most of the time this text will change depending on the users' defaults.

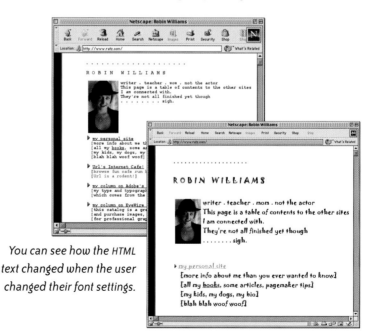

You can see how the HTML text changed when the user changed their font settings.

5

JPEG

JPEG is a compressed graphic file format that can be used across platforms. It stands for **j**oint **p**hotographic **e**xperts **g**roup. If you are unfamiliar with JPEGs, when to use them, and how to make them, you really should read *The Non-Designer's Web Book.*

The JEPG format is typically used for photographs or other images where there are lots of colors that blend into each other, or when there are shades of colors, as in shadows, charcoal drawings, pencil drawings, etc. Compare with the *GIF* definition.

Photographs are typically JPEGs because there are so many colors that blend into one another and the JPEG color palette is much larger than the GIF color palette.

mouseover, rollover

The terms mouseover and rollover are often used interchangeably, although one might argue that technically there is a difference. But it's like the difference between font and typeface—nobody cares. A **mouseover** or **rollover** is when the user's mouse rolls over a button or image or even a blank spot on the screen and something happens— an image appears or changes, the color of a button changes, a list pops up, etc. See Chapter 16 for lots of examples and how to create them.

In this example, as the mouse rolls over a button, the button changes color, an arrow points to the button, and the information in the bottom bubble changes to describe where that link will take you.

nested table

You probably know what tables are (see page 9). A **nested table** is simply a table that is set inside a cell of a larger table. You can put tables inside of tables inside of tables. The technique of slicing up graphics to create more dynamic layouts, as explained in Chapter 12, almost always requires nested tables. You might want to nest a table containing navigation buttons inside the **cell** (*cells* are the individual, rectangular spaces of a table) of a larger table that holds the rest of the design.

one fish		
two fish		
sad fish		
blue fish		
old fish		
new fish		

This table originally had three rows and three columns (nine cells), but we merged the cells in the left-most column into one cell. We made a separate little table for the fish buttons, then placed, or nested, the smaller table inside the largest cell.

ppi

The term **ppi** stands for **p**ixels **p**er **i**nch, and it is one measure of the *resolution* of a graphic image. The more pixels per inch in an image, the more data can be stored in the image. This becomes important when you want to enlarge the graphic, apply filters to it, clean it up, or make any fine-tuning adjustments—the more data you have, the finer tuning you can do.

Graphics for print are typically around 300 pixels per inch, but graphics for

the web are 72 pixels per inch. This is because the *resolution* on paper is completely different from the resolution on a monitor.

The most important thing to remember about ppi is that web graphics should always be 72 ppi; any more ppi is heavy and wasted data. You might start off with an image with more pixels per inch so you can manipulate it cleanly, but you'll always reduce it to 72 ppi before you put it on a web page.

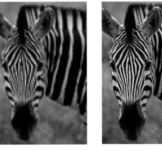

This image is 72 pixels per inch, printed on this page at 2540 dots per inch. On the screen at actual size, it looks exactly the same as the one to the right.

This image is 300 pixels per inch, printed at 2540 dots per inch. It weighs 476K; The image on the left weighs 47K.

raster, rasterize

Raster refers to type or images that are created using dots or pixels, rather than lines defined by mathematical formulas (see *vector*). Any application that uses a paintbrush or an eraser (such as Photoshop, Paint Shop Pro, or any program with the word "paint" in it) creates raster graphics. Whenever you can edit a graphic pixel by pixel, it's a raster image. Both GIF and JPEG files are raster images. Compare with *vector*.

Several years ago browsers could only display raster files, but now we can create and display *vector* files, such as Flash animations (see Chapter 23). When a vector file is turned into a raster image, we say it is **rasterized.** For instance, printers can only print dots, not lines, so when you *print* a vector image, the printer has to *rasterize* the file (turns the lines into dots) before it can print the image. Your monitor cannot really display vector images either—vectors are rasterized to the *screen* for display.

resolution

Resolution refers to how well text or an image is **resolved** through your eyes to your brain. For instance, if you look at a pointillist painting up close, all that your brain comprehends are little, individual dots; if you stand across the room and look at the same painting, the dots are *resolved* into the people and trees and animals that the artist painted. The same thing happens when you **print** a page: millions of tiny dots form the letters and the images. The more dots (dpi) and thus the more finely resolved everything is, the more it fools your brain into thinking the image is smooth.

But resolution on a **monitor** does not depend on how many pixels per inch are in an image. Whether an image appears resolved on the screen depends on the "bit depth" of the monitor—how many colors each pixel is capable of displaying. That is, a 72 ppi image and a 300 ppi image at the same size look exactly the same on the same monitor; in fact, they will look exactly the same on all monitors displaying the same bit depth.

Bit depth translates to the number of colors on your monitor: the greater the bit depth, the more colors and the more highly resolved an image will appear to be.

GIF images use only 8-bit color, which is a maximum of 256 colors, so GIFs usually look just fine on any monitor (except for way old monitors). JPEG files are 24-bit, which means they can display almost 17 million colors. JPEG files will look best on monitors that display millions of colors (24-bit), regardless of how many pixels are on the screen.

If you have a big monitor set to display lots of pixels, you need lots of memory (RAM) to be able to send 24 bits of data to every pixel on the screen.

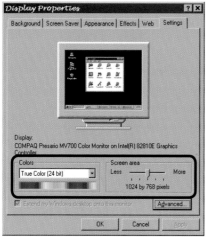

*In the control panels, "Screen area" or "Resolution" refers to how many pixels are displayed on the screen. The more pixels, the **smaller** everything looks; the fewer pixels, the **larger** everything looks.*

*This can make you **think** things are in higher resolution because when pixels are smaller, they appear more highly resolved because there are more of them and they seem "farther away." But this actually won't make photographs "look" better.*

Try this: *Open a photograph on your screen and change the number of "Colors" or the "Color Depth" (bit depth) that your monitor displays; notice how it changes what we think of as the "resolution" of a photograph.*

RGB

The acronym RGB stands for **r**ed, **g**reen, and **b**lue, the colors of the three "guns" in your monitor (or almost any monitor, including television and video) that send varying intensities of red, green, and blue light to every pixel on the screen to make over 16 million possible colors. With all guns off (no light sent to a pixel), a pixel appears black. The full intensity of each color mixed together makes white.

All web graphics use RGB. Every color and everything you see on a monitor is created with RGB; it is not possible to actually see CYMK (printed ink colors) on the screen. A program like Photoshop can mimic what CMYK inks will look like when printed on paper, but on the screen it has to mimic the CMYK with RGB colors.

Mixing colors of light is completely different from mixing paint on a palette; for instance, in the RGB color model, mixing red and green makes yellow.

Just as it's not possible to show CMYK colors on the screen, it's not possible to truly show RGB on the printed page. RGB colors are made of light that goes **straight** *into your eyes, but the color you see here on the printed page is light* **reflected** *off the ink into your eyes.*

server

A **server** is a computer with a full-time connection and special software that connects it to the Internet 24 hours a day and "serves" information, such as web sites, to the Internet. Once you have created your web site, you need to upload the site to a server (using *FTP*) so everyone else in the world can access it.

Actually, you need to establish a relationship with the host server **before** you finish the web site. Several features of a complex site will need particular server information so the programmer can set things up properly. What a server offers can determine what you can offer a client in the way of e-commerce, shopping carts, mailing lists, security, and other advanced features.

Almost any computer can become a server; if you have a full-time connection such as DSL, cable, satellite, or a T1 or T3 line, you can make your own computer a server. In fact, you probably have the software on your computer right now to do what's called "personal web sharing." On a Mac, use the control panel called "Web Sharing." In Windows 2000 or NT (not 98 or ME), use "MS Internet Information Services" from the Start Menu (or load it from the Network control panel, even in 98). If you have a small site you want to serve and you like doing the geeky stuff, try it.

table

A table on a web page is very similar to a table in a word processor or page layout program: it is a rectangular collection of "cells" of various sizes in which you can place text, graphics, and background colors. A table is used to organize your information in a more pleasing arrangement than just in a long, single list on the page.

Without a table, you cannot create columns that actually line up neatly, arrange your elements in anything other than a vertical sequence with maybe a graphic tucked into the side here and there, nor have your links in the horizontal format of a monitor on the left or right instead of across the top or bottom. Very few web pages are created without tables.

One rule about tables: Turn the borders off or go to jail.

Dogs	14	2
Rats	23	6
Tapirs	7	7
Meercats	9	3
Solpugids	83	9

Dogs	14	2
Rats	23	6
Tapirs	7	7
Meercats	9	3
Solpugids	83	9

Borders on.   *Borders off.*

Dogs	14	2
Rats	23	6
Tapirs	7	7
Meercats	9	3
Solpugids	83	9

Dogs	14	2
Rats	23	6
Tapirs	7	7
Meercats	9	3
Solpugids	83	9

Alternatives to turning the borders on.

tile

When you place a background image on a web page, that image is repeated, or **tiled,** across and down the entire web page to fill the space. If you open the web page wider or deeper, the image continues to tile across and down.

If the background image is a small piece, the tiling effect creates a repeat pattern. If the background image is one giant graphic, it may *appear* to be one image as the background, but if you open the page wide enough or deep enough you will see the image repeat, or tile, in the larger space. See Chapter 13 for all the details about background images and ways to take advantage of the tiling effect.

 To the left is a small graphic. Below you can see how that one graphic tiled over and over again to create the background on the page.

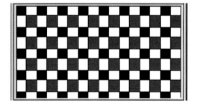

vector

A **vector** graphic is one that is defined by a mathematical formula rather than by pixels on the screen. Illustration programs and draw programs create vector graphics (as opposed to image editing and paint programs, which create *raster* graphics). If the application uses "objects" that you can pick up and drag around on the screen, or if you have points with which you can change the shapes, it is a vector image.

Because vector graphics are defined by math formulas instead of data being stored in every pixel of the image, vector images are smaller and faster-loading than raster images. The images can be resized to any extreme without affecting the quality. They also ignore most resolution issues—they will print at whatever resolution they happen to output on.

You can usually tell vector graphics by their smooth, clean edges. In this example you can see the points with which you can change the shapes, which change the mathematical formula.

web-safe color

Although most computers can display over 16 million colors (even though our eyes can only distinguish a small percentage of these anyway), there are only 216 colors that are common to the different computer platforms. These 216 colors are called **web-safe** or **browser-safe colors.** If you use colors outside of this "palette," you run the risk of your images looking *dithered.*

On the opposite page is a CMYK reproduction of the 216 web-safe RGB colors (remember, CMYK inks can only give a close approximation of the RGB lights that appear on your monitor).

The six-digit sequence under each square is the "hexadecimal" code for that particular color—you can enter that code into any web authoring program or straight into the HTML page.

The three numbers under each square (e.g., 153:0:151) are the RGB values that will create that color. The first number is always the red value; the second number is green; the third number is blue. Enter those numbers in any graphic program to create specific colors.

Hex	RGB	Hex	RGB	Hex	RGB	Hex	RGB	Hex	RGB
990033	153:0:51	FF3366	255:51:102	CC0033	204:0:51	FF0033	255:0:51	FF9999	255:153:153
CC3366	204:51:102	FFCCFF	255:204:255	CC6699	204:151:53	993366	153:51:102	660033	102:0:51
CC3399	204:151:53	FF99CC	255:153:20	FF66CC	255:102:204	FF99FF	255:153:255	FF6699	255:102:153
CC0066	204:0:102	FF0066	255:0:102	FF3399	255:51:153	FF0099	255:0:153	FF33CC	255:51:204
FF00CC	255:0:204	FF66FF	255:102:255	FF33FF	255:51:255	FF00FF	255:0:255	CC0099	204:0:153
990066	153:0:102	CC66CC	204:102:204	CC33CC	204:51:204	CC99FF	204:153:255	CC66FF	204:102:255
CC33FF	204:51:255	993399	153:51:153	CC00CC	204:0:204	CC00FF	204:0:255	9900CC	153:0:204
990099	153:0:153	CC99CC	204:153:204	996699	153:102:153	663366	102:51:102	660099	102:0:153
9933CC	153:51:204	660066	102:0:102	9900FF	153:0:255	9933FF	153:51:255	9966CC	153:102:204
330033	51:0:51	663399	102:51:153	6633CC	102:51:204	6600CC	102:0:204	330066	51:0:102
9966FF	153:102:255	6600FF	102:0:255	6633FF	102:51:255	CCCCFF	204:204:255	9999FF	153:153:255
9999CC	153:153:204	6666CC	102:102:204	6666FF	102:102:255	666699	102:102:153	333366	51:51:102
333399	51:51:153	330099	51:0:153	3300CC	51:0:204	3300FF	51:0:255	3333FF	51:51:255
3333CC	51:51:204	0066FF	0:102:255	0033FF	0:51:255	3366FF	51:102:255	3366CC	51:102:204
000066	0:0:102	000033	0:0:51	0000FF	0:0:255	000099	0:0:153	0033CC	0:51:204
0000CC	0:0:204	336699	51:102:153	0066CC	0:102:204	99CCFF	153:204:255	6699FF	102:153:255
003366	0:51:102	6699CC	102:153:204	006699	0:102:153	3399CC	51:153:204	0099CC	0:153:204
66CCFF	102:204:255	3399FF	51:153:255	003399	0:51:153	0099FF	0:153:255	33CCFF	51:204:255
00CCFF	0:204:255	99FFFF	153:255:255	66FFFF	102:255:255	33FFFF	51:255:255	00FFFF	0:255:255
00CCCC	0:204:204	009999	0:153:153	669999	102:153:153	99CCCC	153:204:204	CCFFFF	204:255:255
33CCCC	51:204:204	66CCCC	102:204:204	339999	51:153:153	336666	51:102:102	006666	0:102:102
003333	0:51:51	00FFCC	0:255:204	3FFCC	51:255:204	33CC99	51:204:153	00CC99	0:204:153
66FFCC	102:255:204	99FFCC	153:255:204	00FF99	0:255:153	339966	51:153:102	006633	0:102:51
669966	102:153:102	66CC66	102:204:102	99FF99	153:255:153	66FF66	102:255:102	99CC99	153:204:153
336633	51:102:51	66FF99	102:255:153	33FF99	51:255:153	33CC66	51:204:102	00CC66	0:204:102
66CC99	102:204:153	009966	0:153:102	339933	51:153:51	009933	0:153:51	33FF66	51:255:102
00FF66	0:255:102	CCFFCC	204:255:204	CCFF99	204:255:153	99FF66	153:255:102	99FF33	153:255:51
00FF33	0:255:51	33FF33	51:255:51	00CC33	0:204:51	33CC33	51:204:51	66FF33	102:255:51
00FF00	0:255:0	66CC33	102:204:51	006600	0:102:0	003300	0:51:0	009900	0:153:0
33FF00	51:255:0	66FF00	102:255:0	99FF00	153:255:0	66CC00	102:204:0	00CC00	0:204:0
33CC00	51:204:0	339900	51:153:0	99CC66	153:204:102	669933	102:153:51	99CC33	153:204:51
336600	51:102:0	669900	102:153:0	99CC00	153:204:0	CCFF66	204:255:102	CCFF33	204:255:51
CCFF00	204:255:0	999900	153:153:0	CCCC00	204:204:0	CCCC33	204:204:51	333300	51:51:0
666600	102:102:0	999933	153:153:51	CCCC66	204:204:102	666633	102:102:51	999966	153:153:102
CCCC99	204:204:153	FFFFCC	255:255:204	FFFF99	255:255:153	FFFF66	255:255:102	FFFF33	255:255:51
FFFF00	255:255:0	FFCC00	255:204:0	FFCC66	255:204:102	FFCC33	255:204:51	CC9933	204:153:51
996600	153:102:0	CC9900	204:153:0	FF9900	255:153:0	CC6600	204:102:0	993300	153:51:0
CC6633	204:102:51	663300	102:51:0	FF9966	255:153:102	FF6633	255:102:51	FF9933	255:153:51
FF6600	255:102:0	CC3300	204:51:0	996633	153:102:51	330000	51:0:0	663333	102:51:51
996666	153:102:102	CC9999	204:153:153	993333	153:51:51	CC6666	204:102:102	FFCCCC	255:204:204
FF3333	255:51:51	CC3333	204:51:51	FF6666	255:102:102	660000	102:0:0	990000	153:0:0
CC0000	204:0:0	FF0000	255:0:0	FF3300	255:51:0	CC9966	204:153:102	FFCC99	255:204:153
CCCCCC	204:204:204	999999	153:153:153	666666	102:102:102	333333	51:51:51	FFFFFF	255:255:255
000000	0:0:0								

This is a chart of the 216 browser-safe colors. Both the hexadecimal code and the RGB values shown are in the order (as always) of red, green, then blue. That is, if the hex code is FFCC33, the value for red is FF, for green is CC, and for blue is 33. If the RGB values are 51:0:255, the value for red is 51, for green is 0, and for blue is 255. Important note: These RGB colors are printed on this page in CMYK! Many of these colors cannot be accurately duplicated in CMYK, so this chart serves only as a general guide.

Resources

Books

Peachpit Press has a wide range of books, training materials, tutorials, and more on all aspects of web design. See **www.peachpit.com.**

Every web designer must read this book: *Don't Make Me Think! A Common Sense Approach to Web Usability,* by **Steve Krug,** published by New Riders.

Elizabeth Castro has a number of well-respected books on HTML, XML, CGI, and Perl. See www.peachpit.com and www.cookwood.com.

Lynda Weinman has a number of great books on web color, graphics, and software packages, as well as several videos on tools such as Dreamweaver and Flash. Check www.lynda.com and www.peachpit.com.

If you are **new to web design,** this book will walk you through the process from beginning (what software to get) to end (how to ftp it to the server): *The Non-Designer's Web Book,* by **Robin Williams** and **John Tollett.**

Online

As you well know by now, web sites about web design abound on the Internet, and their addresses come and go. Here are a few tips:

Go to www.google.com and search for **"web design tutorial"** (put quote marks around the phrase) to find lots of training sites. Search for "web design" to find dozens of focused sites.

Web Page Design for Designers, at www.wpdfd.com, is a site we recommend, and you can buy a number of really wonderful, aliased fonts to use in small sizes in web buttons and navigation.

To find a definition for almost every word in this jargon-heavy world we live in, try **www.whatis.com.** (We don't guarantee you'll *understand* every definition, however.)

The group that makes most of the decisions about what happens on the web technically is the **World Wide Web Consortium.** Keep up with their goings-on at the web site, www.w3c.org.

If you want to see live versions of the examples we created specifically for this book, go to **www.VirtualLastChapter.com.**

Clipart, Stock Images, and Groovy Fonts

How does one acquire content for a web site? In many cases, the client provides most of the content in the form of photographs and text. It's rare, however, that the client gives you everything that's needed.

Our personal experience indicates that web design is much more time-consuming than print design, usually involving technical issues that were either non-existent or easier to anticipate and solve in the print design world. Depending upon the scope of the web project and how sophisticated its functionality, you may need outside help from database experts, multimedia specialists, and various other computer language programmers. Or you may need to use the services of a freelance writer. If your project is that large, there's a good chance you're working with a web development firm that's supplying those resources and more.

But even with a team around you, you may find everyone waiting for *you* to magically supply a large portion of content. After all, you *are* the designer, aren't you? That's when a familiarity with clipart and stock image resources can be invaluable.

Need a parking meter?

At your fingertips

Many web pages are intentionally and appropriately text-heavy, such as research articles, stories, or reports. Sometimes all those pages need in the way of graphics is a headline rendered in a sophisticated type treatment.

But most pages on the web need compelling, informative, or entertaining images to grab and hold a surfer's attention. All this compelling imagery stuff, though, can be very time-consuming if you create it yourself or expensive if you pay someone else to create it.

Fortunately, there are many good sources for great-looking images that are high quality, affordable, and available overnight—or instantly if purchased online and downloaded.

Clip art comes in many different styles, from classical or renaissance to contemporary or futuristic. It's available as photographs, illustrations, cartoons, animated GIFs, digital film clips, and even as animated Flash files.

Clipart and stock images as idea resources

In addition to having all these images available to enhance a page, they're also valuable as idea resources. Browsing through clipart is a good way to generate fresh ideas and to give your imagination a creative jump start. Look at various stock images and ponder how, or if, they relate to your project.

There are two main things you want to look for as you browse through clipart collections and stock photos: 1) An image that fits your project, and 2) an image that may not be appropriate, but gives you a new idea or direction of thinking.

Everyone develops creative habits, and you'll often find yourself in a creative rut, automatically depending upon design solutions that have worked well in past projects. Even if you don't

need clipart for your project, browsing through image resources will help keep the wheels of your imagination turning. After browsing through new images, you'll find yourself experimenting with ideas that hadn't occurred to you before.

The visual reference that inspires an idea may not even be used in the final design, but as long as it initiates a new or different direction in your imagination, it has served an invaluable purpose.

In the example above, the stock image shown to the left provided the inspiration for the design direction and also influenced the color scheme.

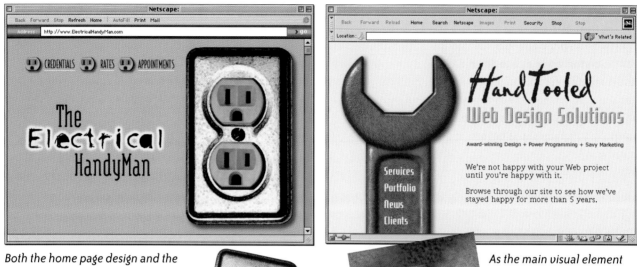

Both the home page design and the navigation of the small site shown above were inspired by a simple stock photo. The visual impact of the image was enhanced by changing the color of the plug receptacles and applying a Photoshop filter (Accented Edges) to the image (from the Filter menu, choose "Brush Strokes," then "Accented Edges…").

As the main visual element in this page design, we used a stock illustration that we edited to our purpose.

This site, which obviously uses a great deal of custom art work, also uses a stock photo for the center illustration. Many of the other product shots were created with a digital camera.

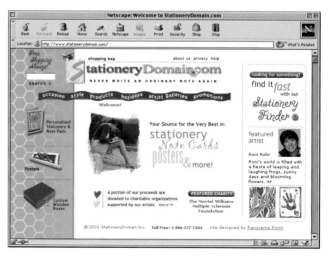

Experiment with free stock images

Several of the popular clipart and stock photo vendors allow you to download low-resolution versions of images **free** for use in comp layouts (a comp layout, or comprehensive layout, is the preliminary one you show the client for approval).

The low-resolution, free image might have a vendor watermark of some kind splashed across it, but with a little retouching it'll still look better than those marker pen layouts we presented to the client in the last millennium.

Use the free images in your comps, and if the client likes one, go back to the site and **buy** the real image, without the watermark or identifying logo tacked on.

You can download free "comping" versions of stock photos and graphics at these sites:

PhotoDisc.com

EyeWire.com (some)

Comstock.com
will send you a CD of thousands of images for comps

Try the stock image lightboxes

If you haven't yet had the sort of client who says, "I don't know what I want, but I'll know it when I see it," you will. The stock image sites are great boons for this challenge.

At most of these sites you can set up your own "lightbox"; you choose images (and at EyeWire.com you can also choose fonts) and put them into your personal lightbox. You tell your client how to get to your lightbox and they can go see the images and fonts you recommend. This is a great resource that can help a client decide what sort of "look" they have in mind for their site. The *client* can also add images to the lightbox to give you ideas for directions to pursue. Some sites let you add notes to the images so your client (or you) can send feedback.

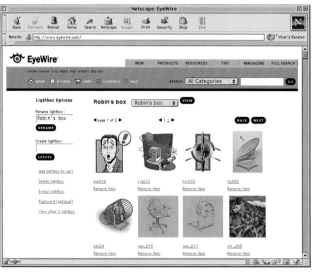

This is a page from EyeWire.com.

This is a page from PhotoDisc.com.

Stock images for buttons

Very nice, but ...

Today's imaging software can make such beautiful buttons automatically that it's very tempting to decorate a site with gorgeous navigation buttons. What usually happens next is you realize that the buttons need to be large to really show off their beauty, not to mention your artistic skill. Before you know it, you've designed a page that looks amateurish, with real pretty buttons.

Don't be seduced by the beauty of a single element on a page. You and I may appreciate the beauty of an embossed, beveled, drop-shadowed button, but most people are looking for relatively simple navigation and information.

Yes, individually your buttons are gorgeous. But on a web site they look horsey and take up more than their fair share of space.

A link doesn't have to look like an actual button. Experiment with un-buttony buttons. Try using clipart or stock photography as links.

While y**our site navigation should complement the page design without competing with the page content,** there's still room for some imagination and creativity.

In these two variations, stock images were used as "buttons," but they also serve as content images.

Above is a sample inside page of this site, picking up the theme of the buttons.

In the design stage of this project, we developed this layout variation in which the descriptive navigation text was hidden until a user moused over a photograph.

This site design uses clipart for navigation icons and also as bright graphics to liven up inside pages that might otherwise be visually dull.

These are pictograph navigation buttons.

We experimented with different versions of the rollover button.

Clipart or picture fonts can lead to fresh new ideas when you lay out web pages or design navigation buttons. In this example for a petroglyph site, we wanted to create a navigation that related to the subject matter, not only visually with pictographs, but also because the symbols do not have words with them. We wanted the first impression to be similar to finding a petroglyph site: curiosity. To be practical, we created the navigation buttons as rollovers so that mousing over the button would reveal text to identify the site section.

Here a font, there a font

You can't have too many

Like most designers, we like to collect fonts, laughing maniacally as our font folder bulges toward the two hundred–megabyte range. Even with this many fonts within mouse reach, we love to experiment with new typefaces. Of the many sources for font shopping, we keep going back to:

> Eyewire (www.EyeWire.com)
> GarageFonts (www.garagefonts.com)
> LetterSpace (www.LetterSpace.com)
> t26 (www.t26.com)
> P22 (www.p22.com)
> FontHaus (www.fonthaus.com)

We're never disappointed with the large selection of fantastic designs from these vendors, ranging from beautiful to innovative to just incredibly cool. A unique typeface can create tremendous visual impact and contribute to a unique personality for your site.

It doesn't take much

These pages show examples from a series of web pages that repeated Robin's newspaper column in the local paper. The text is simple and print-able—the only graphics are the type headlines, with an occasional piece of clipart. A graphic headline makes for a quickly built web page, a fast download, carefree printing, nice clean pages, yet with that special touch that only a spot of graphic type can give.

Artists of Santa Fe on the Web

ARTISTS
of Santa Fe
on the Web

[Check the end of this column for an artists/writers discussion group, a newsletter for visual artists, a new cybergallery, and where to place calendar listings.]

Varying reports call Santa Fe the second largest art center in the United States. Thus it should be no surprise that the Internet is awash with beautiful Santa Fe art web sites.

The online Collector's Guide provides a collector's tour of Santa Fe

High Tech in New Mexico

High-Tech
in New Mexico

Robin Williams

New Mexico is rapidly becoming quite a source of high technology.

Los Alamos National Labs has a rich and beautifully designed site. There you can read the history of LANL, their profile, vision, and mission, take a laboratory tour, and read a first-person account of the A-bomb in Hiroshima from a Japanese survivor. In the Science/Technology section, you can read about the awards bestowed upon people and projects, LANL's work with academia and industry, and opportunities for students and postdoctoral appointments. You can read the Daily Newsbulletin, an online publication for lab employees, which is posted online by 6 a.m.

Native American Sites in Santa Fe

Local Sites of
Native American
information

Robin Williams

There are thousands of web sites all over the world dedicated to many different facets of native peoples. These are some of the nicest local sites.

Where There Is No Name for Art. The Art and Voices of Tewa Children. "The art represented in this web site is not 'Indian art'; rather, it is produced by children whose Pueblo identity is a part of their total life experience." Here you will find artwork and text featured in the book *Where There Is No Name for Art*, authored by

Choosing a Web Designer in Santa Fe

choosing a
Web Designer
in santa fe

Robin Williams

There is a site on the web called "The Web Price Index." Several times a year they ask a variety of web design firms in the big cities what it would cost to have a specific web site built. To have a small web site (20 pages) created in New York City costs $85,000. The same web site in San Francisco would cost $96,000; in Chicago, $19,000. In Santa Fe, the best web designers in town, those who can compete in a world-class market, estimated about $4,000 for the same small site.

A large web site with all the bells and whistles ran from a quarter

Holiday Gifts from New Mexico

Holiday
Gifts
from New Mexico

Robin Williams

Sales revenues on the web in 1997 were $560 million. By the end of 1999 they will ring up at $2 billion. By the year 2002 sales of online goods are expected to be $9 billion a year. It's a happening thing, and it's happening in New Mexico. We have a lot to offer, not only our own citizens, but people around the world. Below are some of the many holiday gifts available online, right here in Santa Fe.

Santa Fe Guests and Locals

SANTA FE
things to do in and around

Robin Williams

This week I spent a lot of time looking at the New Mexico tourist sites on the web. I'm not a tourist here, but I love to travel through our state and I love to poke around our town. The information provided to visitors gives me lots of ideas about what I can do here and what my guests can do. And every concierge in town should know what is available to their hotel and motel customers through the World Wide Web.

Gay New Mexico Online

GAY NEW MEXICO

Robin Williams

There is a nice collection of local web sites that focus on the gay community here in New Mexico.

Gay New Mexico has a great slogan on the site: The Land of Enchantment has a Lavender Edge. This is probably the most important and rich site to begin exploring. Here you will find a professional directory that lists businesses in New Mexico that have gay or lesbian owners, or are gay-friendly. The Events sections lists radio shows, discussion groups, and get-togethers all over the state. Local Hot Spots/Community includes a synopsis of the community spirit in various locales around the state, housing, the job market, and schools. There are addresses for local mailing lists (e-mail discussion groups), including one dedicated to personals.

Land and Architecture

Land & Architecture

Robin Williams

Frijoles Villages is a development that we've all been watching for the past three years as it's gone through the approval processes. For those interested in more details, their new web site is up and includes the master plan, the amenities that will be developed into the village, information about the residential area, a master map, and a location map. A recent angle on the village is the high-tech connectivity that will run throughout the area--Frijoles Village will be totally wired with fiber optics, providing every resident and business in the area with the potential for high-speed Internet connections and teleconferencing.

Small Towns of New Mexico

Small Towns
of New Mexico

Robin Williams

Poking around in the small towns of New Mexico can give you a clue as to just how far the Internet and the World Wide Web are reaching. One might expect such towns as Albuquerque, Santa Fe, Taos, Las Cruces, and Roswell to have an abundance of Internet activity, but you might be surprised to see the activity from Magdalena, Aztec, and Madrid.

The web site at Truth or Consequences (pop. 6221) has links to just about every town in Sierra County. Find out why Chloride (pop. 20) is named Chloride instead of Bromide or Pyetown, and plan to visit the Hanging Tree in the center of Main Street when you visit. But don't plan on going to church, because there's never been one in

New Mexico State Government Sites

new mexico
State Government Sites

Robin Williams

I was so pleased to discover that our State of New Mexico is way ahead of many other states in its web presence.

The New Mexico Legislature has a site that has had more than 27,000 visitors and over 34,000 searches for bills and resolutions since January 21, 1977, the first day of the session! This comprehensive site is updated every night while the Legislature is in session, and as needed in the interim. There is a searchable bill

High Tech in the Marcy Building

high-tech in the
MARCY BUILDING

Robin Williams

The historic Marcy Building on Marcy Street is becoming a little mecca of high technology. Not only does just about every business with office space also have a web site, but the building itself is a highly connected place. Every business mentioned in today's column is at the Marcy Building.

DirectNet Corporation has its New Mexico office in this space and sells T1 access (a very high speed connection) in its T3 line to other businesses in the building. DirectNet provides software, online tutoring, connectivity, and support to schools K-12, and supports the One-2-One Learning Foundation. They are also in the process of setting up wireless 10-megabit networks all over the state to provide wireless Internet and Ethernet services to schools

Tips and Tricks in your Browser

Tips and tricks
in your browser

Robin Williams

This week I'm going to take a break from reporting on what Santa Feans are doing on the Internet, and instead provide a few tips and tricks on using Netscape to browse the World Wide Web.

Enter an address:

Unless you are using a very old browser, you never need to type the http:// part of the address.

To go to a page with an address like www.site.com, all you need to type is site and hit Return or Enter, where "site," of course, stands for the name in that spot. For instance, if you want to go to

Picture fonts

But when you're looking at typefaces, don't forget those picture fonts that give you anywhere from dozens to several hundred images that can be used as clipart.

A picture font is a fabulous way to create innovative buttons with lots of variety, or to use as spot illustrations to create a theme throughout a site, as background images, or to liven up a text-heavy page.

The best thing is you don't have to spend more than the price of a typeface, usually from around $20 to $50, yet you get a whole package of pictures in a similar style. You can't beat it.

Here we took advantage of a picture font of cowboy images to make the navigation buttons, as well as to add interest throughout the site. (The font is ITC DF Wild West.)

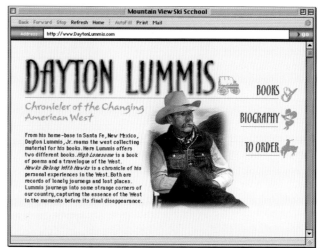

In this example, this playful intranet site uses the font Backyard Beasties for the illustrations. We set one character, the bird in the bath, in an imaging program and painted it, then used other type characters as spot illustrations. Because this is an in-house site for a bunch of wild designers, we could get away with bugs and icky crawly things as "decoration."

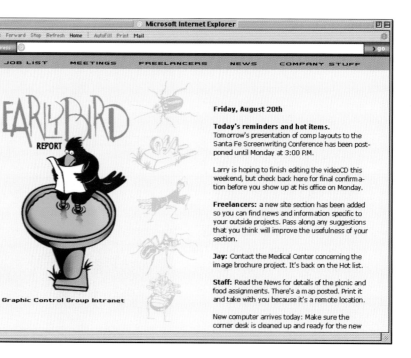

Visual impact of unique fonts

The visual impact of a unique type design can be very powerful and refreshing. Our concept for the entry page shown to the right was to combine elements of simplicity and complexity into one design. We chose the T26 font Droplet for its unique and contemporary personality. A simple click of a Styles button in Photoshop's Styles palette transformed the letter "W" into a colorful symbol representing the richness and versatility of the Web.

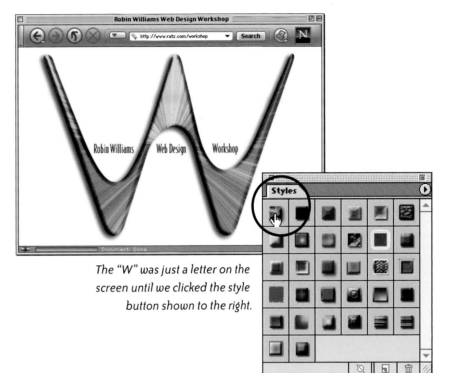

The "W" was just a letter on the screen until we clicked the style button shown to the right.

A typographic layout doesn't have to be dull. The contrast in this design gives it interest and appeal: in addition to the strong color contrast, the messy, hand-drawn logo create an art studio attitude and contrasts with the formal, business-like structure in the navigation area. The cut-out shape beneath the logo is a roll-over that changes as the mouse moves over the navigation.

Resources

Our favorite sources of clipart offer a great variety of styles and subject matter for affordable prices.

EyeWire provides great collections of clip art, fonts, stock photography and illustration, audio files, and digital film footage from a variety of vendors. One of the site features we like to use is the EyeWire Type Viewer. It allows you to type a headline or phrase, then preview it in any of the fonts available from EyeWire in a variety of sizes. **www.EyeWire.com**

ForDesigners.com is a fabulous web site from FontHaus, another of our all-time favorite vendors. Buy on disk or download clipart, stock images, or many thousands of fonts. **www.fordesigners.com**

Clipper, from **Dynamic Graphics, Inc.,** has been known for its high-quality clipart and stock image selection for many years, including the pre-digital dark ages. If you subscribe to Clipper's "Premier Art & Idea" service, you'll get a monthly CD of stock images,

seasonal and holiday art, a layout idea-and-technique how-to publication, and online access to thousands of single images. **www.dgusa.com**

The Bettman Archives are now owned by Bill Gates and can be found at **www.Corbis.com.**

Also check the following:

www.Comstock.com

www.StockPhoto.com

www.GettyOne.com

www.PhotoDisc.com

Watch for messages on web sites that warn you they sell a **license** to use an image **once,** which is very different from **royalty-free** stock images. A license can cost $500 to use a stock photo one time, whereas royalty-free images are typically yours to use as often as you want. Check the agreement before you buy!

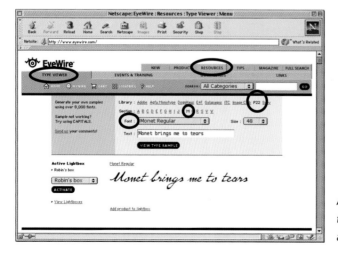

At the EyeWire site, go to "Resources" and find the "Type Viewer." Choose a font design library, a font, type in some text, then click the button.

Spiff up Your Photographs

Unlike print publishing, on the web it doesn't cost extra to publish your photographs in full color. And with the light shining from behind and through a photograph from the monitor to your eyes,* even the worst photo can look pretty luscious (in fact, photos often look better on the screen than in print).

But to make your web site visuals a touch above the rest, here are a number of tips for really juicing up those photos to make them conscious design elements, not just photos plopped on the page.

*As opposed to print, where the light is *reflected* from the ink to your eyes.

Imaging tips

Images add richness

Images can do more than just provide the sometimes necessary visual documentation on a page, such as photos to sell a product. Photo images can also change a page's personality and, either positively or negatively, alter the impact of what the web site is trying to communicate. Adding photographs to a page of text breaks the visual monotony of a page and can make a page more readable and visually more interesting. If a page is visually interesting and catches a reader's eye, it is more likely they will stay on your page and actually peruse your site.

But never forget that your main purpose on any web site is to **communicate.** Be sure that any photo or illustration you add to a page contributes to the overall communication and message. If it doesn't, it shouldn't be there.

A headline graphic can add some visual interest to a page, but a page with this much text could use more visual interest.

A table with a dark color background adds contrast and visual interest to the page.

Adding an illustration to the layout makes the page even more interesting and richer, a big improvement from where we started.

Here the illustration appears to be part of the text block, creating a more unique layout.

A Sizing Reminder

You may sometimes have a reason to place an oversized photo on a web page, but most images (even the largest images on a page) should be reasonably small in consideration of the viewer and the time it will take a page to load. As a general rule (which we break occasionally), we are reluctant to make any image larger than 400 pixels wide in its largest dimension (width or height), for two reasons.

The first reason is **limited window space.** Occasionally, a site's target audience has been identified as having larger monitors, such as a company's internal intranet site. But we usually design a web site with a **monitor configuration** in mind of 800 pixels by 600 pixels because that's currently the most common monitor size and resolution (see Chapter 4). Even though large monitors are increasingly more popular and affordable, laptops are also more popular than ever and the 800 x 600 guideline insures that the visual impact of our complete page design will be visible on most laptop screens.

So, in this minimal monitor configuration, an image that is 400 pixels deep on a web page will occupy more than half of the viewable page area, with some of the space being taken by the browser toolbar and border. Likewise, an image that is 400 pixels wide on a web page leaves only a minimum of space in which to squeeze other content, navigation, the browser border, and scroll bars. In this context, an image that is 400 pixels wide (or tall) is huge.

The second reason, of course, is **download time.** Lest you live in a big city with fast connections and think that surely *everyone* by now has fast connections, know that even here in Santa Fe, the oldest capital city in America, most of us log on at the same speed as in the third world country of Nepal (thanks to QWest). It's very embarrassing.

If a viewer is using an older monitor with a resolution of just 640 x 480 pixels, an image that is 400 pixels wide or tall occupies most of the viewable area.

Even in an 800 x 600 format, a maximum width or height of 400 pixels is huge. It not only takes up a lot of real estate, it takes too long to download.

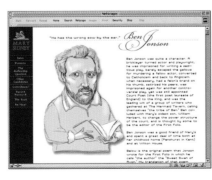

Tilted images

A tilted image can add visual energy to a page and create extra breathing room between the HTML text and the image without having to rely on HTML code to create separation between the image and text.

The JPEG file is not actually tilted on the web page— the image is tilted in the image editing software (like Photoshop).

In a **variation** of this technique, we put a texture behind the photo and behind the illustration on the home page shown below to add richness and visual interest to the page. The texture comes from scanning a piece of art paper.

The tilted images, the textured paper swatches behind two of the images, and the left-edged paper-texture border add warmth and a unique, scrapbook-like personality to the site.

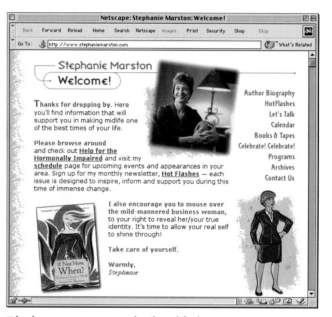

Tilted images give a casual, relaxed feeling to a page, in addition to adding visual interest to the layout.

Silhouettes

You might also want to experiment with isolating one part of a photograph by silhouetting the object. This is especially effective if the object has an interesting shape. The relationship between the negative and positive space of the shape can make your page much more exciting than a square image.

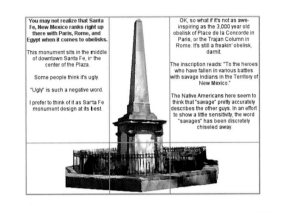

Above you can see the Santa Fe Plaza obelisk in the table; it's sliced into four pieces and positioned in four separate cells in the table. The text is set in two cells on either side to look like it wraps around the obelisk.

(The obelisk looks much prettier in this photo than it does in person.)

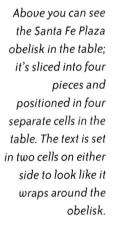

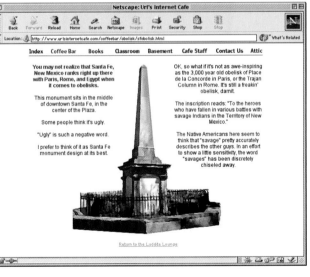

The irregular shape of a silhouetted image automatically adds visual interest and variety to a page.

Cropping

Cropping out unnecessary parts of images can free up a lot of viewable content area on a web page, in addition to speeding up image and page downloads to a browser. Just as important, cropping can enhance the effectiveness of the image by making it more efficient, more focused, or more dramatic.

By cropping the photographs on these pages, we made the images half the original sizes and twice as fast to load, while the main subjects are as large as before.

And as shown on the opposite page, cropping into dramatic horizontal and vertical shapes can add variation and visual interest to the layouts.

It's common to have a reluctance to crop photos, especially if they came from a professional photography source which you assume has already cropped the images to create the best compositions possible. But the fact is that there are many cropping options that work and that create different effects, so crop images in whatever way they are most effective for your particular projects.

This is the original, uncropped image. Since all we care about in this particular photo is the kids and the snowman, we can eliminate the other stuff.

Now we have a faster loading and more visually focused image.

With the tall, narrow photo, we can get a nice contrast of verticals and horizontals in the design. Even though there's enough horizontal space available for a wider photo, the cropping adds visual interest and decreases file size.

Cropping this image not only gets rid of uninteresting parts of the photo, but gives us a more interesting shape.

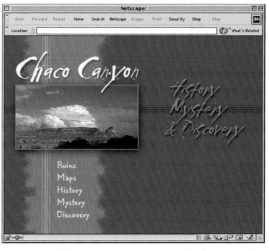

Original image with the cropping marquee shown.

This is the cropped image taken from the photograph above.

We cropped this image to emphasize the horizontal feeling. An image doesn't have to be excessively large to create a strong visual impact.

Creating a sepia tone image

Old photos often look more interesting with a sepia tone applied to them. To capture the photo shown below, we panned across an old photo album with a digital video camera.

After we digitized the footage in the computer, we then exported a single frame as a JPEG image file. We opened the JPEG file in Photoshop to make some image adjustments. Rather than try to color-correct the colors that resulted from filming an old photo in a dimly lit room, we simply desaturated the image, which eliminated all color.

Then we added a monochromatic sepia color, as you can see on the opposite page: in the Hue/Saturation dialog box, we clicked the "Colorize" button and adjusted the "Hue" slider to get the coloring desired. We decreased the color saturation of the image (again) by moving the "Saturation" slider to the left, creating a more subtle and authentic sepia effect.

The original image of John and his twin brother is low quality and an unacceptable color.

We desaturated the image to remove existing color.

To desaturate in Photoshop, go to the Image menu, choose "Adjust," then "Desaturate."

Typically when an image is soft and fuzzy like this one, we apply the "Unsharp Mask" filter to sharpen it. But in this case, the original low-quality image contains JPEG artifacts (lumpy, bumpy, and junky-looking anomalies in the image). As the low-resolution original photo already looked pixelated in places, we knew that sharpening would only exaggerate the pixelation.

Since this original image was rather large, we reduced its size (down to 400 pixels wide) to soften the image: the size reduction blurred the image, minimizing the JPEG artifacts and pixelization. We then applied the Unsharp Mask filter to the smaller, fuzzier photo. (Don't overdo the Unsharp Mask setting—it can make the image look unnatural.)

As a final step we brightened the photo using the "Levels" dialog box, and the image then made a nice web page graphic.

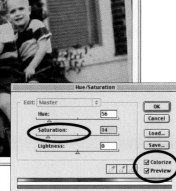

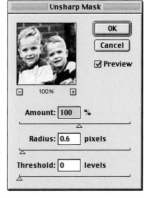

After reducing the size of the image, we sharpened it by applying Photoshop's "Unsharp Mask" filter.

We used Photoshop's "Hue/Saturation" dialog box to colorize the photo and adjust the saturation.

To brighten the image, we used the "Levels" dialog box.

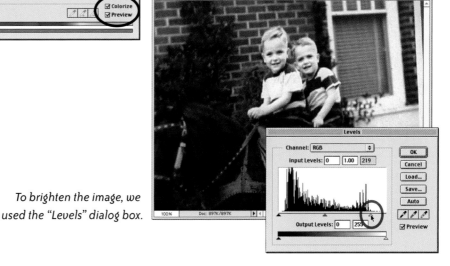

Drop shadows

Drop shadows add a little to the size of an image file, but if your web page isn't already stretching the limits of reasonable download time, drop shadows can add visual dimension and interest to the page, preventing it from looking flat. Another advantage of a drop shadow is that the space around the shadow creates a natural separation between the image and any HTML text that is wrapping around it.

The HTML text on this page is crashing into the image.

We placed HTML tags in the code to force space around the image <HSPACE=10>, but this tag always forces horizontal space on **both** sides of the image, creating a misalignment on the left side.

Photoshop's Layer menu contains "Layer Style" options, including the "Drop Shadow" dialog box which enables you to apply a drop shadow instantly, yet still control many of the shadow attributes.

It's not necessary to drop shadow *everything!* A subtle variety of image effects can be refreshing and help to break the monotony of a text-heavy page.

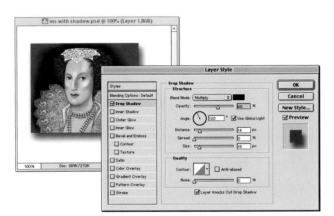

The Drop Shadow dialog box lets you create drop shadows easily, and you can change the settings (and thus the shadow) at any time.

The HTML text is still crashing against the actual sides of the image, but it's not obvious to the viewer.

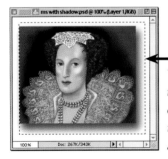

This dotted line is the marquee that indicates where we will crop it. We cropped this image to include extra background on all sides except the left.

37

Have fun with artistic filters

Images that turn too soft and fuzzy after resizing smaller can sometimes be made to look more dramatic and clear by applying an "artistic" filter, such as "Poster Edges" in Photoshop's Filter menu. But the effect of a filter on an image can vary dramatically, depending on the resolution of the image. If your image is low resolution because it's going on a web page, the filter often doesn't look very good because it has limited data to work on. The solution is to temporarily change the resolution, apply the filter, then take it back to the low resolution you need for your final image.

The low-resolution image (72 ppi) shown below is straight from a digital camera. With the limitation of 72 ppi to work with, the image became muddy and lost too much detail when we applied the Poster Edges filter. So we removed the filter and changed the resolution of the image to 300 ppi (from the File menu, choose "Size," then change the "Resolution" to 300). We then re-applied the Poster Edges filter. We were happy with the results and changed the resolution back to 72 ppi. The final image is sharper, more dramatic, and visually more interesting than the original.

With the Poster Edges filter applied to this 72 ppi image, the black edges are too prominent and fuzzy, eliminating much of the image detail.

Notice the difference between the image that had the Poster Edges filter applied at 72 ppi and this image that was set at 300 ppi when we applied the Poster Edges filter.

Create an illustrative look for your images

You can vary the look and feel of images with Photoshop filters. You can even make a photograph look like an illustration. Some of our favorite filters in the Artistic filter collection are Watercolor, Dry Brush, and Paint Daubs.

In the example below, we used the Watercolor filter, but that filter usually makes the shadow areas of an image very dark. To show more detail in the shadow areas, we lightened the midtones by adjusting the middle slider in the Levels dialog box (from the Image menu, choose "Adjust...," then choose "Levels...").

But when we lightened the midtones, we lost much of the contrast. To help compensate for the flatter contrast, we increased the color saturation in the Hue/Saturation dialog box (from the Image menu, choose "Adjust...," then "Hue/Saturation...").

Then we sharpened the image slightly using the Unsharp Mask filter (from the Filters menu, choose "Sharpen," then "Unsharp Mask..."). The final result is an image with rich texture and a painterly feeling.

Don't get carried away with filters, though! Some obvious filter effects are overused and have become cliches. This distraction could prevent your message from communicating effectively.

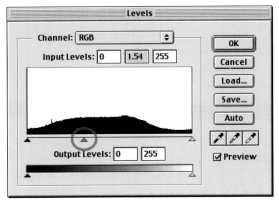

Use the midtone slider in the Levels dialog box to lighten and bring out more detail in the midtones of an image.

Using a filter, such as this watercolor filter, on every image would look tedious. Special effects work best when used sparingly for visual impact and contrast with other images or page content.

Brighten your images

Many photographic images can benefit from adjusting the "levels" of an image, especially if they've been scanned on a desktop scanner. You'll be surprised how often an image looks perfectly fine until you try adjusting the brightness and then realize just how dark it really is. In Photoshop, use the "Levels" dialog box (from the Image menu, choose "Adjust…," then "Levels…").

In the example below, we moved the midtone slider (the gray triangle in the middle) to the right, but it's far more common to

brighten an image using only the highlights slider (the white triangle on the right).

The advantage of using the Levels dialog box over the Brightness/Contrast dialog box is that Brightness brightens *all* of the pixels in the image the same amount, while Levels allows you to adjust only the highlights (white areas), midtones (gray areas), or shadows (dark areas) individually. Each image is different. Experiment with different settings, using either the midtone slider, the highlights slider, or both.

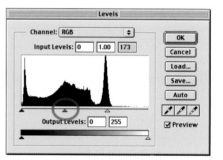

Adjusting these settings can work wonders with dark images.

We thought this image looked pretty good on the monitor, until we experimented with brightening it.

We were surprised how dark the original looked after we created this version.

Soft proofing

Images usually appear a little darker on PCs than they do on Macintoshes, so if an image looks too light on your PC, it'll look even lighter on a Mac. Or if an image looks borderline dark on your Mac, it'll look even darker on a PC. Photoshop allows you to preview images in both of these environments with a technique called "soft proofing."

Open an image in Photoshop. From the View menu, choose "Proof Setup," and select "Windows RGB" or "Macintosh RGB." The document's title bar will display the name of the proof profile you've selected. To see both Mac and PC proofs of the images at once, select "New View" from the View menu; the original image and its duplicate can now be assigned different proof profiles for comparison.

The title bar indicates which platform the image preview is simulating.

The Windows preview displays a slightly darker image. The goal is to find a balance so the photo is neither too light on a Mac nor too dark on a PC.

Select a soft proof model: from the View menu, go to "Proof Setup."

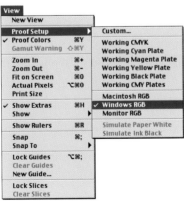

Use Saturation Tools (global)

Scanned images and photographs downloaded from digital cameras sometimes look a little dull or not as colorful as you'd like (or not as colorful as you remember). We use the Saturation tool on many photo images to enhance the color of either the entire image (shown below) or to enhance specific areas of the image (opposite page).

To globally saturate all the colors in the photograph of the dog enjoying the Annapurna sunrise, we opened the Hue/Saturation palette (from the Image menu, choose "Adust," then "Hue/Saturation…"). We dragged the "Saturation" slider to the right. Adjustments like this are more dramatic on a monitor than they are on a printed page, so the effect may look more subtle here than it does on a web page.

Everyone and everything enjoys the magical sunrise at the base of the Annapurnas.

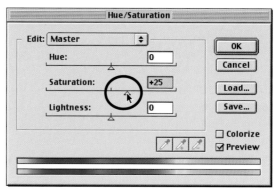

Drag the "Saturation" slider to the right to juice up the colors.

Use Saturation Tools (local)

Instead of saturating an entire image, you can saturate just specific, local areas.

In the photograph shown below of a web designer posing with a young girl from Bhaktapur, we selected Photoshop's Sponge tool from the Tools palette and set its "Mode" to "Saturate" (it can also be set to "Desaturate"). We set the percentage of saturation ("Pressure") to 20% and began manually saturating the girl's dress and the man's hat by scrubbing over those areas with the sponge tool. The increased color saturation created more visual contrast between the desired focal impact of the image and the secondary, background elements.

Because design is playful and experimental by nature, we couldn't resist carrying this a step further. We reset the Sponge tool Mode to Desaturate and *removed* color from the background. Although the image was obviously altered from reality, the effect fits nicely with the theme of our web site text: Nepal is a surreal place.

After you select the Sponge tool (left), the menus above will appear in your toolbar.

This is the original image, a web designer (disguised as a Nepali Sherpa) and his friend.

We cropped the image, saturated certain areas, then desaturated and blurred the background to create more visual impact and contrast with the foreground subjects.

Add wild styles to text

The styles in Photoshop's Styles palette are not just for buttons or boxes—apply them to type, letterforms, or any selection of pixels. If the usual colored, drop-shadowed headline just isn't wild enough, try applying a style to it.

If none of the preformatted styles in the Styles palette appeal to you, you can apply your own choice of effects (or combination of effects) to a headline: use the Layer Style choices from the Layer menu (Drop Shadow, Inner Shadow, Outer Glow, etc.). After achieving an effect you like, save the settings as a New Style in the Styles palette popout menu.

Just because you can turn a headline into abstract art with the click of a button doesn't mean it's always a good idea. But it's fun and effective if you use good judgment and a degree of restraint. Also remember: just because it's in the Styles palette doesn't mean it's usable.

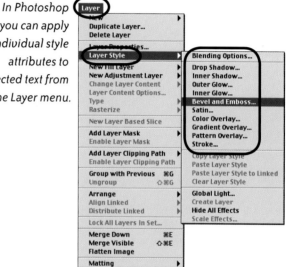

In Photoshop you can apply individual style attributes to selected text from the Layer menu.

Or you can apply multiple style attributes at once by clicking on a style swatch in the Styles palette. If you choose, you can edit any of the style settings, then save the edited version as a "New Style."

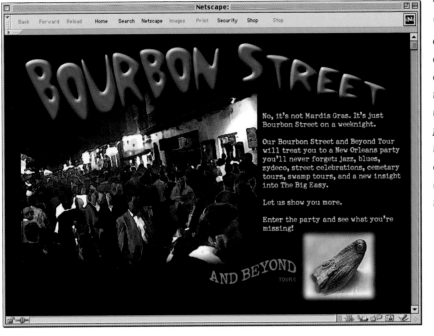

Type can be used as a visual element.
With Photoshop's Style palette you can create obnoxious or sophisticated text effects instantly. The three-dimensional effect of the type on this page helped to separate the headline from an otherwise flat page. The distorted casual font added a festive atmosphere, and the polished rendering of the type contrasted nicely with the photograph. (We applied the "Accented Edges" filter to the photograph.)

To establish visual continuity throughout the site design, this site's secondary pages use various type treatments from Photoshop's Style palette.

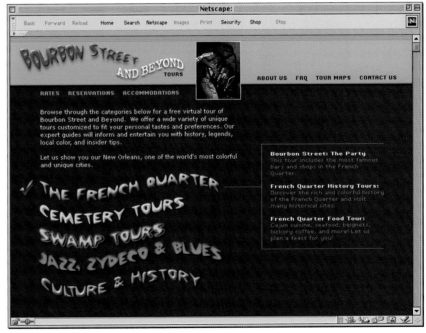

Thumbnail images

Thumbnail images are useful as enticements to jump to linked pages that contain larger versions of the thumbnail images. A thumbnail image can be very small and the quality can be rather marginal since you're linking to a larger, nicer version of the same image on another page. For the thumbnail page, the main prerequisites are small file size (in bytes) and fast loading. The Robert Burns page shown below contains a lot of thumbnails, but all together they contribute less than 60 kilobytes to the page weight (approximately 4K each).

When you've created an image that's incredibly beautiful, you'll want to make it really large. Right? Yes, you'll want to, and no, don't do it. At least not until the telecoms have provided all of us with unlimited bandwidth. Even if someday the telecoms give us unlimited bandwidth and blazing speed, you're still going to be paying a server to store all of your files, and if your files are excessively larger than necessary, you'll be paying for more server space than necessary.

Okay, maybe you've got a good reason to have huge images on a web site. If so, at least provide a page of small thumbnails that link to individual large-image pages, each page containing no more than one huge graphic. (You can always tell if a designer has a lightning fast Internet connection by how many large images he's willing to put on a single page.)

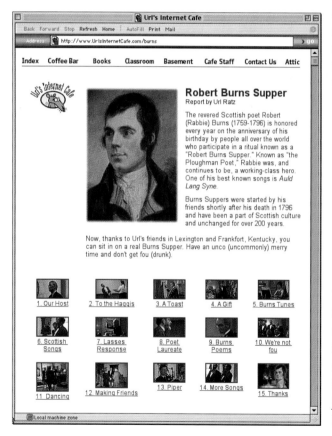

Thumbnails can be very small and still be an effective visual clue to help the reader decide whether or not to follow the thumbnail's link. Large thumbnails can be irritating when you realize that the image you've clicked through to is just slightly larger than the thumbnail image. Thanks for wasting my time.

There's always an exception

Now that we've chastised you for using large thumbnails, here are examples of exceptions. These thumbnails aren't just visual hints to a link, they're actually product shots, so it's important to have a clear, readable image. The large thumbnail links to a page with a slightly larger image, but the page contains other information that wasn't available on the first page, making a click-through worth the effort.

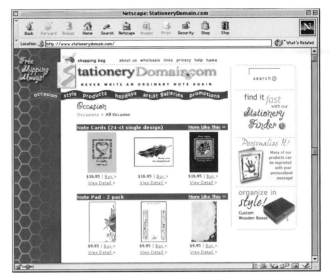

These thumbnail images of note cards are large enough to interest the viewer, but not large enough to read. Clicking through to another page is a better choice than having a page full of large note cards that would take too long to download.

There should be a reward for the user if they make the effort to click-through on a thumbnail. Don't disappoint them.

Web Photo Gallery

Your client is across town and needs to see the photos you've chosen for her web site in the next five minutes. You're in luck—another Photoshop feature, Web Photo Gallery, can create simple, multi-page web sites within seconds from a folder of your images. A mouse-click will create a simple web site containing a home page of thumbnail images, each of which links to a separate page for each image, and includes navigation buttons on each page. The file name appears below each image. This quick and simple site can be created and uploaded to a private folder on your web site within minutes, accessible from anywhere. Your client will think you're a genius.

From Photoshop's File menu, select "Automate," then "Web Photo Gallery." In the dialog box (shown below), choose the "Source" folder where your images are currently, the "Destination" folder where you want the new web pages stored, and the page layout "Options." Then click OK.

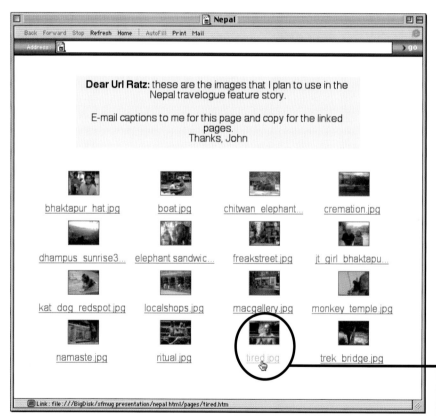

You can customize a number of settings using the "Options" menu, including thumbnail and image sizes, source folder, and destination folder.

This web site, which consists of 17 pages, including this home page, was automatically created with Photoshop's Web Photo Gallery feature. It was built within seconds from a folder of images and is ready to upload to the web for the client to see.

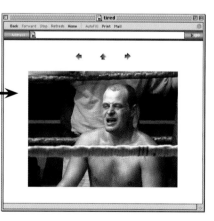

Paste a Photoshop Web Photo Gallery
into an existing web page

UrlsInternetCafe.com occasionally features a story that includes a gallery of photographs. We sometimes use Photoshop's automated Photo Gallery to create the first page of thumbnail images.

The work of creating the thumbnails and placing them in a table takes just a few seconds because Photoshop does that part automatically. We can then paste the table that Photoshop created into a cell of a table on our existing HTML page. For more examples, see the following pages.

After we pasted the automatically created table into our HTML page (using Dreamweaver in this example), we changed the captions from file names to descriptive copy.

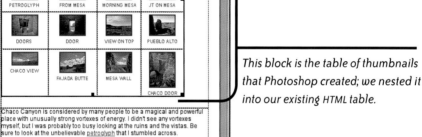

This block is the table of thumbnails that Photoshop created; we nested it into our existing HTML table.

More on Web Photo Gallery

The layout shown below was designed with an open space where we planned to place an HTML table of thumbnails. We planned to nest the thumbnail table into a larger table that already contained the headline and body copy.

We nested this Photoshop-created table into the existing page table.

To this end, we used Photoshop's automated "Web Photo Gallery" dialog box, as shown below. We understand that in most cases we'll still have to clean up or alter the HTML file after it has been created, but to begin with we'll let Photoshop do most of the work.

After we designated a *source* folder of images and a *destination* folder for the new web pages, Photoshop created the thumbnails by resizing the original images. It also automatically created a web page, placed those thumbnails on the web page, and linked each one. Each link went to another automatically created web page that held larger images of the photographs, along with "Back" and "Next" links.

We opened the HTML thumbnail page in Dreamweaver and changed the thumbnail captions from file names to more descriptive labels.

In addition to designating a "Source" folder and a "Destination" folder, the Web Photo Gallery dialog box lets you have some limited control over the page layout.

A closer look at our thumbnail table

The Web Photo Gallery page, as it appeared in Dreamweaver, included a banner that contained a headline. For our purposes, we ignored the banner, copied the HTML table containing the thumbnail images, and pasted it into the HTML table that we had created for our Bangkok page. We considered any other changes we wanted to make to the table, such as text color, table cell padding, table cell spacing, or horizontal and vertical alignment of cell contents.

Shown below is the web page in Dreamweaver where you can clearly see the nested thumbnails table. We had also created a navigation table and nested it into the table cell at the top of the page. The blank table cells contain spacers, transparent 1 x 1–pixel GIF files, that have been sized to stretch to the dimensions of the table cell to help hold the overall table shape and avoid the unwanted resizing of table cells that is a common problem in HTML production. When you

use programs such as Adobe ImageReady or Macromedia Fireworks to slice a layout and automatically create HTML files for you (see Chapter 12), you can specify whether a table cell will contain an image or a spacer.

Photoshop's automated Web Photo Gallery creates HTML page files with an extension of .htm. If you usually use .html file name extensions instead of .htm, be sure to check that all links into a Photo Gallery page use the matching .htm extension.

This is the original HTML page as created by Photoshop; shown in Dreamweaver.

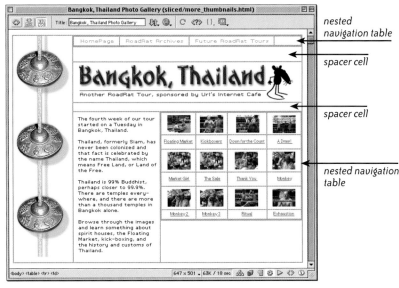

nested navigation table

spacer cell

spacer cell

nested navigation table

This is the nested Web Photo Gallery table as seen in Dreamweaver.

We deleted the banner, changed the captions, and altered the spacing between the rows so the captions would be closer to the images they belong to.

Make client meetings a little easier:
Contact Sheets

Designers and art directors used to browse through all the images for a project by spreading out the photos on a desk or putting lots of transparency slides on a light box. They would then sort through the images, creating separate stacks of which images to use and which images to put back in the file. This was cumbersome and awkward.

Today, it's even worse. You may have 100 images on your computer that were either scanned by you, digital files given to you by the client, or perhaps you downloaded photos straight from a digital camera. Opening each of these images on your monitor to show the client is very cumbersome to do, and the files are awkward to keep track of during a meeting.

Rather than deal with that digital mess, we like to put all the images in a folder (and in sub-folders if it helps simplify the overall organization of files), then have Photoshop automatically create contact sheets of all the images.

In Photoshop, from the File menu, select "Automate…," then select "Contact Sheet." Define your preferences in the "Contact Sheet" dialog box, click OK, and Photoshop will create the necessary number of contact sheets to show all your images. Your client can review the contact sheets on the computer's monitor, or you can print the pages out, either in color or grayscale. You can even convert the contact sheet to a PDF file and send it to the client.

You can automatically create a color contact sheet from a folder of images to help you organize your project and review images quickly.

Make client meetings even easier:
History Palette Snapshots

Designing a home page in Photoshop can result in a lot of design exploration and experimentation. In other words, your Photoshop document may ultimately have dozens of layers. This is very convenient because you can turn layers on or off to simulate different design variations. But when the client is looking over your shoulder, fumbling through fifty layers can be extremely confusing and time consuming. To simplify the process (and impress your client), create "Snapshots" of your document at any state with the History palette.

Before the client arrives, turn on the layers that need to be visible to present various layout versions. In the History palette, click the popout menu button (upper-right side of the palette) and choose "New Snapshot...." Give the snapshot a memorable name.

Next, turn on the layers necessary to show another layout variation, or to show what a button looks like when you mouse over it, etc.

From the History palette popout menu, select "New Snapshot...," and name that new History state snapshot.

Repeat this process for as many file variations as you want to show. When the client arrives, you only have to click on the snapshot names in the History palette to show the different variations of the file. This is also a useful technique to use as you experiment with design and layout—making occasional snapshots makes it easy to backtrack to earlier versions as you evaluate design decisions.

Be aware, however, that **snapshots are temporary** and will not be saved when you close the document! If you do want a permanent record of the Snapshot History states, make a screen shot of the document window in each state.

By selecting different items in the History palette, we see snapshots of our layout versions.

Weighted optimization

When an image has been "optimized" for the web, it has been saved in a format suitable for the web (a GIF or JPEG file format, for instance) with customized settings for compression, dithering, and color palettes. Usually these settings apply globally to an entire image, but Photoshop's software enables you to vary these settings in different parts of the same image by using an alpha channel.

The goal is to have higher quality settings applied to the important areas of an image, such as someone's face, and to have lower quality settings applied to the less important areas, such as the background.

The resulting file looks high quality, but since some areas of the image have been optimized with high levels of compression (a lower quality setting), the overall optimized image is smaller than if the entire image had been optimized with high-quality settings. And the general quality of the overall image is better than if we had compromised with a medium-quality setting in an attempt to reduce the image file size.

Give the Lasso tool a feathered edge so the compression variations will not be hard-edged. In this example, we used a Feather amount of 6 pixels. Lasso around the area(s) where you want to apply higher quality optimization settings.

Select the Quick Mask button in the Tools palette to automatically create a temporary "alpha channel." The red mask indicates what area of the image is being masked; this separates the image into two areas, inside and outside the selection.

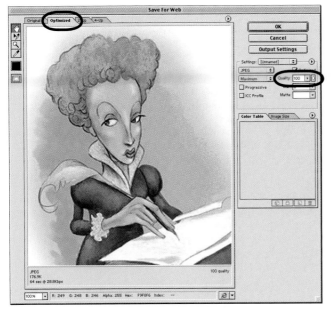

From the File menu, choose "Save for Web." You'll get the window shown above. Click the "Optimized" tab to view the optimized image. Click on the tiny channel button to the right of the "Quality" edit box.

You'll get the "Modify Quality Setting" dialog box, as shown to the right. From its "Channel" menu, select "Quick Mask."

Define the quality range by setting the sliders for the **highest** level of quality to be applied **inside** and the **lowest** level of quality **outside** the selection you lassoed. Click OK to name and save the file.

This enlargement shows how the different compression levels have affected different areas of the file.

The face area looks good because it has been set to a low-compression/high-quality setting. The rest of the image has been highly compressed with a low-quality setting. The hand is obviously pixelated, but the background handles the high-compression/ low-quality setting very well.

While you can take advantage of this technique on any photo, it works best on images that have undetailed backgrounds that will not easily show the effects of high- compression/low-quality settings.

Photoshop tips and shortcuts

Since so much of the design work is done in Photoshop, knowing a few Photoshop tips can increase your efficiency during the design stage of a web site project. Here are some of the tips and shortcuts we use most often when working with image files.

Keyboard shortcut to change numerical entries

When you're exploring different numerical values for a selection in a palette or dialog box, you can highlight the numerical field in the palette, as shown to the right. Press the keyboard's **UpArrow to increase** the value and the **DownArrow to decrease** the value.

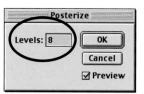

In the type size example shown to the right, the UpArrow or DownArrow will increase or decrease type size in one-point increments. Hold down the Shift key to change point sizes in ten-point increments.

The specific incremental value depends on which edit box is selected at the moment.

Keyboard shortcut to change type sizes

You can also use a keyboard shortcut to resize text in a Photoshop document without opening the dialog box:

Select the text with the text tool. To increase selected text in two-point increments, hold down the Command and Shift keys (Mac) or Control and Shift keys (Windows), then tap the GreaterThan symbol (>, same key as the period); each tap will enlarge the type two points. To decrease the selected text in two-point increments, hold the Command/Control and Shift, then tap the LessThan symbol (<, same key as the comma).

Add the Option/Alt key to either operation to change text sizes in ten-point increments.

Another way to easily change type size is to highlight the value in the Font size value field, then use the keyboard's Up and Down arrow keys to change the value in one-point increments. Press the Shift key with the arrow keys to change the value by ten-point increments.

Merge layers

When working with multiple layers in Photoshop, you can use a keyboard shortcut to merge any layer with the layer directly below it: select the top layer and press "Control E" (PC) or "Command E" (Mac).

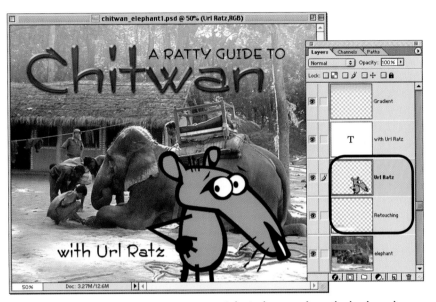

Select a layer and use the keyboard shortcut to merge the selected layer with the layer directly below it.

Experiment with anti-aliased text colors

Experimenting with many different text colors can be fast and easy when the text is on its own layer:

If the text is still in text format and has not been rasterized, select the text, then type Command H to hide the high-lighted selection bar that appears over the selected text. Click on a color swatch in the Swatches palette to see the text update with your color selections. Even if the type has been rasterized (is no longer an editable text format) and is still on its own transparent layer, select the layer the type image is on, then press Option Shift Delete. The swatch color will be applied to the type selection or to any pixels on that layer.

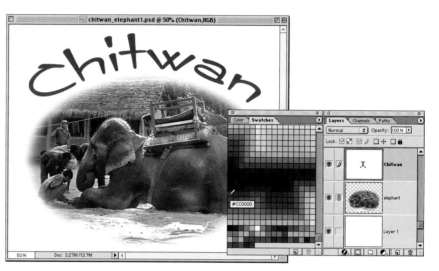

Experimenting with different text colors can be as simple as selecting the type layer and clicking on swatches in the Swatches palette.

Color it perfect

But don't make the mistake of using the Magic Wand tool to select rasterized type, then selecting a color and filling the shape using the Paint Bucket tool. If you do so, it will fill every pixel with solid color, including the anti-aliased pixels around the edges that make type look smooth instead of jaggy. The result will be an aliased, jaggy version of your type. The colorization of the anti-aliasing will vary, depending on the tolerance setting of the Magic Wand tool, but the overall effect will be unsatisfactory. If the type you want to colorize has been rasterized and merged into a background color, it's better to recreate the type on a transparent layer, then color it while it's on that layer.

Selecting rasterized type with the Magic Wand tool and coloring with the Paint Bucket can result in this dreadful effect.

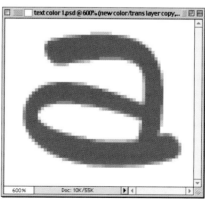

Correctly colorized type preserves the semi-transparent edge pixels.

Quick and easy retouching

Often images need minimal retouching. Rather than spend a lot of time with the Airbrush Tool or the Rubber Stamp, let Photoshop do all the work.

Use the Lasso tool with a small feather radius (2 pixels, for instance, to keep from creating a hard edge around the shape you draw) to draw around scratches and artifacts in an image. From the Filter menu, choose the "Dust & Scratches" filter. This technique works best in areas that do not have a lot of detail.

When you select the Lasso tool, the "Feather" options will appear in the toolbar. Yes, you do want a checkmark in "Anti-aliased" for this procedure.

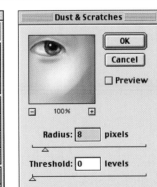

When scratches or dust appear in undetailed areas of an image, Photoshop's "Dust & Scratches" filter is a fast and easy fix.

The preview box (the box with the eye visible at the moment) shows a live update of the slider settings. When the slider adjustments look good, click OK.

Get rid of the text highlight selection

The highlight selection obscures your view of the changes you're making. When the Type tool is selected, you can toggle between showing and hiding the highlight bar that indicates selected text: press Command H (Mac) or Control H (Windows).

You can't see the results of your text effects when the text is obscured by the selection slug (the dark highlight). Use the keyboard shortcut to make the selection slug disappear, while leaving the text actually selected so you can apply effects and formatting.

Hide the marquee

To have a better view of your selection, hide the shimmering marquee: press Command H (Mac) or Control H (Windows).

Hide palettes

Sometimes your screen becomes so cluttered with palettes that you can't see your project. To temporarily hide all the palettes, make sure you are not in the Type tool, then press the Tab key. To bring all the palettes back, hit the Tab key again.

Hide all palettes except Tools

Sometimes you want to get rid of all the palettes but you need the Tools palette still available. To do this, hold the Shift key down and hit Tab. To show the palettes again, hold Shift and hit Tab again.

Use the keyboard shortcut to hide all palettes (below, left) or all except the Tools palette and ruler (below).

It's a Horizontal World

Whether you design print materials professionally or simply as the default person who puts together flyers and newsletters in the office, you are probably accustomed to a vertical format, such as the typical 8.5 x 11–inch page. But web sites are viewed on monitors that have a more horizontal shape, and it takes a bit of an adjustment to wrap your design into this shape.

Why horizontal?

Web pages present a unique design challenge: think horizontally. Traditional print media has conditioned us to think of design in a vertical format. Most magazines, newspapers, brochures, and books exist in this vertical space, and all designers, ranging from professional artists to school kids making posters, are accustomed to working in this format. Since web pages are viewed on horizontally constructed computer monitors, you need to visualize your page design in a horizontal format. Even if a web page ultimately is an extremely vertical, scrolling page, **the primary visual impact of the page design** should appear in the visible, horizontal content area of the browser window.

Even though many people have monitors large enough to see this much of the home pages, we played it safe by designing the page so that all the primary visual content would appear intact, even if viewed on a 640 x 480 pixel monitor.

This shows how much of the home page a user with a smaller monitor would see. Even though they have to scroll down to see the rest of the page, at least they get the full initial visual impact of the design.

Design around a standard size

Most of our site designs are based on a horizontal format that is 800 pixels wide by 600 pixels high. This is a size that is common to a large number of monitors, and it ensures that our design will fit comfortably on the largest percentage of monitors possible (17-inch monitors).

Some clients request that a site be designed to fit within 640 x 480 pixels to accommodate their target audience, those with 14-inch monitors (like many schools, as well as the millions of computers in corporations around the world) and laptops that can't display higher resolutions. While more and more large corporate site designs assume their audience has at least 17-inch monitors, you can't totally ignore the fact that many people, especially in other countries, are going to hang on to their 14-inch monitors (640 x 480) until the last pixel is dead.

*If you need a **screen ruler**, go to shareware.com and search. On a Mac, we use Screen Ruler. On the PC we like to use Reglo (from Basta) because you can set the size of the window in the ruler and apply a hotkey to it, then whenever you want to see a window in exactly that size, just hit the hotkey and the browser window jumps to that size.*

Is your monitor bigger than mine?

As a designer, you may be tempted to ignore these size and format limitations that we outline in this chapter. If your page design is really beautiful, it's a shame to have to alter or miniaturize it just so it will fit on a smaller monitor. After all, you say, many people have large, 21- and 22-inch monitors, making it easy enough to stretch open the browser window to accommodate a vertical or extra wide page design. But in reality, even though these large monitors are more popular and more affordable than ever before, the majority of monitors in homes and businesses are much smaller than 21-inch.

And don't forget that laptop computers are also more popular and affordable than ever—even the largest laptop screens are small (although the newer ones have more options for higher resolutions). And if you've ever seen a web design presentation or given a presentation yourself with a projection system, you know that many projection systems are limited to the 640 x 480 resolution. If the web site you're presenting doesn't fit into that space, it can make the entire presentation difficult. So in most cases it's best to get over it and design your pages in a size and format that makes viewing and navigation easy for everyone, even those with limited monitor environments.

Screen real estate dilemmas

Within the limitations of a typical monitor, we have other considerations that affect the actual size of our content area. On a Macintosh, approximately 20 pixels of monitor real estate is occupied by a menu bar at the top of the monitor screen, and on PCs the browser window has the application menu across the top of the window, also taking up about 20 pixels. If a user is browsing the web using America Online, even more of the vertical space is taken up by the AOL menu bar.

Even the computer's operating system uses some screen real estate for menu bars, which impacts the amount of screen space left for the browser window and its toolbar.

Unpredictable browser variations

On all computers, a certain amount of a browser's viewable content area is occupied by the browser's border and tool-bars. The exact amount of available content area varies depending on which browser is used and which browser "View Options" are used.

For instance, if a user chooses to show both text and icons in the toolbar, that toolbar occupies more vertical space than if a user chooses to show text only. Millions of users don't know *how* to change their toolbars and just live with the default, which is usually the most space-consuming arrangement.

The horizontal real estate of a web page will give up 25 pixels of usable design area to the browser's border and a scroll bar. Even more of the actual content area can be lost if the browser is set to display special function tabs on the left side of the browser. Below you can see the how the different menu bars affect the space visible on a web page.

Don't put your important navigation at the very bottom!
At the bottom, it may not be visible unless you've planned for the worst-case scenario concerning viewable browser area. Don't make the user scroll to find the navigation buttons.

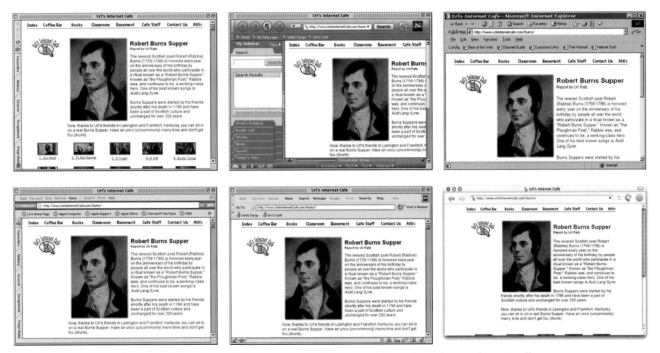

As you can see, a user's personal browser settings can change the presentation of a web page dramatically.

Be conservative and safe

The bottom line is that you can't be sure how much space anyone is going to allow you in their personal browser. Our conservative design approach is to assume that most browser setups will allow us the following amount of space *for the initial pre-scrolling content area* of our page design:

14-inch monitor—about 600 pixels of width; about 360 pixels of height .

17-inch monitor—about 760 pixels of width; about 520 pixels of height .

We make certain that the *initial visual impression and the main navigation* is visible within the pixel dimensions outlined above (depending on which market you choose to cater to).

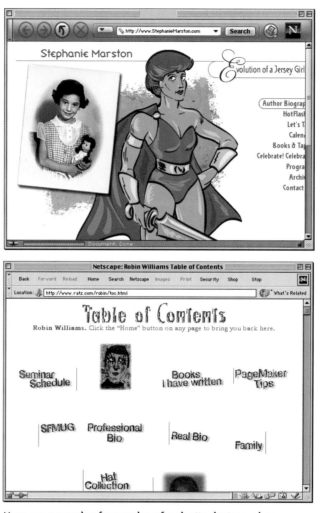

*Here are a couple of examples of web site designs where the **initial visual impact** is **not** contained within a limited browser window. What you see here is what many typical users around the world might see if you design your pages too large. Don't make people scroll to find the main navigation buttons.*

*Here are a few examples of web sites whose **initial visual**
impact is neatly contained within a limited browser window.*

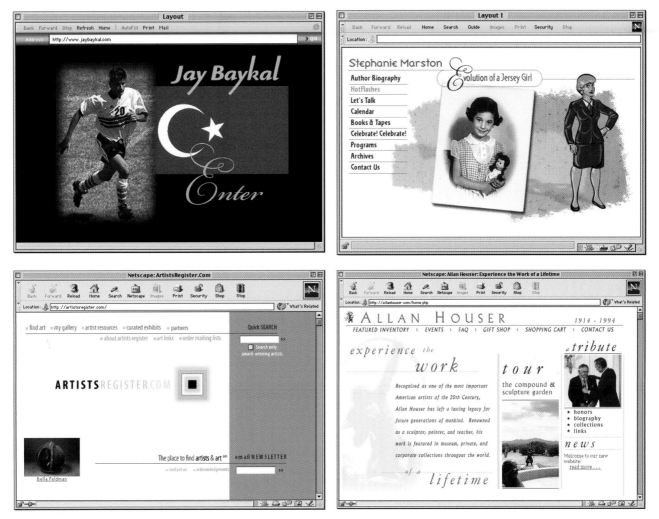

*Even though interior pages of these web sites scrolls down, the initial visual impacts
and their navigation bar are all contained within the limited browser space.*

How to design within the limitations

Use image editing software as a visual design tool

Web authoring and image editing products, such as Adobe Photoshop or Macromedia Fireworks, provide powerful tools for constructing and building web pages. These programs are not only valuable as production tools— they're also indispensable design and layout tools.

Some designers and programmers take pride in their ability to write HTML code from scratch. This is tremendously impressive to those who have a limited knowledge of HTML, DHTML, JavaScript, and various programming languages. The other impressive thing, we think, is how easy it usually is to identify web sites that have been written in code from scratch by a genius programmer: it's functional; it's got bells and whistles; it's way ugly. Or at least visually uninteresting.

More often than not, an HTML coding approach to design results in layouts that are what we call the "HTML box," also known as "first-generation web design": layouts that look like they were created when the web first appeared.

The first generation of web pages used simplistic and unimaginative layouts because the web page technology of that time was very limiting. A designer with fantastic technical programming knowledge—or none at all—can design more creatively if using a visual approach: **solve design problems visually, then use technical knowledge to make the design functional.**

A web page design built in the "HTML box" is usually unimaginative and modular.

Design with the browser in mind

We always start a layout by placing a screen shot of a browser window, sized to 640 x 480 pixels or 800 x 600 (*outside* dimensions), on a Photoshop layer. This gives us a visual reference for the image area that we need to design within. Since we know that a web site will always be seen in the context of a browser window, this enables us to always see our design in the same context, and it adds a constant dose of reality as we play with design. We even go so far as to create additional Photoshop layers containing screen captures of various browsers so we can simulate what the page design will look like in more than one browser.

When a client reviews our site layouts, the sites they see look more finished and realistic even while in Photoshop if the layouts are presented within this fake browser interface.

Advantages of working with layered files

Using a program such as Adobe Photoshop for design allows you to create variations of design elements which can be placed on individual layers, to be turned on or off (made visible or invisible) as you evaluate design options. The Layers palette of this layout file allowed us to choose between several navigation designs, whether to use a small or large portrait as the main visual, and the option of making other layout elements visible or not. Working with layers like this will give you more flexibility and make it easier to try different combinations of various design elements. Client changes are relatively quick and easy if you keep a layered file of your layout as a backup.

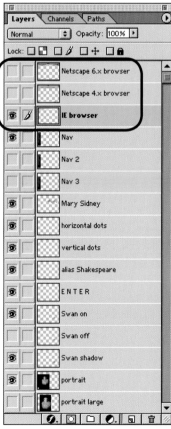

Notice that the Layers palette contains several browser layers that enable us to simulate what our layout will look like in various browser. We keep two different layered Photoshop documents as templates to use when designing web page layouts: one document is 640 x 480 pixels and contains various browser types on separate layers; the other document is 800 x 600 pixels and contains similar layers. Sometimes a client has a specific request that a certain browser be considered, and we add it to our Layers palette.

Love those layers

Inevitably, either you or the client will want to make changes to the initial layouts. Once again, this technique of designing within an image editing program comes in handy. After the client approves the design, the layered Photoshop document serves as our main source file, where we can return to make changes much more easily and quickly than if we had designed the sample site in HTML code.

A layered Photoshop source file may contain a very large number of layers by the end of a project. We sometimes make a copy of the file and eliminate some of the unnecessary layers, **but we always keep the original file,** just in case.

When we show a client the design variations, we verbally explain our design decisions to help prevent design-uncertainty from the client later on. If the client knows that your design decisions are based upon good judgment rather than arbitrary flights of fancy, doubts about the validity of the design will be minimized.

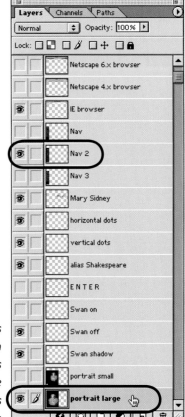

The ability to easily experiment with design changes is a powerful feature of robust image editing programs. To alter this layout, we turned on a different navigation layer, a new background color layer, and the large portrait layer.

We place variations of page elements on individual layers. This allows us to evaluate different design versions with a few mouse clicks.

Source file management

We like to create separate Photoshop files for the home page and for a typical interior page. These two page types usually look slightly different, because the home page serves not only as a way to navigate through the site, but also as an introduction to the site. Most interior pages have a similar, consistent look to aid in site identification, familiarity, and ease of page navigation, even though they usually have slight design variations from the home page.

If we want to design other distinctive pages, we create *another* Photoshop source file. Using separate files for various layouts is easier and less confusing than trying to use one huge Photoshop file with an unreasonably large number of layers.

If a design goes through too many variations and the number of layers becomes hard to handle, we save the source file with a new name, then delete or merge as many layers as possible. If we need one of those deleted layers later, we can return to the original source file.

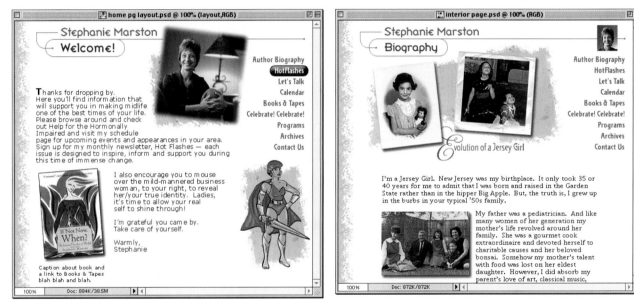

We created a layered Photoshop source file for the home page layout.

This is a separate layered Photoshop source file for secondary pages.

Breaking the rules

There are exceptions to the sizing rule, of course. If you've identified your target audience as one that has large monitors, you could design around a larger format and not be concerned with how your site looks on smaller monitors. Or if you're designing a corporate intranet site which is accessible only to the target audience, you can design around the size limitations of the monitors being used on the intranet network.

Section Two: 2 Plan that Site

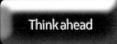

Think ahead

My cat could've built that website. In his sleep.
With one paw tied behind his back.

—Web developer discussing
   the sophistication of a website

Design is Not the First Step

Design may be the fun part, but it's not the first step on the web development journey. To do it right, you've got to do your homework and build a foundation for your concept.

Make a plan

At the beginning of a web project, sometimes you just want to dive in and start designing the home page before anything else. You've got so many creative ideas just waiting to be unleashed on this project—what could possibly be more important?

As tempting as it may be, *design is not the first step in this process.* Before you create the visuals, you need to create a plan.

A solid plan is the secret to any effective web site. If you take the time to consider a few things beforehand, you'll save yourself loads of time in reworking later. The planning process will allow you to gain the knowledge to create not only a great-looking site, but one that is highly usable and is right for the target audience. It's as simple as educating yourself and your team about the client and the people who will be using the site. If you are first able to understand those two groups and what motivates them, you'll be prepared to create a site that works well for everyone.

So, what does this plan actually look like? In our experience, it usually takes the form of a **written document** that describes our own understanding of the project combined with our recommendations for the site. It contains an overview of the categories and pages to be built and a visual diagram of the site architecture (see Chapter 7). It describes exactly what features the site will have, how many pages it will contain, and how much it will cost to develop.

Depending upon whom you ask, this document might be referred to as the "proposal," "contract," or "specification" ("spec"). In many ways it's like a recipe or blueprint for the project.

The process of creating the site specification will allow you and your collaborators to focus on necessary details apart from design and prepare for the project ahead. It also serves as **an agreement** between yourself and the client so both sides have a common understanding of what will and will not be included for the quoted price.

We recommend that you **bill the client** for the planning phase and the resulting specification document (spec) on an hourly basis, separate from your bid for the actual development process. The reason for this is simple—it's darn near impossible to accurately price the project before a comprehensive plan is created. A detailed spec will allow you to knowledgeably prepare a fair bid based on the true scope of the project and the number of hours you believe it will take to complete.

If the client chooses not to accept your bid, they keep the spec, you keep your money, and everyone is happy.

Planning is one of the most valuable aspects of web development, so be sure that you charge your clients for your time and effort—a good specification is worth every penny!

Before you can actually write the specification, you'll need to roll up your sleeves and do some homework to learn about your client and their customers.

But first...

Educate yourself

Take the time to educate yourself about the site before you begin. **The most effective web designer is an informed web designer.**

Keep in mind that in most cases when you're designing a web site, you're probably not the typical user of that site. Based on limited information, you may try to *imagine* what an appropriate solution would be, but without understanding who the audience is or what they want you'd just be making an uneducated guess. Just as you bring your design expertise to every project you undertake, you also bring your biases, opinions, preconceptions, and misconceptions.

Research

Research is the best way to prevent your personal biases from taking the design in the wrong direction. The design should be heavily influenced by the needs of the *target audience,* tempered with the *client's* wishes and goals.

Do some of your own market research and you may find out things that your client didn't even know about their customers concerning their web habits and preferences.

First of all, **get a feel for the target market.** Read your client's company literature and review their print materials. Look at the competitors' sites and see how they address the audience. Your research may tell you what you *don't* want to do as often as it points you in the right direction.

If possible, talk to people who are or could be **potential users** of the site and find out what's important to them. What kind of information do they need most?

What kind of images do they respond to? What colors work for them? Are there similar sites that they like? If you involve a few people at this early stage, they will be a valuable resource later on when you begin to design. Their feedback can identify potential interface problems and help ensure the site works correctly. But more about that on page 89, "Usability."

Don't forget your clients

Learn about your clients' design preferences. Often they have subjective likes and dislikes that will influence your design. Clients may tell you they can't stand the color yellow or they absolutely love pages that use the Arial typeface. You may not always agree with their preferences or quirks, but it's your responsibility to either get them to see things your way or find a way to interpret and accommodate their wishes in a way that makes both of you look good.

Keep in mind that clients often have very good ideas. A helpful exercise is to ask your clients about their favorite web sites and *why* they like them.

If clients don't have much hands-on web experience, it's not uncommon for them to approach the site design from a print perspective. You will need to educate them about the practical limitations of the web medium and how it differs from print. Help them develop an appreciation for the elements of effective web design.

Talk with your clients about their goals for the site and what their target audience expects. *Make sure they understand the difference between what* **they** *want and what the* **audience** *needs.* Your job is to convince your client that for their web site, it's in their best interest to give their *customers* what they want and need.

In the end, it is *their* web site and they need to feel good about the final product. How a client feels about their finished web site can largely depend upon how well you listened, educated, and responded to them in the planning phase.

Branding and tie-in with existing identity

Be aware that your client may not be asking you to reinvent the wheel when contracting for your web design services. There may already be an existing corporate identity that they want you to adapt for the web. Sometimes the look you create for the web will define your client's corporate identity, but most of the time, it will need to tie in to the established identity in some way. Logos, typefaces, colors, or shapes can all contribute to making a site look like it's in the same family as the other company materials. Talk with your client and find out their level of openness to incorporating some fresh design ideas into the site, while maintaining the established visual look. The goal is to make a web visitor feel like they are entering a familiar place, with a few well-placed visuals that they may have seen before in a magazine or on TV. If it's a company the public is not familiar with, you'll want to ensure that the web site makes a good introduction and establishes a look that people will see and recognize elsewhere in the future.

Even with an existing brand, by necessity, you will need to create visual elements that are unique to the web such as navigational buttons or spot graphics. These "new" elements can't look tacked on—they need to integrate seamlessly with the established branding mainstays. Make sure that any new typefaces and colors work well with the corporate logo or standard tagline.

Sometimes even the corporate logo, as sacred as it usually is, may need to be applied in a slightly different way than it has been in other media. For example, some logos, while interesting, were never designed to introduce the brand on a home page.

To achieve instant comprehension, the logo may need a supporting graphic or tagline that bears the load of introducing the company name or concept. This is probably not as important for established brands, but for new or lesser-known entities it could mean the difference between a visitor staying to explore or leaving in confusion.

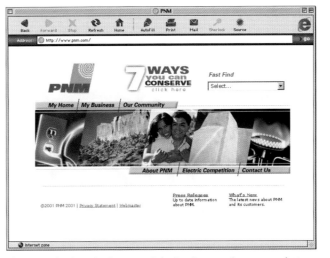

The use of color, the logo, and the background watermark tie this design to the existing corporate identity of PNM.

What would you recommend?

Your client depends on your expertise to recommend features that will make their site more interesting, useful, or profitable. These features could include adding audio or video, animation, a survey, message boards, a database, e-commerce, photography, custom illustration, and the list goes on. (See Chapter 6 for explanations of many of the features you might or might not want to recommend to your client.)

Anything like this that requires special programming or additional content development should be conceived of and recommended during the site planning stage. If you wait to suggest your brilliant idea until development is in full swing, you may jeopardize the deadline or the budget; even worse, the contractor you need to do the work probably won't be available on short notice. Your client may really like the new ideas but become frustrated wondering why you didn't bring them up earlier when they could have been more easily accomplished.

Avoid the trap of adding gratuitous bells and whistles just because they're cool. Historically it's been a weakness of web designers to become enamored of the new technology of the month and want to try it out on the first victim, er, customer they can find. Their enthusiasm is admirable, but many of these new, cool technologies are best left to experimental projects. You may be able to sell a trendy, yet ultimately useless, feature to an inexperienced client, but you'd be doing them a disservice and throwing away their money.

Every feature on a web page should support the overall goals of the site. It shouldn't be too hard to determine what those features are if you clearly understand your client's goals and the needs of their customers. Of course if your client has a burning desire to enhance their image through some gratuitous, cutting-edge web technology, then go full throttle and consider yourself lucky that you could help them accomplish that goal.

Knowing all the pitfalls, if a special web feature makes sense to you, your client, and their budget, then don't hesitate— it'll probably make for a better site and will be fun to work on as well.

Working with a development team

Many web designers work alone and are quite talented at a variety of sophisticated tasks. Still, there may come a time when a project is simply too complicated or extensive for just one person. At that point, the lone designer may find herself in a team situation and working with several others to complete the project. If you land a job with a web firm or advertising agency you will, by necessity, need to understand how to work within a team. The team may be comprised of people with titles like account executive, project manager, copywriter, site architect, content manager, programmer, and quality assurance manager.

In Chapter 8 you'll find a detailed description of how a team works together. For now, keep in mind that only the simplest of web sites are created by the lone designer, so you might want to start cultivating relationships with others in your area who can help fill the needs of your clients.

You may need a programmer

As a web designer and project coordinator, you may be occasionally asked to take on a project that requires some skills you don't possess. Back-end programming is the most common example of a skill that most designers don't possess. This includes the ability to add features that allow a site to communicate with a database or conduct credit card transactions, or that enables the client to make their own page updates without knowing HTML.

In these situations, make sure you find a **capable programmer** to partner with *before you start anything.* The programmer will likely have several valuable, cost-saving ideas about how to plan and build the site. Besides, you'll need to know how much they will charge and how long it will take them to complete their work.

The very worst thing you could do

is wait to contact the programmer until you've gone down the path of bidding the job and creating the pages. At that point they may be unavailable to do the project, be more expensive than your bid allows, or won't be able to finish the project before your deadline. They probably will even tell you that the pages you've laboriously built have to be reworked to accommodate the back-end features.

Decide on a host

If the proposed web site requires high-end features such as e-commerce or database integration, your programmer might also need to recommend a web hosting solution appropriate for the type of site you're producing. Sites that provide credit card transactions or database access may require a different hosting server than ones that contain only HTML pages.

Guidelines for selecting a web hosting solution:

Along with your client, you should determine:

1. How much traffic is anticipated?
2. How much can the client afford per month?
3. What is the level of service and reliability needed?
4. What hosting environment does your programmer recommend (UNIX or Windows NT?)
5. What kind of data needs to be logged for site traffic reporting?

The technical influence

What influences and informs a design

As a designer, your job (and hopefully your passion) is to create and communicate. The quality of the web sites you create is influenced by an unlimited set of variables, unique to you and your design and life experience. This is the basis of your individuality and unique design perspective. It shows in your style and the choices your make in your designs.

While your design **influences** are more or less innate, any truly effective web design must be **informed** by several conscious considerations. Among these are the technical limitations and opportunities of HTML, the need to tie-in with existing branding identity, and (not least) accommodating the needs, wishes, and personalities of other people.

Learn to compromise

From one perspective, you might say that the path to arriving at the most appropriate web interface is marked by a series of **compromises.** There are compromises with your client, the audience of end-users, and the technology.

If you accept the notion that your original design ideas are always the best solution, then each time you have to compromise for whatever reason, you may feel that something is lost in the process. But if you think about it further, you'll realize that in letting go of your preconceptions and taking in other points of view, you actually get closer to a more appropriate solution.

While there's always a danger of diminishing a great design by letting "too many cooks" get involved, you don't have to let that happen. Under your expert direction, you'll find that these "compromises" aren't really losses— they're informed choices that result in a stronger interface design.

Technical influences

The web medium offers so many possibilities for interactive communication, often going way beyond what is possible with print. Unlike the printed page, the web isn't one-way communication. Web users can often interact with the content of a site, with the ability to easily search and find the precise information they are looking for, and sometimes to add their own ideas and comments. Web pages can be colorful or muted, fun, sophisticated, or edgy, and visually convey the same range of feelings as any effective printed piece.

As good as the web is, it does have its limits, forcing a designer to consider things they would never otherwise have to think about with a printed page. When designing a web interface, you'll need to work within the technical realities of several areas: HTML, bandwidth, browsers, and platforms. Each of these factors should influence your design decisions because if you ignore any one of them, you run the risk that the site's message will not reach a portion of the intended audience. Your goal is to create a site that will work consistently and perform well with most any browser, computer configuration, or Internet connection speed.

HTML

Since it's the glue that holds every web page together, it's important to be very familiar with HTML and know its strengths and weaknesses. By itself, HTML does a good job of defining the basic layout of your web page and displaying images and text, but it doesn't do it as precisely as you may want. Plain HTML pages may display slightly or even dramatically differently depending upon the browser or computer used.

If you need more control to position page elements down to the pixel level, specify point size and leading for fonts, and other picky details, you'll also need to become familiar with DHTML, CSS,

and JavaScript. The addition of these scripting languages will allow you to overcome some of the inherent shortcomings of plain old vanilla HTML.

While creating a design, consider how it could be efficiently built with the technologies at hand. There are many fantastic design possibilities that will work perfectly fine in HTML, but there can also be designs that don't lend themselves at all to the web format. Sure, you can achieve most any visual look on a web page if you try hard enough, but it may cost you in either browser compatibility or download time (as explained in the following section of this chapter).

The browser influence

Browsers

Designing consistent pages for 4.0 level browsers and up is much easier than for their 3.0 and earlier distant ancestors. Beginning at the 4.0 level, Internet Explorer, Netscape, and America Online all provide some support for DHTML and cascading style sheets (CSS, see Chapter 19). You will be free to designate layers, pixel-level positioning, and use CSS to control your type. You'll have the ability to make your pages behave like you want them to.

If, however, you find that your client or the target audience needs 3.0 browser compatibility, be prepared to make lots of compromises in your design. These earlier browsers don't support layers or style sheets, and don't even think about pixel-level positioning. In this situation, the easiest thing will be to tailor your design to the 3.0 level so that the site will (theoretically) look good in any browser, old or new.

If your client has extra money to spare, you may want to convince them to create two sites, one compatible with 3.0 browsers and one that takes advantage of the advanced 4.0 or greater features. It's a challenge to maintain two versions of a site, so think hard before suggesting it. You may just want to try talking your client out of supporting 3.0 altogether, because it's a real pain in the you-know-what!

Common 3.0 browser limitations include:

- Poor margin control: In Netscape, you can't set your margins to zero, so there will always be an eight-pixel offset between the edge of the browser window and where your page content begins.

- No cascading style sheets: You're pretty well stuck with the basic HTML relative type sizes. Be prepared for your HTML text to look bigger on Windows computers and smaller on the Macintosh.

- No layers: Don't have your heart set on achieving any complex graphic alignments; you may be able to pull it off on one browser but not the others.

- Limited JavaScript support: 3.0 browsers do support JavaScript, but not to the degree that current browsers do. You may see some JavaScript error messages.

- Slower page loads: Older browsers often aren't as snappy at loading a page compared to the newer models.

- Bugginess: Older browsers still contain bugs that newer releases have since corrected. Be aware and tell your client that there will be some display problems or other quirks that are not fixable.

Older browsers aside, even the newest browsers tend to have their own quirks and may display pages differently from one to the next. Sigh. It's all part of the fun of being a web designer.

Printability

Some clients will want their web pages to be printable so that users can retain a hard copy. While this is possible, browsers are notoriously bad at faithfully printing web pages. Web pages are optimized for the computer monitor, not a printed page. Usually, the more interesting or complex the design is, the more difficult it is to print. Often, type will be cut off and some graphics will not print at all. You may have to make your page narrower than you would like in order to allow it to print correctly within an 8½ x 11 sheet. By default, browsers do not print background graphics, so the resulting printout may look a little weird. Framesets are a particular problem—most users don't know how to print an individual frame, so they will inevitably be confused when the wrong one emerges from their printer.

If reliable printing from a site is very important, you may want to suggest the creation of alternate printable pages for some sections. This can be designated by a "Print this Page" button that links a page from the screen-friendly version to a more sparse print-friendly version. This is more expensive for the client, but it does solve the problem.

The bottom line is: Don't expect too much from a browser printout, and be sure to advise your client of this fact.

Bandwidth

Since the beginning of the web, the pursuit of quick load times has shaped the way pages are built. Web designers learned long ago that if a page takes too long to download, people won't wait around. Slow dial-up connections have made it necessary to keep graphic file sizes small and HTML code efficient. Even with the current popularity of broadband connections like DSL and cable modems, it's still important to keep your file sizes small. People are impatient—they want instant gratification and will rarely wait longer than fifteen seconds or so for a page to load unless they know what they're in for. When designing, don't choose a path that will result in a beautiful page that takes five minutes to load. Not many people will ever see it.

There's a certain satisfaction when you create a page that looks complex, but takes mere seconds to load. Lots of designers can create a nice-looking, but slow-loading web site—being able to make it efficient and attractive is the mark of a good web designer.

Plug-ins

You may decide to include some cool features on your site like streaming video, audio, or even Flash animation. That's all well and good, but remember that these features may require the end user to take additional time (and expertise) to download a plug-in or helper application. It's not necessarily a bad thing, but be aware that many people are not willing to download additional software to see bells and whistles, cool or not. A good rule of thumb when using these features is to make them optional.

The platform influence

We hate to burst your bubble, but if you thought the list of incompatibilities ended with the browser software, think again. Differences in computer hardware and operating systems will also keep you up late at night compensating for visual inconsistencies on your pages.

Monitor sizes

Along with variances between web browser software, you should also be aware that web pages display differently depending upon the computer they're viewed on.

The most common computer variable is screen size. Monitors come in many sizes from the small 14" screens, all the way to 22" and even beyond. As we discussed in Chapter 4, 17" monitors are the most common size these days with a screen resolution of 800 x 600 pixels. If you design for the 800 x 600 space, remember that a small percentage of people will either have to scroll left and right to see the entire page on their 640 x 480 screens, while others on 1024 x 768 monitors (or above) will see massive amounts of dead space surrounding the design (if the browser window is maximized).

While it is possible to program certain pages to expand or contract to fit the browser window, many designers prefer to stay with a fixed width. Doing this preserves the integrity of their design and keeps text line lengths from being too long to read easily.

There is no perfect design solution to accommodate all monitor sizes, but if you stay with the 800 x 600 ratio, your interface will be easily viewable by the vast majority of your target audience.

Gamma: Mac vs. Windows

Have you ever noticed that the same web pages displayed on Windows and Macintosh computers don't look the same? If you compare side by side, Windows pages are darker, Mac pages are lighter. The reason for this is that each operating system has a different saturation or gamma setting: Windows is preset to 2.2 and the Mac is 1.8.

While this isn't a big problem, you should be aware that this will affect your color choices. Photographs that look just fine on a Mac may be dark and muddy on a Windows PC. Images created on a PC could look dandy, but just plain washed out on a Mac. This goes for flat colors, too.

You'll need to compensate for this discrepancy by viewing your colors and images in both environments and adjusting to find a middle ground. Photoshop, ImageReady, and Fireworks all allow you to preview your graphics in a simulated mode that shows what they will look like in either a Mac or Windows monitor. Also see Chapter 10 about testing your web site.

The web-safe palette

Another technical consideration in web development is the browser-safe palette of 216 colors. These rather limited color choices represent the colors known to display accurately and consistently across computer platforms, in browsers, on 256-color monitors and above.

Colors outside of this palette may shift, sometimes dramatically, when viewed under different software and hardware configurations. Photoshop and Fireworks include this 216-color palette with the program and make it easy to select a web-safe color for flat color areas of a page.

Photographs are less likely to color shift because there are so many colors involved, and thus are exempt from the browser-safe color palette rule. As time goes on and more computers can display 16.7 million colors or more, the browser-safe palette may become unnecessary. For the moment, it's still a good idea to play it safe and use these colors in your designs.

This screenshot was taken on a Mac: resolution of 1024 x 768, millions of colors, browser window size of 800 x 600. Notice the text is smaller than on the PC, the navigation links can't even be read, and the images are lighter and brighter.

This screenshot was taken on a PC: resolution of 1024 x 768, millions of colors, browser window size of 800 x 600. This was obviously designed on a PC because the text size is optimized for a Windows machine. The overall look of the page is darker.

Fonts

On a purely technical level, web pages are capable of displaying any typeface you throw at them. Just include the name in the font tag or style sheet and it'll show up on the page in all its glory. Simple, right?

Yes, but the problem remains that most folks out there don't have all the same typefaces on their computers as you do. When you specify an HTML text block to display in Super Colossal Extended, it may look fine on your screen, but the rest of the world will see the usual Times New Roman (or whatever their defaults are set to).

Of course, you can use any typeface in the world if you turn it into a **graphic** and place it on the page. But the only way to make sure everyone has a similar look to any **HTML text** is to use fonts that are common to most every computer out there when building your web site.

The most common fonts found on the average computer are the familiar Times New Roman (serif), Arial (sans serif) and Courier New (monospaced). If you specify any of these on your page, nearly everyone will see them in the same consistent (but somewhat boring) way. The popularity of the Internet

Explorer browser has added a few other fonts to the mix. If you have Explorer installed on your computer, it's a good bet that you'll find Georgia (serif), Verdana (sans serif), Trebuchet (sans serif) and several others from that package. It's usually a safe bet that most people will also have these IE fonts installed and if you include them in your design, your type will display in the way you intended.

See Chapter 18 for a chart of cross-platform fonts and suggestions for specifying fonts that will maximize their chances of showing up clearly.

This page uses three fonts (ITC Tremor, Frutiger Light, and the ornament is a character in the font ITC Bodoni Ornaments). If you have these fonts loaded on your computer, this page will look just like you see it here.

Anyone who does not happen to have those same three fonts loaded will see the text in their default font (Georgia, in this case.)

Usability

Find a balance

Usability, as it applies to the web interface, has been a much-debated topic in recent years. In the search for the most usable interface, the extreme viewpoint seems to dictate a bland, vanilla-flavored web environment—highly usable, easy to understand, but devoid of any visual character. The opposite end of the debate favors the design aesthetic over all else, promoting complex, breathtaking pages at the expense of such practicalities as intuitive navigation and clear communication. While both sides make valid points, we tend to favor the pursuit of balance. Finding the right mix of creativity and user-friendliness is the approach that will best serve the end-user and will make for an enjoyable web experience. So, the question remains, how do you go about finding that balance?

Do your homework

Designing a site to be attractive and usable requires you to study how the real-world users of the site will actually interact with it and how they will most easily comprehend the message. Based on that knowledge, you then arrange, or rearrange, the page elements accordingly.

To make a site highly usable is the ultimate show of respect for the end user. You're putting their convenience and comprehension above all else, perhaps above even your own visual ideas. It's like saying, "I've taken the time to understand you well enough to know what you really need to do here and this design will save you some time and effort."

People love sites that are easy to use and they keep coming back to them. Unfortunately, there are enough convoluted web interface designs out there to make the good ones stand out.

To begin your usability research, talk to people who are or could be potential users of the site and find out what features they think are important. It's critical to test your initial design ideas and sketches with as many people as possible to see how well they understand what you're trying to communicate. Often what is plainly obvious to you can be confusing to uninitiated users. If someone has to spend more than a few seconds trying to understand how to use your site or determining what the site is about, then there's a problem that requires you to make some modifications. You should keep getting feedback and modifying your design until you're satisfied that most people will know how to use the site without an instruction manual!

The audience knows best

Unless you perform usability testing, your target audience won't have much to say about your design choices before the site is launched. For that reason, there's a danger of forgetting the most important person in all of this, the web customer. This is the person who will ultimately decide whether the site works correctly and communicates its message. You and the client would do well to listen to the web audience feedback and make any necessary changes. If your client doesn't listen to their customers and their needs, there's a competitor who will.

If you have to change your design to make it more usable, so what? It may be hard to swallow, but it's more important for people to be able to use a site easily than it is for you to win a design award. While it *is* possible to do both, always keep the interests of the end user in mind.

For large web projects, you may want to convince your client to allocate part of the budget for usability testing. Thorough testing takes time, but if done correctly (see Chapter 10) will be more than worth the money spent to do it.

You may want to even consider bringing in an outside consultant or company to conduct the testing for you. In recent years, web usability has become something of a specialized pursuit and there are many knowledgeable specialists out there who can assist in obtaining the feedback you need.

It's important to remember that when you help end users by creating an intuitive web environment, you are also helping your client build a good relationship with their customers and supporting their business goals.

A great book we highly recommend is *Don't Make Me Think, A Common Sense Approach to Web Usability,* by Steve Krug, published by New Riders. In fact, every web designer should read it and follow Steve's advice.

Working with clients

No two expectations are exactly the same

Unless you're one of those lucky designers doing web development to please yourself, you've probably come to the realization that you need to work with clients. The premise seems simple: you design a web site for someone, he pays you, everyone is happy. But unfortunately, it's often not that easy. Between those basic steps, plenty of misunderstandings can occur unless you take precautions. You need to establish limits, because your client most certainly will not.

For the most part, web clients are decent, understanding people. They've decided they need a web site and were smart enough to select you as their designer. But—in your role as a designer and project coordinator— you need to prevent mismatched expectations. It's common that *you* will understand the scope of the project to be one thing, while your *client* believes it is quite another—

Client vs. designer expectations

usually bigger and grander than their budget allows. If you allow this mismatch to continue through the project, you'll likely have an unpleasant surprise at the end. Your once-happy relationship with your client can deteriorate into a prolonged and unhappy argument.

In the absence of defined parameters, clients usually make assumptions. Something like, "I see my site has only 20 pages—I assumed there would be at least 75!" In situations like this, you will almost always lose time, money, or your temper.

Clients will be subjective

As mentioned before, there are many useful principles of design that, if applied, will help you make the right decisions and end up with a balanced page layout. Still, the process remains a highly subjective undertaking by any measure. The question is always there: "Will the client like it?" Welcome to the one of the great mysteries of the design process—client reaction.

There's just no way to quantify or anticipate the exact emotional response people will have to any given design. Usually they either like it or they don't. Or they like some parts of it and despise others. To make matters worse, their dislike may be vague or even irrational. "I don't know what it is, but I just don't like it," your client may say as you feel your blood pressure begin to rise. But before you lose your cool, remember that this is all a typical part of the process to determine the best design solution.

The fact is, clients will *always* like some things and dislike others. While you have little control over that, you *can* guide the process to a satisfactory solution. If you find that your client has issues with your proposed design concepts, identify and focus on the things the client does like and try to understand why. You may get some insight about their design preferences. Try to determine if it's a subjective, personal opinion thing ("I don't like goats or green neckties") or if it's related to external communication ("I'm concerned that our customers won't understand the photo of the goat in a green necktie").

The more you discuss the design with your client, the more likely it is that you will learn how to create a solution that will make them happy. However, if you discover that what they really want is undoubtedly the worst idea you've ever heard, then you may have to resort to persuasion.

That's when it comes in handy to be able to express design concepts verbally, as Robin talks about in *The Non-Designer's Design Book*. If you can't express in words what makes a particular concept succeed or fail, you and the client will simply have a tug-of-war of "I like it this way" and "Well, I like it that way." Good luck.

Selling your ideas

Most designers we know don't think of themselves as sales people, but during the design process you do need to know how to "sell" your ideas. Usually your client has seen and likes your design style before you begin work on their project, but that doesn't mean they won't make their opinions known when they see your initial ideas. If they challenge your choices, you need to know how to stand your ground and convince them why your way is the best.

Remember that your client most likely doesn't know the things you do about creating an effective site. In theory that's the reason they came to you in the first place. Yet, despite their absence of web knowledge and experience, you may encounter certain clients who will forcefully tell you what their site needs to do and how it should look, even if it contradicts what you know to be right for the end user.

A common situation involves a client who has no experience with the web, but has worked extensively with print. This could work against you if they try to apply their print design logic to your web interface. What a printed piece has to accomplish is quite different from the function of a good web site, but to a client, they may only judge its worth by the design appearance, the aesthetics, and overlook the usability factors.

As the designer and project coordinator, it is your responsibility to educate clients about the limitations and possibilities of the web medium. They'll need to hear why the site should be usable instead of just attractive. Explain the underlying design principles of your layout and how your choices support their overall goals. Remind them that you both want to create an effective site.

You may not always win the battle, but it's important that you articulate your position and at least try to make your client come around to your point of view.

Making yourself happy

Lastly, don't forget yourself. You deserve to be happy with the final product. You've worked and probably reworked the interface design until everyone was either satisfied or worn out. External factors may occasionally get you down, but the end result should be something you're proud of. If you stand your ground and are confident of what you know, then it's likely you'll be allowed to create a site that pleases everyone, including yourself.

PUT IT IN WRITING

It is clearly the designer's responsibility to manage the clients' expectations. This can be accomplished by taking the time to explain your process and describe exactly what you will do and *not* do for them. This meeting should be accompanied by a **written document** that details the responsibilities of both the designer and the client. You'll be very happy you took the time to do this when you encounter some of the situations listed below. We suggest you create this document even for (or especially for) pro bono work or web sites for friends.

Common misunderstandings can be about:

1. How many pages will be produced.
2. When the site will be completed.
3. How much the site will cost.
4. When payment is due. (On bid projects, we like to ask for ⅓ up front, ⅓ after the interface design has been approved, and the final ⅓ prior to site launch.)
5. The number of different design ideas the client will see.
6. Which browsers will be supported.
7. The degree of content design on individual pages (number of photographs, any custom illustrations, text formatting, etc.).
8. The extent of changes the client can make after the site is finished.
9. "Feature Creep" is not free. (e.g., "I know it's not in the plan, but can we add just one more . . . .").
10. Assumptions about what features will be included in the initial site development bid. ("I thought search engine registration was included!")
11. The extent to which the client is allowed to rewrite their text (the text they provided) after pages have been built.
12. Forgetfulness. ("Oh, I don't remember hearing you say that e-commerce wasn't included in the price . . . .")
13. When the client's text, photos, and other content is due.
14. When a client is scheduled to provide feedback to a design.
15. How much work is involved in "small" things. ("Just paste one of those little 'Submit' buttons on the form.")
16. Who is responsible for proofreading the final pages, and what is the procedure and responsiblities for fixing grammatical and spelling problems after the project is complete.
17. How printable the web pages will be.
18. Who is going to update and maintain the site, and how often.

Provide for a bail-out

It doesn't happen very often, but there is the possibility that after you spend 30 or 40 hours on a design concept, you and the client realize it is impossible to work together. For this potential situation, make it very clear, in writing, how to proceed in such a case. For instance, the client might say, "I haven't gotten anything usable from you!" And you might say, "Well, that's because you are mean and rude and negative and Athena herself couldn't make you happy!" You want to keep the ⅓ deposit because you spent 40 hours trying to please this obnoxious rat, and he wants his ⅓ deposit back because he "didn't get anything." Your fee for having created work the client won't use is actually called a "kill fee" and is very typical in other businesses, like freelance writing. Having it in writing earlier will not entirely solve the problem, but it will at least give both of you a place from which to mediate the issue.

Design tips

Here are a few tips to consider when you actually begin work on the design. There is more about the design process in Chapter 9 (as well as every other chapter, of course), but this should whet your appetite until you get there.

Some design concept pointers

The **home page** is not a magazine cover, but in part, it needs to function as one. It's not a table of contents, but it does need to present an overview. Find the balance between the aesthetic and the functional aspects.

Every element and arrangement on a web page should have a **purpose.** If you can't easily justify something in your design, then it probably shouldn't be there.

Create a **visual hierarchy** on your page so that you lead the user through the content in order of most important to least. It's often useful to have a dominant graphic on the page that provides an important visual cue as to what the site is about. The visitor should be able to instantly understand the visual hierarchy without having to study the page.

The **navigation links** are important, so don't shove them to the sidelines. You'll need to work to integrate them into the overall design so that they can be easily recognized and used. In fact, you should consider that the navigation is the most essential part of your site.

Avoid visual clutter. Simplicity on a web page is a virtue (compare Google.com to Excite.com). Too many elements can create a confusing presentation and overwhelm the user.

Avoid animated or conceptual introductory pages that precede the actual home page. Unless there is a very good reason to do this, forcing the users to sit through a mini-presentation with flying type or a techno soundtrack can be a frustrating barrier that prevents them from reaching the information they seek. Many may even leave before they reach the home page. And often they don't want to come back again because they know they'll have to sit through it again.

If a home page must **scroll,** the initial viewable area should constitute a complete design concept. Don't make a user scroll to fully see and understand your design. Put the most important information in the first screen view and leave the rest below the scroll.

It's all about expectations

You've got a new client who wants a web site. Where do you start?

Your client may be a total stranger, a friend, or a even a relative. Before either of you has made a commitment of money or time, there are several critically important things that should be discussed, such as budget, deadlines, and who will be responsible for certain aspects of the project. The client needs to realize that official approvals at various stages of the project means that subsequent changes will affect the budget. Spell out in detail exactly what pages will be created, what content will be provided, what content you'll create, and what technology enhancements and special features are going to be included (original illustrations, animated GIFs, interactive forms, e-commerce, rollovers, image swaps, Java, JavaScript, Flash, database integration, etc.). You may need estimates from a programmer or other specialist. All of this information will help you to develop a realistic estimate.

If you're new to web development and you've been a designer in the print media world, estimate your hours as if it were a print project, then triple them (at least). Not because web design is more valuable, but because it's more problematical and less predictable. And it's the only chance you'll have of ever coming close to covering your time spent on the project.

If you have an amicable relationship with the client, you'll be tempted to forego this time-consuming and potentially stressful conversation, assuming that everyone will be nice and understanding and willing to work things out as they occur.

Wrong.

And it won't be a issue of whether you or the client is unreasonable— it's all about expectations. Unless you spell out *exactly* what the expectations are on both sides, a conflict is inevitable.

While you're working away on design and layout and creating HTML pages, you'll assume that the client's expectations are similar to yours. The client assumes yours match his.

Wrong again.

Half-way through the project is a bad time for both of you to realize how wrong you both are. The only way to avoid a conflict is to decide *at the very beginning* what will and will not be included for the proposed budget.

- Make sure your client contact is the final decision maker. You can sometimes be taken in the wrong direction if you deal with a go-between employee and not the Big Boss with final design approval authority.

- Decide what will happen when new or unanticipated pages have to be added later that weren't included in the original budget, usually called a "change order": a per page price or an hourly fee may work for simple additions.

- To meet the project deadline, plan a design and production schedule that incorporates intermediate deadlines through various phases of the project.

- Get signed client approval at the completion of each phase of the project so that it's clear what changes can be charged for.

- Set deadlines to receive materials and content from the client.

- Set dates for client approvals.

- Explain to the client that failing to meet their deadlines means rearrangement of the planned schedule because other clients' schedules can't be changed.

- Decide who will be responsible for proofreading pages. The client may prefer to do it rather than pay for your time. (If the client does it, we guarantee they're going to want to make editing changes; decide long before this point how that will be handled.)

- Your bid should include time for testing the site in various browsers and on different platforms at several times during the project.

- Agree on a payment schedule. Clients who have worked with print designers and advertising agencies have historically been conditioned to think they have 60 to 90 days after a project is completed before payment is necessary. A common approach among web development firms is to request a down payment of one-third to one-half at the beginning of the project, another payment upon approval and completion of the design phase, and the remainder due before the final files are uploaded to a server.

- Agree on a plan for maintenance. Most web sites need some sort of updating occasionally, if not constantly. An hourly fee for maintenance may be arranged, or a monthly retainer fee may be an option if maintenance is expected to be a substantial, ongoing part of the project. Some clients want to maintain and update their sites in-house. This could mean that providing some training is necessary.

- Even if the in-house web maintenance person is experienced, you may need to add consulting time to the budget to familiarize a maintenance person with the site.

It's better to work through all these details at the *start* of the project, even if the client is a good friend. Perhaps we should say "especially" if the client is a good friend.

When the client is presented with a realistic picture of what will be required to create the site he envisions, he may have second thoughts about moving forward. Or he may decide to go with the "nephew who does web sites" type of solution. Either way you'll remain friends and probably get to hear some good nephew stories later.

We practically guarantee:

The client is going to want more on their web site than they originally thought.

It's going to take you longer than you think to create the site.

The client is not going to understand why it costs so much.

Pre-design checklist

This is an encapsulation of the pre-design work you should cover before you start designing actual pages.

- Explain your approach to the development process and payment terms to the client before starting any work on the project.

- Research your client and their customers. Talk with your clients, learn all about them, their existing branding, what they want to achieve with this web site, etc.

- Get very specific with the client about the site: do they want printable pages, motion graphics, browser compatibility back to 2.0, etc.

- Learn what all the available options are that can help your clients achieve their goals with this site. If you're going to need programmers, contact them now.

- Choose a web hosting server. Together with your programmer, make sure the host can accommodate any special features and technologies in your site plan.

- Understand your audience and the usability factors that will make a difference to their comprehension of the site.

- Technical factors will influence your design decisions. Learn how browsers, bandwidth, and computer platforms will have an impact on the ultimate design of your site.

- Anticipate the need for assistance on the project. If you think you'll have to enlist the help of a programmer, HTML producer, or even a full development team, book their time early so they'll be available when you need them.

- Set your client's expectations prior to embarking on the design process. Agree upon the scope of the project beforehand to avoid any misunderstandings later on.

- Make a detailed plan, a written specification document that describes the project, categories, pages, features, etc. Have the client sign off on the plan. Remember, creating the plan is billable work!

Enhanced Functionality

Web sites have obviously come a long way in a short time. Often, the best solution is still a simple one: text, images, links. But the possibilities exist for enhancing the communication with a wide variety of features and techniques. In this chapter, we'll explain the most common enhancements that you might want to offer a client. And we'll give you some ideas to consider for determining whether or not you need a particular feature, plus where to go to get it done if you can't do it yourself.

Techno rampage

If you're developing a non-commercial web site, the need for enhanced functionality may not exist. Many commercial sites are exceptionally attractive and informative without using specialized features and sophisticated programming.

However, the fact remains that some sites can benefit immensely from the growing number of existing and developing interactive web features and technologies. Amazing things are happening in the back rooms of the Internet as engineers and visionaries plan how the Internet will work in the future. Just about the time most of us become aware of Future Technology 1.0, those goofy, wacky programmer folks are working out the bugs in 4.0.

You should have an awareness of the mainstream enhancements that are most common so that you can recommend them when it's appropriate. To *implement* enhanced functionality in a site, you will most likely need to contract with a specialist who has experience with a particular language or technology.

Any topic in this chapter deserves an entire book (at least one, if not more), so we can only hope to give you a quick glimpse of each and let you decide which ones may benefit your projects.

Animation

Animation is a fabulous attention-getting technique, whether it's a simple, basic, animated GIF or an amazing Flash movie. The technique you use or recommend will depend on your expertise, the budget, or both. See Chapters 22 and 23 for more details about animation.

Animated GIFs: Animated GIFs are easy to make, and you can become an Animated GIF Master in an hour or two. Especially if you read Chapter 22. This techique usually doesn't send people scrambling to your site to see the animation, but it's very affective for adding a little visual interest or entertainment in a web site.

Large GIF animations are impractical since their raster format is less efficient than Flash's vector format. GIFs are best used as smaller enhancements to a page.

Flash: Macromedia Flash has pretty much set the web world on fire with its fast-loading, visually stunning, vector-based animation effects.

Flash uses a vector format that enables files to be *very* small in file size and thus fast to download. (It can, when needed, also handle raster files, such as GIFs and JPEGs.) With Flash you can create full-screen movies, which were unthinkable just a while ago. You can even create entire sites in Flash.

Amazingly complex animations can be created more easily than most of us would have ever imagined. Even simple animations that enhance the look of navigation can be almost mesmerizing, due to Flash's animation power.

Thanks to the incredible Macromedia software and brilliant user interface, you don't have to be a programmer to learn Flash. However, it's not one of those programs that you'll learn in a day or two. So if you'd like to learn Flash for a project, plan for at least a small learning-curve delay.

Special Flash plug-ins are required so browsers can interpret and display vector data, but all current browsers have the plug-in built in. According to research, a high percentage of people using older browsers have manually downloaded and installed the Flash plug-in; therefore, a high percentage of viewers can see Flash movies, but still not everyone. See more about Flash in Chapter 23.

DHTML: Dynamic HTML can also create animations of a sort by having static images, or even animated GIFs, travel across the screen on a pre-determined path over a specified time frame. Unfortunately, older browsers cannot see DHTML animation at all, and even the newer ones are inconsistent in their display. See Chapter 20.

Watch this bee!

In this DHTML animation, the honey bee on the left flaps his wings and flutters to the right to land on the flower.

Automated features

In today's web site world, any delay in communication gives a negative impression of how important and professional a site may be. Because viewers have become accustomed to instant response and gratification, you might improve a site's image and save yourself a lot of work by implementing a few automated features.

List management: Large and small web sites that harvest information from visitors through submitted forms need a way to manage the responses or to compile email lists of customers. A newsletter site that solicites subscriptions (free or otherwise) often wants to automatically notify e-subscribers of a new issue online, or may even want to automatically send the current issue to subscribers as email or as a PDF (Portable Document Format, a multi-platform file format).

Some small sites with this need compile e-subscriber lists and manually email a newsletter to the list. Larger sites that have large lists need more automation, especially since they often have many kinds of lists and mailings.

Professional programmers are one solution for more complex list management, but you can also pay third-party list management companies to supply the software and server space for list management services. A popular such service is www.SparkList.com. Search the Internet for "list management" (with quotation marks) and you'll find many other options.

Auto-responders: An auto-responder automatically sends an email response to a viewer when they submit an email or a form from your web site. Auto-responders can be very simple, such as an email that says, "Thank you for participating in our survey," which requires only a few minutes to accomplish. They can also be very complex, requiring skilled programmers and an integrated database. For example, if you've ordered products from a web site, you've probably received an email confirmation of the order listing your purchases, the credit card charges, an address verification, and shipping information.

Setting up a simple auto-responder can be easy and free. Most commercial host servers offer POP email addresses, email aliasing, email forwarding, and auto-responder features with a web hosting account. Commonly, once you've signed up for a web hosting package, you'll have web access to something like a "control panel" on the host server which will enable you to configure email and set up multiple auto-responders without any programming knowledge.

A typical auto-responder form looks like this.

Autoresponders:

@urlsinternetcafe.com	File to Send	Reply To	Who to Notify
rattyadvice	thankyou.txt	urlaa@urlsinternetc	url@urlsinternetcaf

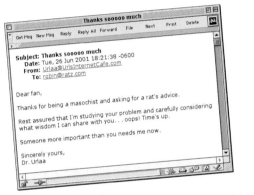

An auto-responder sends out a polite email form message.

The form instructs any mail addressed to "rattyadvice@UrlsInternetCafe.com" to receive an automatic, generic response, such as, "Thank you for your interest." We created and placed that response on the server in our home directory with the rest of our web site files. We typed the name of the response file in the "File to Send" field, added our email address to the "Reply To" field, and entered an alternate email address in the "Who to Notify" field. We can use the web host's Control Panel to change any settings necessary, at any time, from any computer.

Auto-responders help to fulfill the web visitor's expectations of instant communication. Immediacy is one of the things all users have come to expect from web sites, especially commercial sites that are competing for attention.

Chat rooms and guestbooks

Chat rooms, message boards, and forums are web-based discussion software.

Message boards usually can be searched by the date a message was posted.

Forums can be followed by date, the threads of discussion, or the replies and comments concerning a particular topic.

Guestbooks are usually not much more than that: a place to sign in and leave a brief comment.

Live chat rooms are viewed by many people as frivolous entertainment, but they can also be a useful and powerful tool for real-time customer interaction. Businesses large and small can take advantage of enhanced corporate communications by implementing chat capability. And online communities can experience real-time community communication.

Web hosts often offer chat room software that's easy to set up and works well with their particular server. Whether or not chat software is available or not may depend upon the hosting package you've chosen. If you've bought an economical, web-starter package, you may have to upgrade the service to use a chat feature. Most servers count chat data transfer against the amount of data transfer allowed for a specified price—an active chat room can add substantially to that total, which may affect how much your monthly server costs will be.

Third-party chat, message board, and forum software solutions are also available for a fee, but there are also some very nice solutions that are free: Search the Internet for "chat rooms," or ask a programmer for a recommendation.

Some solutions require databases, some are written in Java or PHP. The best solution will depend partially on what works best on your host server. These are some sites to check:

> CGI-Factory.com
> DrB-Software.com
> DigiChat.com
> Phorum.org
> Volano.com

Beware: Unfortunately, this wonderful open communication system is vulnerable to obscene and unkind comments from people who don't have enough to do. For this reason, we hesitate to implement any of these systems unless there's a real benefit involved, such as the potential for gathering or disseminating useful information for a group; for semi-private business communication through a private intranet; or unless password protection is used to provide privacy, exclusivity, and to help ensure politeness and responsibility. But used in the right circumstances, message boards or chat rooms can be great community-building features.

Fill out the fields below to generate a guestbook.cfg file	
Options	**Settings**
Send Mail when someone adds an entry	○ Yes ● No
Use Logging	● Yes ○ No
Link Mail in Guestbook	○ Yes ● No
Type of Separator	○ Line Break ● Paragraph Break
Automatically Return to Guestbook after adding entry	○ Yes ● No
Entry Order of New Entries	● Newest First ○ Newest Last
Send Mail to user who added to Guestbook	○ Yes ● No
Add Line Breaks to comment field	○ Yes ● No
Submit	

Setting up a guestbook for a site can be as simple as choosing "Install guestbook" from the host server's tech support page, then choosing configuration options from a setup window such as this one.

Pop-up menus

Another nifty and relatively easy site enhancement is to add **DHTML pop-up menus** to your navigation. These aren't just eye-candy—they are a valuable visual aid to help users understand the depth of content in a site and to be able to navigate more quickly.

The way they work is simple: when a visitor mouses over a navigational link, a small menu pops up and displays links to all of the pages within that particular section. If they click on a link from the menu, it takes them directly to that page. When they mouse off, it goes away.

Pop-up menus not only facilitate navigation, but they also help reduce visual clutter on a page. They're visible when you need them, but gone when you don't.

From a design and usability standpoint, it's good practice to use them to keep your pages simple yet quite useful. The main thing we like about DHTML pop-up menus is that you can allow users to see all of the link options in a site without leaving the current page.

There are shareware JavaScripts available on the web that can enable pop-up menus, or you can use Macromedia Fireworks 4.0 or later to install and design any variety of pop-up menus. As with any other JavaScript or DHTML, make sure you test your pop-ups in multiple browsers so that they work consistently and reliably on any computer.

Forms

Forms can be simple interactive tools to collect data and provide feedback. Or they can be very complex, involving e-commerce, credit card verification and approval, inventory status reporting, and shopping carts.

Either way, forms can encourage the submission of information and automate the processing of that information. Any size site can benefit from their convenience and functionality.

Programmers or third-party solution specialists (e-commerce or database integration experts) should be contracted for planning complicated projects, but most basic form functionality can be handled by non-programmers, as we discuss in Chapter 24.

It's amazingly simple to add stylized pop-up menus to your pages using FireWorks: from the Insert menu, choose "Pop-up Menu...." FireWorks will guide you through each step to create DHTML pop-ups without hand coding.

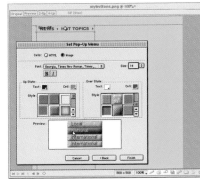

CGI scripts

(also known as CGI applications)

CGI (**c**ommon **g**ateway **i**nterface) is a standard for interfacing external applications with information servers. In plain designer's language, it's a method for passing data back and forth between the user, the server, and back to the user again. The CGI application on the server is responsible for passing data back and forth and processing it.

CGIs can be written in a number of languages, including Perl, C, C++, Java. Alternatives to CGI include Microsoft's ASP (**a**ctive **s**erver **p**ages), which requires a Microsoft web server, or PHP, which can run on Unix and Windows servers.

CGIs can work on multiple platforms and can execute varied applications, not just the processing of forms. For example, CGI scripts can power shopping carts, message boards, and even browser detection.

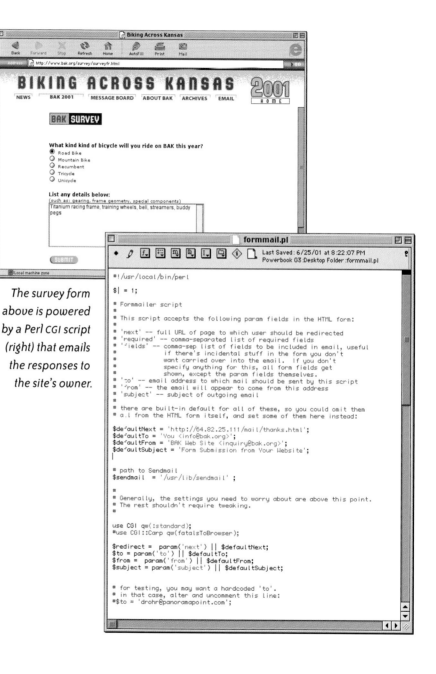

The survey form above is powered by a Perl CGI script (right) that emails the responses to the site's owner.

Database integration

Database integration allows a web site to go beyond simple communication and become a tool for research, shopping, or content delivery. While many sites won't ever need them, databases are the best solution for searching and delivering massive amounts of information over the web that would otherwise be impractical to present on a static page.

A database-driven web site is a good example of "dynamic content"—custom information requested by a user and delivered on-the-fly. Sure, the same information could be contained on a regular web page, but the process of clicking through hundreds of individual pages to find a specific piece of information would be a navigational nightmare and way too time-consuming for the average user. Searchability is a key attribute of a database, giving the user the power to easily and quickly make associations between often unrelated bits of information.

Databases are in use everywhere on the web, from online banking to book retailers, genealogy research, news content delivery, and search engines.

If you decide you need one for your site, you'll need to partner with database programmers who know their stuff and can configure the data structure and server. A good programmer will not be cheap and it's likely that the database work will cost more than your design or production fees.

You may want to consider some of the tools on the market that can make database integration easier, such as Dreamweaver UltraDev. While it doesn't eliminate the need for an experienced programmer, UltraDev gives more control to the web designer and can simulate the database configuration for offline testing purposes.

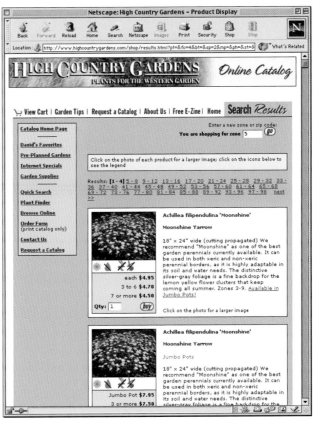

Catalog sites like High Country Gardens rely on a backend database to allow their entire inventory to be fully searchable down to the smallest attribute.

In this case, we searched for yellow or orange flowers that take full sun in our climate zone. We wound up with an abundance of choices.

E-commerce

If your client has a need to sell a product or service online, you will likely be the one to recommend and implement the necessary e-commerce technologies. These can be as simple as a form mailer CGI script or as complex as an integrated product database with a shopping cart.

As we mentioned on the previous page, e-commerce sites are usually, but not always, tied to a database. If there is a large number of products involved, say over 30, you'll want to recommend the utilization of a database so the end users can search for and quickly find the products they are looking for.

If your client has only a few products and doesn't intend to expand, your programmer may be able to create a custom order form without a database. Other **low-cost pre-fab solutions** are the Yahoo Store which offers clients the ability to set up a small or large web store for a monthly fee, or PayPal which provides credit card processing services for small online stores.

Online shopping carts have become the preferred way to allow customers to select, compile, and then order merchandise on the web. There are many types of shopping carts on the market and while they all are designed to accomplish the same thing, each one has its own unique features. Many are custom-built and designed to fit the needs of one particular business model. Others have more generic feature sets and are sold as complete off-the-shelf solutions.

The cost to implement a shopping cart will probably be a deciding factor for your clients, so you may want to offer them the choice between a customized and thus more-expensive shopping cart, or a generic one with fewer features but ultimately less expensive.

Security is another issue you'll need to incorporate into your e-commerce solution. Web customers want to be assured that measures have been taken to protect their personal data and credit card information. To accomplish this, you'll need to purchase a "secure certificate" under your client's name or arrange for them to tie into the certificate of someone else. A secure certificate authenticates your site and lets the browser and visitor know that you are who you say you are.

Purchase secure certificates from Equifax (equifaxsecure.com), VeriSign (verisign.com), Thawte (thawte.com), and others.

Real-time **credit card processing** is by far the best way to implement e-commerce if your client is willing to pay for it. By enabling this feature, your site will be smart enough to either authorize or deny a customer's credit card during a transaction. This way only correct, authorized orders will be completed and processed; customers who use an invalid card number or make a data-entry error will be told to try again. VeriSign is one of several companies that offers online credit authorization. You'll want to research the setup and maintenance costs before recommending any of these solutions to your client.

Consult with your programmer before recommending an e-commerce solution to your client—the programmer will have suggestions for the best technical solution and most cost-effective way to proceed within the budget.

Content management systems

A content management system is a combination of technologies designed to simplify site maintenance, allowing the content of a site to be altered or replaced without directly editing the HTML code. A CMS is most useful on a large site that needs be maintained by a client who has little experience with HTML and probably isn't going to learn.

There are many degrees of content management, from customized systems that administer the text on a single page to expensive pre-packaged software that can accommodate an entire site. While there are major differences in approach, the central idea behind them all is that the content of a page (text and images) is handled separately from the overall HTML page structure. In most cases, the content is stored in a database and can be changed through an administrative control interface. You (or the client) can make changes to the content through a web browser form or from within a commercial client database package such as Access or FileMaker.

There are also commercial software packages that offer CMS solutions, including UserLand's Manila (on the less expensive side, userland.com) or Vignette Content Management Server (in pricier territory, vignette.com). This type of system is usually more expensive to set up initially, but there are considerable cost savings over time (by giving the client more control over their own site). The design integrity of a site with content management in place is less likely to be compromised by a novice client because they only have control over the content and not the structure. This is especially beneficial to you as a designer because you can sleep easier knowing no one will inadvertently trash your hard work.

Implementation of a content management system is quite complex and is best left to those who know what they're doing. You'll definitely want to consult with a programmer before selling this to a client.

These two screenshots are examples of web-based content management forms.

Any changes made from these forms reflect immediately on the live web site.

Sound and video streaming

There are few things more compelling on a web page than the added dimension of motion and sound. As broadband Internet connections become more of a reality, we're all likely to see increased demand for video and audio clips on the web, so it makes sense for you to know how it's done.

At this writing, the main web video/audio **technologies** you should be aware of are QuickTime, Real, and Windows Media (AVI). Each one has its own proprietary way of compressing and streaming video and audio content, but the premise is pretty much the same with all: Video and audio files tend to be quite large and prohibitive to download all at once, so these technologies first compress them to a smaller size and then allow them to "stream," or play as they go. Once a portion of the clip is downloaded to a computer it begins playing while the rest is still coming down the pipe.

There are **two options** for getting video and audio into a digital format suitable for the web. You can either do it yourself (if you have the right equipment and software) or you can go to a professional service and have them work their magic while you focus on other web challenges. No matter which way you get your files digitized, you should be very sure that you are allowed to publish them. As the folks at Napster found out, copyright laws are upheld in court, so if you don't own the rights or have explicit permission, don't even think about posting that video or audio clip on a web site. And no, not even if your client tells you to!

If you go the route of creating your own video or audio clips, you'll need some hardware and software to get it into the desired digital format. There are entire books devoted to this subject so we can't get into the nitty gritty right here, but you'll need to invest a small chunk of change to do anything worthwhile.

Starting with **hardware,** you may want to consider buying a DV (digital video) camera to make your own movie clips. A good DV camera will capture both high-quality video and audio and can transfer the data right into your FireWire-enabled computer (FireWire is also known as IEEE 1394). Prices on the DV cameras have really come down in the recent past and there are many options to choose from. If you're only interested in audio, an inexpensive computer microphone may do the trick.

The hardware mentioned above will capture the source files, but you'll need the right **software** in order to edit and save the files into an appropriate web format. Apple Computer has some outstanding video editing software offerings for the Macintosh with iMovie (bundled free with new Macs) or the full-featured and pricier Final Cut Pro. Adobe Premiere is also a solid option—a long standing digital video editor for both Windows and Mac.

Although many people now have high-speed broadband connections, you should still keep your **video file sizes** small, usually around 240 x 180 for 56K modems and 320 x 240 for higher speed connections. If you have the luxury of time and money, you may want to provide the option of multiple sizes and let the users pick the right one for their Internet connection speed. The QuickTime format is still our favorite because the image quality is simply superior to the others and the player is nicely designed to boot.

Once you have your digital clips saved and ready to go, **embedding** them into your web page is quite easy and requires very little HTML coding. Programs like Dreamweaver or GoLive can do the job for you or you can refer to a site like WebMonkey (webmonkey.com) to get how-to instructions.

Finally, make sure that you use video and audio for **the right reasons.** If it helps communicate the site's message and deepens the user's understanding or enjoyment, then it's right on the mark. If it's added as an afterthought or contains confusing, extraneous, or downright boring content, you're better off leaving it out.

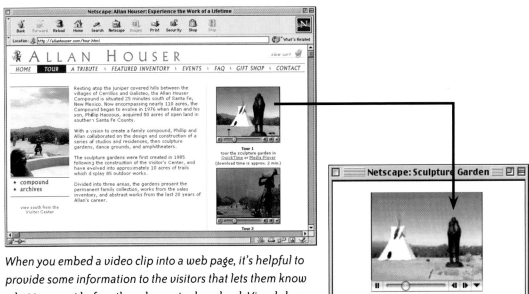

When you embed a video clip into a web page, it's helpful to provide some information to the visitors that lets them know what to expect before they choose to download. Visual clues— such as an image of the first frame of the clip or a warning of the approximate download time—will prevent users from getting unwanted surprises.

XML

XML (ex**t**ensible **m**arkup **l**anguage) is another powerful language spoken only by programmers. It is similar to HTML in that it uses markup tags to describe the contents of a page. While HTML mainly describes text and graphics in terms of format (how they're to be displayed), XML also describes a page in terms of data (information) about items on a page. This makes it possible for a computer, or other display device, to show, share, or interact with associated data in various ways, depending on the device being used.

XML is a method of putting information from spreadsheets, address books, financial transactions, medical charts, etc., into a text file, similar to an HTML text file. Like HTML, XML uses markup tags, but rather than using defined markup tags, XML leaves the definition and interpretation of tags up to the programmer.

For instance, a web page with information about Native American tribes may have tags surrounding various categories of information such as <pueblos>, <petroglyphs>, or <ceremonies>. This enables a computer to extract that information from an XML page and use it elsewhere.

XML works with other technologies to extend its powerful potential. DTDs, XML Schema and Namespaces, XSLT and XPath, XLink, and XPointer are some of the technologies that combine with XML to take full advantage of its power.

Even though XML files are text files, they're not meant to be read by mere mortals, only programmers. Text files are easier to debug and an expert programmer can use a simple text editor in an emergency to fix a broken XML file.

XML files are less forgiving than HTML files in accepting incorrect code. In fact, XML is completely unforgiving. While an HTML file allows or tolerates incorrect code (such as a missing tag or missing quotes around an attribute), XML files explicit do not allow broken code and will issue an error message upon encountering bad code.

The term "extensible" in XML means that its capabilities can be extended by users (programmers) who can define new data types (to meet specific application needs) and create new markup tag definitions.

XML is a cross-platform, W3C (World Wide Web Consortium) technology and, as such, is license-free. For more information, search the Internet for "XML." Some of the resources available include:

XMLresources.com

IBM information:
www.software.ibm.com/developer/education/xmlintro/xmlintro.html

The XML Cover Page:
oasis-open.org/cover/sgml-xml.html

W3C architecture domain:
w3c.org/XML

To learn how to program with XML and also take advantage of those related technologies, read **Elizabeth Castro's** book:

XML for the World Wide Web: Visual QuickStart Guide

PHP

PHP is a script language that could be described as HTML on steroids, providing a whole new family of tags that support another level of page instruction. The name is derived from its earliest version which was called Personal Home Page Tools.

Like CGI, PHP is an alternative to Microsoft's ASP (**a**ctive **s**erver **p**ages). PHP code is embedded anywhere within an HTML web page and creates dynamic pages whose content varies based on the PHP script and its interpretation. It can perform sophisticated mathematical calculations; provide user network, platform, and browser information; and much more.

Its database interfacing capability is powerful, and it supports a large portion of the most popular database

servers available, including MySQL, Oracle, Sybase, mSQL, Generic ODBC, and PostgreSQL. PHP is favored by many web developers whose sites track customers, merchandise, online purchases, and credit information.

HTML pages that contain a PHP script are usually given a file name extension of ".php," ".php3," or ".phtml." If your host server supports PHP, all you have to do is add the proper PHP tags to your documents that contain correct scripts.

PHP is used primarily on Linux web servers, although it's cross-platform. It's offered on an OpenSource* license, which means it's free.

As with most software, doing it isn't hard—learning what it can do is the hard part. There are numerous books on PHP and you can learn a lot from

the PHP web site, **www.php.net.**
Other resources include:

    Developer Shed

    DevShed.com

    Zend

    Zend.com

    LinuxWorld.com

*OpenSource software (OSS) is software developed with a philosophpy which maintains that source code of programs should be available to all people. Or, to be more exactly practical, to all programmers. The idea is that people (programmers) will modify it, improve it, fix the bugs in it, and cause it to evolve as useful, powerful software many times faster than if just a few privileged programmers get to see the code and work on its development. The Linux operating system was developed with this philosophy, and so was CGI.

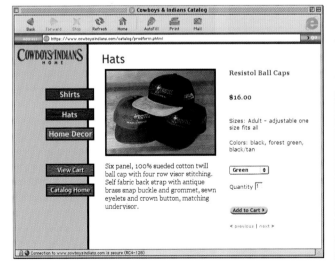

PHP enables the pages within this ecommerce site to display dynamic information extracted from the database.

This is an example of the PHP code that inserts the required information into the page template.

Java

Java is a powerful **programming language** developed by Sun Microsystems that can be used to write complete standalone applications that run on either a single computer or that can be distributed among a network of servers and clients (other computers on the network).

Java is often used to create small application modules (applets) to be used on web pages. Applets provide a way for web page users to interact with the page. Java applets are fast because they are executed (run) on the client's computer instead of on the client's server (remote computer on the network). You've surely seen Java applets before: stock market tickers that scroll across the page, sports messages that keep you up-to-date, or headlines from your instant messenger.

Java programs are portable, meaning they can be used in an operating system other than the one in which they were created, if the user's computer has a Java virtual machine that compiles the Java code into executable code on the user's computer. All major operating systems contain a Java compiler, and a Java virtual machine is included in both Netscape and Internet Explorer browsers.

Some web resources for more information about Java are:

Sun MicroSystems
java.sun.com

The Java Directory at Developer.com;
search for "Java" on the web.

JavaScript

JavaScript is not Java. It originated at Netscape, it's easier to learn than Java, and it's less powerful than Java. But its simplicity makes it ideal for many kinds of web page enhancements, such as: automatically changing a formatted date on a web page; making a page appear in a pop-up window; causing a graphic image to change during a mouseover or an image swap. JavaScript can display a predetermined message in the bottom of a browser border or as a marquee message on a web page.

JavaScript can be interpreted by web browsers and doesn't need a compiler or virtual machine to be functional. Macromedia Dreamweaver and Adobe GoLive generate JavaScript to execute their built-in DHTML (dynamic HTML) features.

Other than the JavaScript enhancement features that are built into popular HTML editing software, there are many interesting and useful sites on the Internet providing sample scripts for adding all sorts of features and functionality to your web pages. Do a search for "JavaScript" or visit these sites:

A Beginner's Guide to JavaScript
JavaScriptGuide.com

Matt's Script Archive
WorldWideMart.com/scripts

JavaScript.com

JavaScriptSource.com

WebCoder.com

WebReference.com/javascript/

Developer.com; search for javascript

SVG

SVG (**s**calable **v**ector **g**raphics) is just starting to make its presence known, but it promises to be a major player. It's an XML-based language for web graphics from the World Wide Web Consortium.

SVG works with vector graphics to provide fast-loading, dynamic content with greater interactivity potential. Since SVG is scalable, SVG images are suitable for viewing in a variety of devices, such as digital cell phones or PDAs (personal digital assistants, like Palm or Handspring). Users will be able to zoom or pan SVG graphics on a web page without waiting for extra graphic data to download. Maps will pan and zoom in high resolution without accessing the server (thus slowing things down).

Mousing over a map or other graphic will cause descriptive information to appear. Online brochures and catalogs will have the same high-quality professional graphics as their print counterparts, with dynamic behavior and interactivity added. In short, the web experience will be faster, richer, more powerful, and higher visual quality.

SVG allows text within images to be recognized as text, enabling search engines to locate and translate such text. Imagine a web search being able to find a restaurant featured in a local or regional map. Adobe is one of the major software companies that has made a commitment to supporting SVG across its product line.

For more information about this fascinating technology, refer to:

> Adobe.com/svg
>
> The World Wide Web Consortium: w3c.org/Graphics/SVG
>
> SVGmagic.com

For a **demonstration** of the scalability and panning feature, as used in a CAD program, visit the CAD Standard web site at www.cadstd.com/svg, or go to www.VirtualLastChapter.com to find the example of Url holding the map, shown below.

If you haven't already installed the Adobe SVG plug-in in your browser, at the CAD site listed above you can click on the "Adobe" link to download it. Click on one of the thumbnail views of a CAD drawing and the SVG version of the image will open in a new window. Place your mouse over the new window and use the Control key to zoom in, or the Control Shift keys to zoom out. The Alt key will allow you to pan across the drawing using the browser hand icon.

The enormous usefulness of this technology for technical, engineering, and map sites is obvious, and the potential for developing other uses seems unlimited.

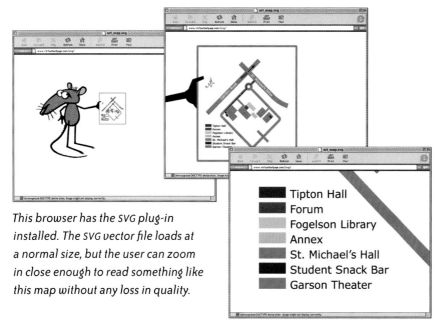

This browser has the SVG plug-in installed. The SVG vector file loads at a normal size, but the user can zoom in close enough to read something like this map without any loss in quality.

115

Checklist

Whew! Over the last few pages we've covered a lot of possibilities for enhancing your site. Use our handy feature checklist below to help you make sense of it all.

Dynamic Functionality

Animated GIFs

Flash and LiveMotion

DHTML (Dynamic HTML)

Automated Functionality

Email list management

Auto-responders

Message boards (BBS)

Guestbooks

Pop-up menus

SVG graphics (scaleable vector graphics)

Video and Audio clips

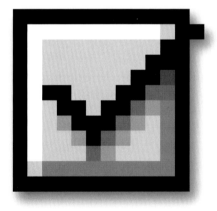

Organizing Your Content

One of the greatest challenges of any web site development project is to organize the content in an intuitive, intelligent manner. On the scale of importance, **information design** is right up there with **visual design,** and success of the site is riding on your decisions.

Create an effective site architecture

Your job as a web designer could be described as the act of making order out of chaos. You literally have to take a scattered pile of images, words, and concepts and arrange it all in a way that makes sense to the people using the site. The web designer is the filter and interpreter for the client's ideas and goals and it's the designer's job to put it all in place.

In more formal terms, **information design** or **web site architecture** is the process of structuring a site's content (text, photographs, etc.) and making decisions about how it's presented to the end user.

The two stages of site design

When you get right down to it, there are really two stages of site design, the informational and the visual. The visual part is obvious because it's what the user sees and reacts to first. The informational component is less noticed by the casual user, but it completely influences the way they use the site. *Make no mistake, a site's architecture is just as important as the way it looks.*

If you take the time to notice, a well-structured site is easy to spot: the purpose of the site is easily apparent from the very first page, information is easy to find, and you don't get lost in the depths of the site. This is the kind of site people will bookmark and return to time and again.

On the other hand, there are many examples of sites where architecture seems to have been an afterthought—or worse yet, given no thought. These are the sites with either a jillion links scattered across the page or maybe only one or two with obscure titles. There has been no effort to pre-digest the information into logical groupings and sections. This hodge-podge approach is confusing and provides little clue as to what is or isn't present in the site. Sometimes the only way to locate something is by a page to page search—and who wants to do that?

Know your subject

To begin, research the subject matter and learn as much as you can about the content and the client. At this point, there's no substitute for knowledge. To organize it, you've got to understand it. (Also see Chapter 5 for more ideas on researching your subject.)

You'll want to talk with your client about how their information has been communicated in the past with print and other media. Find out the questions their customers ask on a regular basis. Are there any recurring queries? If you're redesigning an existing web site, ask to see the web usage logs to learn which pages are visited the most and the least.

Take a look at successful competitors' sites to see how they structure their information. If you like what they've done, think about how to improve upon it for your site.

Have your client provide as much text and photography as they currently have so you can begin to get a sense of how it might all tie together. You may decide that more copywriting or photography is needed to fully communicate the site's message.

Finally, imagine yourself in the end-user's position—the ones who will actually be using the site. Based upon what you've learned so far, write down the information that seems most important, then next important and so on. Pretty soon you'll end up with a working hierarchy of information that will serve as the basis of your site structure.

Site map for designers

The process of creating an effective site structure is real brain work. You'll need to comprehend, organize, and associate large volumes of data. It requires logic, intuition, creativity, and a good measure of patience. If you do your job right, the end result will look easy to the target audience.

Putting it together

Now that you've become an expert on the targeted subject, what do you do with it? It's now time to create a **site map** that identifies all the sections and pages of the site and shows how they relate to each other. This site map is similar to a flow chart.

Structure

For your map you may consider a **pyramid structure,** with broader content at the top levels and more specific content as you move further down into the site. This way, the user doesn't get overwhelmed with unnecessary information at the start, but can still drill down to find more if they need it.

You could also do a **star structure** with the broader information near the center becoming more specific as you move outward.

Indicate relationships

In addition to the hierarchy, you will also want to indicate **relationships and linkages** between different sections of the site. One of the web's strong points, of course, is the ability to place hyperlinks within information that will instantly transport the user to a related topic. This non-linear approach will serve to strengthen the site's usefulness and allow a user to discover related content in your site without spending too much time or effort.

There's more than one way to make a site map. Depending on the extent of the content, you can choose a pyramid (left) or a star structure (right).

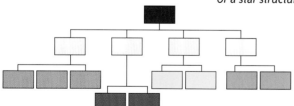

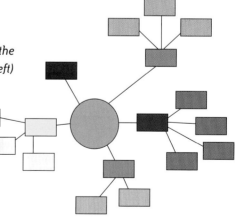

Start with broad categories

Starting with the top level, you'll want to create broad categories that will accommodate and contain the more specific information. If your site has more than one targeted audience of users, group subjects together that pertain to each specific target.

For example, on an e-commerce site, you might put all consumer links within one section, wholesaler links in another, and investor links in yet another. Base the category structure on what you learned from your research with the target audience.

Build for the future

Look ahead and make sure that your structure is extensible so that future content can be added easily. One of the most common client requests is to add more categories or subcategories to a site. If there's no logical place to add another category or link, you may have to do more restructuring than you or your client would like.

Limit the top-level links

For the best end-user comprehension, limit the number of top level links to seven or so. If that's not possible, then group the links into more manageable subsets of about five to seven.

It's much easier for people to understand and retain a short list of links than it is to scroll through a long list. With too many top-level choices, at some point the visitor will probably become confused and possibly give up on the site altogether.

Short link names

This is also when you will select names for your navigational links and page titles. Do your best to keep the link names short—one word is best. If one won't cut it, go with two or three short words but try to leave it at that. Sentences don't make good buttons!

Don't worry about link names not explaining enough about the section they represent—think of them as directional pointers instead of introductory paragraphs. In that one word, the link should convey enough information to give the user an idea of what to expect when they click it. Once they've clicked through, you can present them with as much text as they need to read or you feel the need to write.

Include hidden pages

Don't forget to include "hidden" pages such as search result lists or response pages that only appear if the user fills out a form. *Every bit of information in the site should be accounted for and have a place somewhere in the site map.* The site map will prove to be your most important planning document when you begin building the site.

What does a site map look like?

Below and on the following pages are examples of what site maps might look like, with endless variations, of couse, depending on your particular project. All of these maps were created in the software Inspiration, from Inspiration Software, Inc. (By the way, this program is also great for plotting your novel, conceptualizing your brilliant ideas, outlining your thesis paper, brainstorming your public relations plans, and much more besides site maps.)

Your completed site map will not only help you better understand the full extent of the web site, it will also serve as a blueprint for the client. Besides, if you've clearly identified all the site's pages in the map before you begin development, the client won't be able to sneak in pages later on.

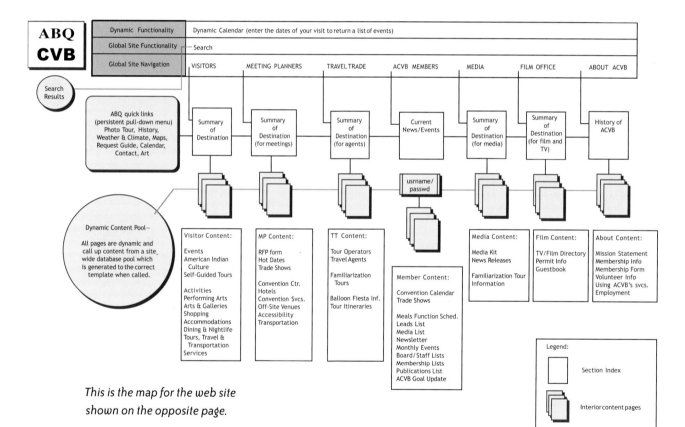

This is the map for the web site shown on the opposite page.

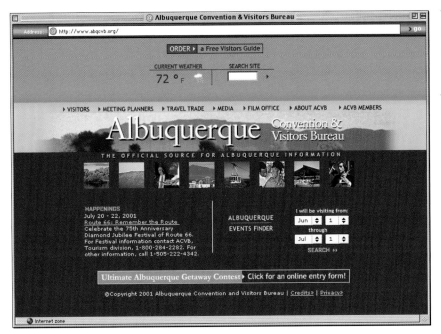

The Albuquerque Convention and Visitors Bureau site map (shown on the opposite page) illustrates the structure of the content management database.

As with most sites, the home page (left) shows only the top-level links, while subsequent interior pages (below) also contain sub-navigation that is specific to the particular section.

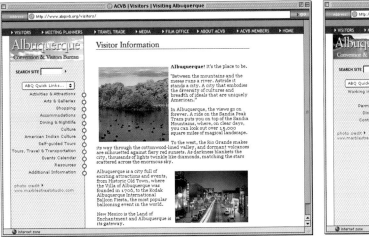

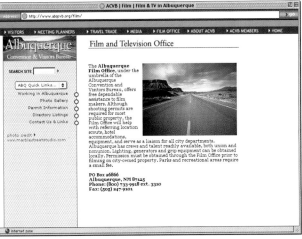

Be specific

The more detailed and specific you can make your site map, the better it will be when building the site. These three maps for the web site StationeryDomain.com illustrate three different aspects of the overall concept.

StationeryDomain.com   Universal Site Map 10/27/01

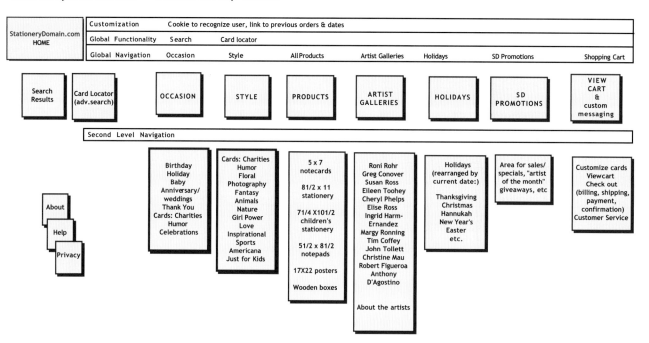

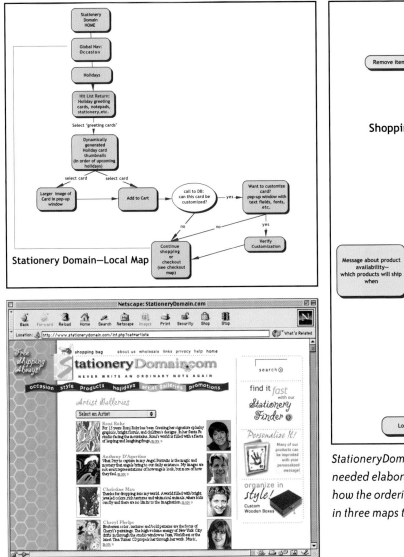

Stationery Domain—Local Map

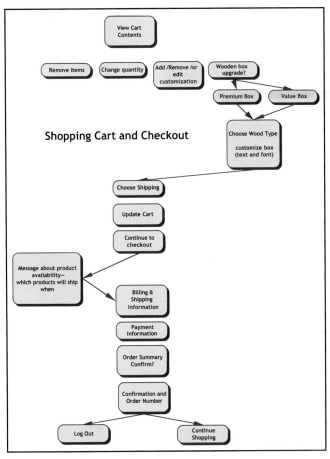

Shopping Cart and Checkout

StationeryDomain.com, a database-driven e-commerce site, needed elaborate detail in its site maps to illustrate exactly how the ordering process would work. The results are shown in three maps that depict both structure and flow.

Software helpers

As we mentioned ealier in this chapter, a site map can be presented in several different ways. To help with this, you may want to consider a charting software package like **Inspiration** or **Visio,** designed to help visualize informational hierarchies. They are especially good at diagramming relationships between individual pages in several different sections of a site. They also can designate colors to different categories to help you distinguish them from each other. The greatest advantage of using this type of software is the ease with which you can change relationships and structures of information.

For larger sites, flowchart software may be a necessary timesaver, but for smaller sites, you can at least use a pencil and paper, a large sheet of paper with sticky notes, or draw it in any draw or illustration program you happen to have.

www.inspiration.com
(Mac and Windows; download a free trial version)

www.microsoft.com/office/visio
(Windows only)

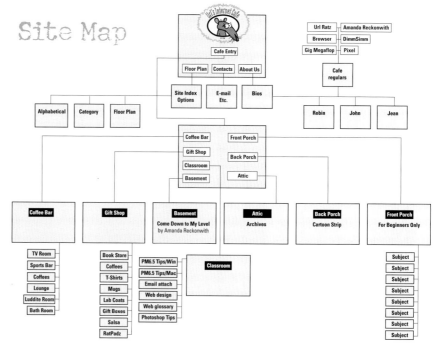

This site map was created in Illustrator. It's definitely not as flexible as Inspiration—you have to redraw boxes, move links, and do all the rearranging manually. But for a small site, a draw or illustration program is an option.

Organizing the Work Flow

When you **work alone,** it's clear how a web project is supposed to go. You start, you do every last bit of work yourself, and then the project is finished (well, as "finished" as web sites get). The lines are blurred between the tasks of design, production, consulting, and project management. You simply do what has to be done and you probably like it that way.

The minute you start involving other people in the process, things change dramatically. You quickly realize that it's not just you anymore and you'll have to learn how to **share the workload.** This is actually a good thing for the project, but it may take some getting used to. Remember, the more help you have with other parts of development, the more time you will have to spend perfecting your designs.

Team workflow

As part of a **web design team,** the most important skill for you to possess is the knowledge of how to communicate with others. When working on large sites, web development is truly a team sport and cooperation is key to success. To work effectively on a development team you need to understand the responsibilities of each member and how you fit into the mix.

Who is on the team

A **web development team** can be as small as two people or it might involve dozens. It all depends on the scope of the site being developed and the technologies required. It should be no surprise that a large site with lots of pages and complicated programming requires the involvement of many more people than a small, modest site.

If you normally work alone, a special project may require a team no larger than just two members—yourself (the designer), and a programmer you've chosen to partner with. However, if you're employed by a development company, you'll likely be part of a larger team whose members have very specific duties.

The following is a breakdown of the possible members of a web development team and their responsibilities. Not every team will need to have all the members listed here, but their collective duties must be covered in any web project.

Sales

The primary function of the **salesperson** is to convince the client that this is the right company and the right development team for them. They must be knowledgable about the entire process and be able to communicate the value that each team member brings to the table. They also must be a good listener and understand what the client wants to accomplish with the site.

The salesperson is the initial point of contact and liaison between the client and the development team. He or she must be able to effectively communicate to both sides so that each has a good understanding of what is needed and the potential solutions.

Client

It may seem unusual to include the **client** on the development team roster, but their participation is absolutely vital to the process and they have unique responsibilities that no one else can assume. They must be available throughout the process to provide content, feedback, and approvals. The team literally can't do it without them.

Account Manager

For ongoing business, an **account manager** is assigned to look out for the interests of the client and help them formulate a web strategy. The account manager is aware of the big picture and works with the team to strategize and accomplish the long-term goals of the client. They are also available to troubleshoot and ensure the client's long-term satisfaction.

Project Manager

The **project manager** is responsible for coordinating the members of the development team and ensuring that the project moves ahead on schedule and under budget. The project manager is typically the client's first point of contact during the development process and serves to relate information to the team. They also sometimes coordinate and write parts of the site specification and other planning documents.

Content Manager

A **content manager** is responsible for gathering and accounting for all the content that needs to be displayed in the site. This includes text, photographs, illustrations, video, audio, animations, and anything else that will appear on the web pages. If additional content is needed, they will work with the client or contractors to develop this.

Site Architect/ Information Designer

A **site architect** analyzes all of the content to be presented within the site and determines the best way to organize that information. They determine information hierarchies, as well as identify how the sections of the site should relate and link to each other. The end product of their efforts is a detailed site map, a flow chart that illustrates the page structure of the entire site. This is the blueprint the designers and producers will follow when building the pages.

Usability Consultant

For larger sites, a **usability consultant** is helpful in making recommendations and testing the proposed site architecture. They may recruit testing groups to review the proposed page designs and note the features the testing groups did and did not understand. They may contribute descriptions of typical user scenarios to the specification document. In the end, their recommendations will help make the interface design more understandable and easy to use.

Interface Designer

Finally, **here you are!** As the **interface designer,** YOU are responsible for the outward appearance of the site. Taking all of the planning information and recommendations from the site architect and usability consultant, you design a workable, attractive, visual interface for all of the pages of the site. (For more details, read all of the other chapters in this book!)

HTML Producer/Developer

The **HTML developer** is the person who takes the project from design concept to finished web site. They are proficient with HTML and a number of other relevant web technologies. The developer uses several different applications to get the job done, including image editors, HTML page and text editors, and sometimes motion graphics programs like Flash. They work closely with the designer to ensure that the final product is faithful to the design plan.

Programmer

The designer may determine how a site looks, but the **programmer** is responsible for how it functions. The programmer handles interactive forms, databases, shopping carts, content management systems, web hosting configuration, and many other coding tasks both great and small. They work closely with the HTML producer to integrate the back-end programming functions with the front-end appearance of the site.

QA Tester

There can be multiple **quality assurance testers** assigned to a particular project. Their job is to perform thorough testing on every page and function of the site and report any problems back to the producers and programmers. They also will look for spelling or grammatical errors in the site text.

Site Marketer

Site marketers are in charge of making the site known and available to the general public, or at least to the target audience. The marketer does search engine registration and works with the HTML developer to optimize the pages so that they can be more easily catalogued by the engines and directories. The marketer may also track the site usage and deliver monthly reports concerning the number of visitors to the site and which pages are most frequently visited. Often they work with the client to devise an audience development plan that helps drive more visitors to the site.

One more time?

In case you got confused back there, here's a **brief overview** of who does what in a team-based web development process.

The web development process is always initiated by either the **Salesperson** or the **Client.** After they find each other, the Salesperson convinces the Client that their two companies are a good match and can work together effectively.

If the Salesperson is successful in her efforts, the Client is introduced to an **Account Manager** who is the Client's advocate and primary point of contact in all future interactions. The Account Manager prepares a contract and oversees the preparation of the specification documentation.

Along with the Account Manager, a **Project Manager** is assigned to ensure that the project moves forward on schedule, on budget, and works as described in the specification. The Project Manager coordinates all of the members of the development team and keeps them all focused on moving the project forward.

Sometimes the team has a **Content Manager,** a person who gathers the text and images. The Content Manager also may subcontract with a **Copywriter, Photographer,** or **Illustrator** to provide additional content.

The **Site Architect** reviews all the content and organizes it into a cohesive structure for optimal communication and ease of use.

The Site Architect may enlist the help of a **Usability Consultant** who recommends changes to make the architecture easier to use.

When the pre-planning decisions have been made, the **Interface Designer** (that's you!) finally gets his or her hands on the project and creates a web interface that is both dazzling and usable.

On the heels of the design phase, the **HTML Producer** and **Programmer** are called upon to build the site according to the design and functionality specification.

To make sure the end result is as polished and error-free as possible, the **QA Tester** combs through the new site to identify any mistakes or problems.

Finally, when the site goes live, the **Site Marketer** works to drive customers to the site and make sure it's listed in the search engines.

The Design and Development Process

In this chapter we discuss design from a procedural perspective rather than a visual one. The following overview of the design and development process includes guidelines and advice for getting through this stage of site development efficiently and successfully.

Gather your tools

Web editing applications

In the market for some new web tools? As we've mentioned before, there are several good choices on the market depending on your budget and needs. Below are some of the most popular and dependable.

BBEdit and HomeSite: Two of the best HTML editors (for creating web pages with code instead of visually, or for editing your pages) on the market are BBEdit on the Mac and HomeSite for Windows. Both have been specially developed for web programmers and have many features that save coding time and automate repetitive processes. Both have features that go beyond just HTML editing and can benefit users of JavaScript, Perl, and other scripting languages.

Adobe Photoshop: Photoshop sets the standard for all others in the image editing market and is an excellent choice for creating web graphics. It now comes bundled with **ImageReady,** a specialized application for slicing, compressing, and animating web graphics. Between the two, you can do almost anything in the web arena.

Adobe Photoshop Elements: This is a smaller, less expensive version of Photoshop (less than $100). It lacks some of Photoshop's advanced features, but retains a lot of power for the price.

Macromedia Fireworks is a relative newcomer to the image editing scene but unlike Photoshop, it exists solely to process web graphics. It has many powerful editing features and can even outdo Photoshop with a few features such as vector editing and the automation of certain JavaScript functions. It's a great choice for the budget minded—it's almost half the cost of Photoshop.

Macromedia Dreamweaver: Since it was first released just a few years ago, Macromedia Dreamweaver has become a major player in the WYSIWYG web editing market and is one of our favorites. It is capable of creating just about any kind of web site and will suit the needs of both the beginner and the seasoned professional. Most people find it intuitive to use and extremely easy to learn, despite its ability to create complex DHTML pages or implement sophisticated JavaScript behaviors. It works well with hand-coded pages and will not rewrite any HTML code created outside of the program. It also is designed to work seamlessly with other Macromedia applications like Fireworks and Flash.

Adobe GoLive, NetObjects Fusion, Microsoft FrontPage, and other web authoring applications are used by thousands of people, all of whom passionately support their product of choice. If you don't have an application already, check each vendor's web site for details and choose the one that suits you.

Thumbnail sketches

You've planned, you've researched, and you've prepped—now it's time to put it all to use and design your site! By this time, you've undoubtedly got a lot of great ideas in your mind about how the site should look, so the best place to start is with some quick sketching to get it all out on paper.

Thumbnail sketches

We usually make small thumbnail sketches of possible home page layouts—nothing too detailed, but just enough to establish a visual structure and hierarchy for each separate design concept.

After creating 8–10 thumbnails on a single sheet of paper (or on your computer if you wish), you'll have the opportunity to look them all over and make side-by-side comparisons, evaluating the overall interest and impact of each design. You may find that you favor two or three concepts from the batch and want to give them further refinement. It's also possible that you don't really like any of them yet. If that's the case, you should go back to the drawing board and keep sketching until you're satisfied with at least a few.

The beauty of creating rough thumbnails on paper is that you can quickly conceptualize a web interface, make changes, combine the best elements from different layouts, and evaluate what you've done, all in a matter of minutes. Speed is essential here. The thumbnail step will save you the trouble of creating detailed concepts too early in Photoshop or Fireworks and discovering that you've gone down the wrong path only after you've invested a large chunk of time on it.

These are for your use only—you don't have to show these to the client!

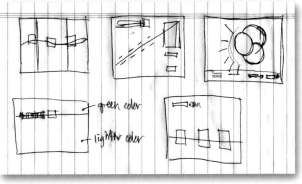

Thumbnail sketches are not meant to look pretty—they're a form of visual shorthand that provide a rough way to explore concepts without getting caught up in the details of creating graphics. Sometimes it's easier to see potential in a layout if the details are vague and undefined.

Get some design training

Unless you're working on your own experimental web site, remember that commercial web design is typically not about self-expression. **Your main goal is to create effective visual communication.** A web site can be a thing of beauty, but its aesthetic qualities shouldn't dominate at the expense of the message. Like in print, a good web page structure follows the time-tested principles of design. If you attended design school, you'll still need to use what you learned about alignment, repetition, proximity, and contrast and all those other helpful rules.

If these concepts are unfamiliar, we suggest that you read a book or take a class and get up to speed on the basics of design. Too many people think that writing code or knowing how to use the software is a substitute for design principles—it's not. Learning the fundamentals will definitely have a positive impact on your ability to make sound design decisions.

In this book, *Section III: Idea Source,* includes a variety of design possibilities and suggestions. You might also want to take a look at the books listed below, as well as the huge number of design books available at any bookstore:

> *The Non-Designer's Design Book*
> *The Non-Designer's Type Book*
> *The Non-Designer's Web Book*
> *Robin Williams Design Workshop*

Don't forget the navigation

Don't wait to tack on the navigation towards the end—it's an integral part of the page and you'll need to work it out now in the thumbnail stage. Treating navigation as a secondary concern would be like a car manufacturer putting the dashboard controls in the back seat for aesthetic reasons. Navigation exists to be used, so don't make it hard on the people who visit the site! Site navigation doesn't have to command the most attention on a page, but it does need to be obvious.

You're ready to move on

When you feel like you've created a few strong concepts, you can now take it to the next step and begin building finished design concepts or "comps" (comprehensive ideas) on your computer. We use Photoshop to build our comps, but you could just as easily do them in Macromedia Fireworks or Adobe ImageReady. As long as you construct the page in an application that supports layers, you'll have the flexibility to make changes throughout the design process.

The design comps

Computer comps

We like to make our design comps look as much like the envisioned web page as possible so our client understands exactly what is being proposed. While it's important that the comps look good, *they shouldn't look any better at this point than they will after being built in HTML.* That usually means setting body copy as aliased text to match the way it will look in a web browser. Of course you should also use web-safe colors (as explained in Chapter 1) and adhere to the appropriate screen width and height (as explained in Chapter 4).

Besides serving as a visual blueprint for the site, design comps also allow the client to participate in the process and provide their opinions and feedback. As a designer, it's important that you take firm control of this part and make sure you communicate well with your client and set boundaries on the comping process (like how many will be created within the budget). If you don't, the client may run away with the situation and you'll be stuck doing countless iterations without a clear direction.

Limit the choices

Don't inundate your client with too many design choices. We usually choose to show only three to five of the strongest design comps of the bunch. Any more than that can tend to be confusing and make it that much harder for the client to make a selection.

On the flip side, you should provide at least three distinctly *different* page comps for evaluation. Any less than that may leave your client feeling that you are giving them no choice in the matter and they will probably ask you to show them more. Variations on a single theme don't count—make sure the comps you show have very different looks.

In the first round of the comp presentation, we usually only show representative home pages for consideration, holding off on any interior or secondary pages. We've found that it's better to wait and see which visual direction the client prefers for the home page before going to the trouble of making companion interior page designs.

Once the client has made their home page selection, you'll then need to create a few interior page comps that coordinate with the selected look before you start designing the entire site.

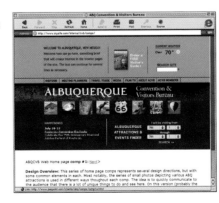

ABQCVB Web Home page **comp #1:** Next >

Design Overview: This series of home page comps represents several design directions, but with some common elements in each. Most notably, the series of small photos depicting various ABQ attractions is used in different ways throughout each comp. The idea is to quickly communicate to the audience that there is a lot of unique things to do and see here. On this version (probably the

ABQCVB Web Home page **comp #4:** < Back | Next >

Design Overview: The version above features a dominant central photograph, in this case the river and the mountains. Most scenic photographs should work in this space. The navigation and other features are arranged on either side.

How many rounds?

You may be lucky on your first try and create a design the client absolutely loves without any changes (ha!). But more often than not, clients will usually have ideas on how to make your design "better." It may be in the form of very minor adjustments to color or page elements, but you should be prepared for even more dramatic directives.

If your preliminary client meetings included a discussion of color and type-face choices, you may be able to avoid having initial designs be rejected or reworked for those reasons.

Frequently, a client will like elements from several different versions and want to incorporate them all into one super design comp. This can work sometimes, but it's up to you to draw the line if you think it will result in a disaster. With a little innovation on your part, you may be able to accommodate their wishes without compromising your design sensibilities.

Our typical comping process lasts about three rounds, give or take an alteration here and there. Round one is when a client reviews your initial three to five comp ideas. You should expect that they will select one or maybe two favorites

from the bunch and ask for changes to those. This constitutes round two, a refinement of the original concepts. If there is a round three, it usually consists of a few very minor alterations to just one of the comps. Of course there is no real limit to the number of changes that can be made to a design, so to preserve your sanity you'll need to make the process clear with your client up front. Tell them that you have budgeted time for three (or however many you want) rounds of design comps and that anything beyond that will be done at an extra cost. Setting these limits will likely discourage your client from being indecisive and drawing out the entire process longer than it needs to be.

These images (and the two on the previous page) are examples of progressive comp iterations created for the client's review. These are JPEG images placed on HTML pages, then posted on the Internet for client review. Notations for the client below each JPEG are in HTML text.

Interior comp pages for this same site are on the following page.

Presenting your ideas

In person

If you are located in the same city as your clients, it's usually a good idea to have a face-to-face meeting with them to present and review the proposed comps on a computer monitor. Not only is it a good business courtesy, you will be much more likely to win them over to your ideas if they hear your design rationale first hand.

During the presentation, go through each proposed design and explain *why* you made the choices you did and *how they will work* to meet the client's goals. You will also want to cover the usability features you incorporated and discuss *why* these features will help the end users. **This means you must know the answers to these questions before you meet with the client!**

Don't worry about boring them with too many details about your process—your client will be impressed that you have given their site so much thought and effort.

Online

While an in-person design review is the best, there are many times when you and the client may be in different cities or even different continents, making it impossible for you both to sit down around the same monitor to discuss the site. In this circumstance, you'll have to post your ideas on the web. It's important to be well prepared so you can be sure that your visual ideas come across in the exact way you intended.

We typically begin by saving each Photoshop page comp as a single JPEG file and then insert that file into a blank web page. We add copious notes about the design below the image and summarize what we would have said in person. When displaying several comps of the same page, we add navigation links to each so the client will have an easy time jumping from one comp to another and back again.

We've found that it's also beneficial to allow your client to first review the proposed design ideas online by themselves in the privacy of their own office. Often, their initial reaction is not their final word, so it's best to let them think about it a bit before responding to you. There is always going to be discussion about the design concepts, so if you let them hash it out in their own offices, let them go ask their friends and uncles and the plumber who happens to be there that day what *they* think, then the clients can get back to you with a cohesive written account of what they did and didn't like—all without having to waste your time.

After all that, we upload the files to our own web server and email the special, private URL to the client. If you're a small business and don't own your own server, this process can be as simple as uploading a folder of the pages to your own domain site and giving the client the address, such as "www.mysite.com/clientname" (another good reason to own your own domain, no matter how small your business is). No one else but the client will know to enter that particular address.

Some web development firms have a "clients only" staging section of their site that clients can access with a password to allow them to view pages in development. Once inside the staging site, the client can call the pagesup in a web browser and review them at their own pace.

After the client reviews the pages online, we always like to follow up over the telephone and answer any immediate questions they may have and point out any details they may have missed.

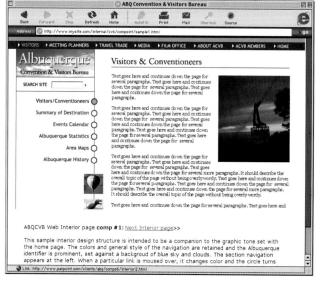
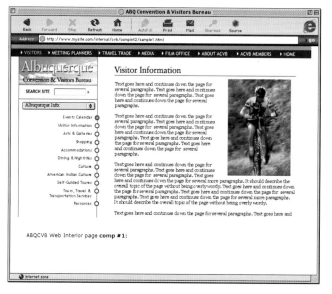

These two examples are interior pages that were posted during the client approval process as described on the previous pages.

Client feedback

If your client has feedback for you (of course they always do), it's critical to request it **from the client** in the form of an email or a fax. This does two important things:

1. It makes the client focus and collect their ideas in a cohesive manner.

2. It provides a clear written reference detailing the changes they would like to see.

If you rely only on a verbal feedback session, you take the risk of missing something critical or having a subsequent misunderstanding about what was or wasn't said. It's much harder to dispute what was written on a piece of paper than what was said verbally.

Get signature approval

After several design rounds, if you're very lucky, your client just may sign off on final web comps. This is the point where they agree that the comps fully meet their expectations and they authorize you to begin constructing the pages in HTML.

When that day comes, **don't rely on their verbal approval**—*have them sign on the dotted line!*

We make color inkjet prints of the selected comps (two sets of the home page, interior template, any other key pages) and have the client *sign each page in both sets.* Then both the client and the design firm can walk away with an approved set to keep on file.

By having a signed comp approval, you protect yourself against requests for any unpaid production changes. It's not unusual for a client to later change their mind about some aspect of the selected design comps and often will want you to make the changes for free. Without the presence of that signed piece of paper, some people can be very vague or flat-out mistaken about what they did or did not approve. Plan ahead and avoid this potentially unpleasant situation.

Production

This book is about the *design* of a web site, and we assume you know how to actually *produce* pages. But if you're part of a web team and won't be producing your own designs, you need to make sure that the pass-off is smooth and you communicate well with the HTML developers.

Pass-off to the production team
If you want the developers to produce the site as closely as possible to your original design, sit down with them, go over the comps, and make sure they have all the original Photoshop documents, fonts, and content files necessary to complete the project. If they're missing any one of these items, they won't be able to finish the site without your help.

It's usually helpful and often critical to create a **style guide,** a printed document that serves as instructions for the HTML developer or anyone else who will be maintaining the site in the future. The style guide lists every relevant detail about the site: fonts and colors used, file names, cascading style sheets, standard headings, navigation, rollovers, JavaScript, and anything else necessary to communicate how to build and maintain that particular site. It doesn't have to be long, just thorough.

As the designer, you should stay informed throughout the production process and do some quality checking at the beginning, middle, and end. Problems are always much harder to fix at the end than early in the process. It's important to remember that no one will be as particular about your design concept as you, so stay involved for the duration.

Production applications

There's more than one way to build a web site, and if you're producing HTML pages, you'll need to select a method that suits your needs. Many web sites are still programmed using a basic text editor by patient and proficient developers who wouldn't think of using a visual program to do the job.

On the other hand, visual or WYSIWYG web authoring applications are available for the rest of us who may know some HTML but would rather work directly on the web page as seen in a browser than with the code. Both methods have their strengths and shortcomings depending upon who is doing the work and what application is being used.

Get familiar with HTML

Even if you prefer to use Dreamweaver, GoLive, or some other visual editing program, you should still understand and be able to edit HTML code. In web work, there's just no substitute for a good foundation in HTML and it's simple enough for even mere mortals to learn. The best way to pick it up is through doing. You can start by studying the HTML source code from existing pages, reading tutorials on the WebMonkey site (webmonkey.com), or reading an HTML book.

> *HTML for the World Wide Web: Visual QuickStart Guide,* by Elizabeth Castro.

You may typically use a program like Dreamweaver almost exclusively, but we guarantee that at some point you'll have to roll up your sleeves and edit some HTML to make your pages work and look the way you want. Web editing applications do a great job, but they just can't assure compatibility with every page in every web browser on the market. It always takes a little manual HTML tweaking to squeeze out that last one percent of compatibility.

Checklist

So here is a checklist of steps to follow as you begin the development process. Good luck.

- Read Chapter 5. Do your market research and get to know your client and their mission.

- Read Chapter 6 and decide which special features your client needs in their site (if any). If you're going to need a programmer, find her now and explain your plans so you can work it into the budget.

- Work out a written agreement with the client as described in Chapter 5.

- Create a site plan as described in Chapter 7.

- If you have no design training at all, please acknowledge this fact and spend a day or two in the library (not on the client's budget) perusing books about design. If you plan to design web sites for a living, please take some classes.

- Spend some time sketching ideas on paper.

- Create a number of comps in your image editing application.

- Present your ideas to the client.

- Get client feedback and make design alterations.

- When the client is happy with the design concept of the home page and a couple of sample interior pages, print up proofs and have the client sign off on them. Keep a copy in your files.

- Read Chapter 11 to make sure you build in features to help search engines find the site.

- Start the HTML production of the web site.

Test Your Web Sites

10

We've known more than a few web designers who have created beautiful web sites that looked world-class on one computer (the one in the designer's office) and terrible on another computer. It can be quite a shock to see your design expertise trashed by an unfamiliar operating system or browser.

Some HTML editing software writes code that's more compatible with one browser than another; some browsers are more sympathetic to web designers than others. And some designers are actually scared to test their pages in other browsers and on other platforms, fearing what they might see.

Personally, we understand, but it's best to put your big-boy pants on and test the daylights out of your site.

Why test a site?

Browser compatibility testing and quality assurance (QA) have got to be two of the most underrated and overlooked aspects of web development, while at the same time being two of the most important parts of the development process.

Many times developers will skip over compatibility testing completely and not even budget time for it in the process. If it's done at all, testing is often an afterthought, something to spend half an hour on before site launch.

Probably the main reason for the apparent lack of interest in web testing is that it's not glamorous work. It's definitely not what designers dream about doing after they graduate from art school, and awards aren't given for the most well-tested sites in any competition. To make matters worse, clients rarely request it and will frequently question the necessity of any testing when reviewing a development bid.

Even though it's not exactly the most popular activity in the development scene, thorough site testing is the mark of a true web professional. If you care about how your site looks and functions, this is a no-brainer—it's got to be done.

Start testing now

The time to start testing is *not* after the site is already built, but at the beginning of the page construction phase. This is the best opportunity to catch any potential problems and fix them before they duplicate throughout the site.

When one or two HTML page templates have been completed, you should take the time to run them through the browser gauntlet and make sure they stand up to the challenge. You'll be surprised how different the same page looks in a variety of browsers. Additional testing should also be performed in the middle of the production process and again after completion.

What to look for

In the actual testing, you'll be looking for any inconsistencies in color, font usage, composition, or alignment. Some of the most typical **browser incompatibilities** include:

- ¤ Font sizing problems
- ¤ Margin alignment
- ¤ Inconsistent style sheet handling
- ¤ JavaScript errors
- ¤ Color saturation problems in photographs
- ¤ DHTML layer misalignment
- ¤ Frame sizing discrepancies
- ¤ Form text fields that are either too large or too small
- ¤ Gaps between images that have been sliced and placed into tables

Download times: You'll also want to make sure that the page download times are acceptable. If you use a high-speed line in your office, make darned sure you see how the pages perform coming through a slower modem line. Download times of over twenty seconds per page are questionable, so you'll want to make adjustments and possibly use more compression on your photographs and graphics.

Links: All the hypertext links should be tested to ensure they are directed to the correct pages. Broken links are unacceptable and should be fixed immediately.

Media: If you are using Flash, video clips, or some other embedded media type on your pages, you'll want to preview each one to uncover any possible glitches.

Text size: If you aren't using cascading style sheets (CSS), be aware that Windows browsers display HTML text larger than Macintosh browsers because each platform deals with font sizes differently. If you want web text to look the same on either platform, you'll need to use CSS tags (see Chapter 19).

Proofreading: Don't forget to proofread your pages (although this might be the client's job, if you made that clear earlier in the planning stage). Spelling errors and bad grammar are just as unwelcome on the web as they are on the printed page—even more so because they're more easily fixable on the web. You may want to print each page so you (or the client) can mark any misspellings or grammatical errors.

Printing: If your client requires that their web pages be printable, now is the time to make sure they are. Printing from browsers is notoriously unreliable and some graphics won't show up at all on paper. The important thing is that the body text is fully readable when printed from each browser and isn't cut off in the margins or printed in a color too light to read.

How to test sites

To achieve optimal compatibility, you'll need to test in quite a few browsers. The best place to start is with the primary browser on your development computer, which should be the most current version of either Internet Explorer or Netscape. Take notes and list problems on a page by page basis. In the end you may not be the one to make the changes and corrections, so be as specific as you can so that someone else will understand what you mean.

Also, be aware that you, as designer and perhaps HTML producer, may be too close to the project and have a more difficult time spotting errors than an outside observer. It's good practice to enlist the help of people who are unfamiliar with the project and have them take the site for a test drive. It's always interesting to see the kind of errors they spot.

Be sure not to be a back-seat driver when someone unfamiliar with the project is testing the site—you can't be saying, "No, no, click here," or "See, we invented this new navigation system so you have to first download a small text file to learn to use it," etc. You have to sit on your hands and keep your mouth shut and just watch what they do, where they get confused, what they miss, etc. And take notes.

These days, we typically only develop for and test in browsers that are version 4.0 and above. The 4.0 level marks the point where most browsers began supporting advanced features such as DHTML layers and cascading style sheets. If we're feeling particularly daring, we will sometimes review our pages in something like Netscape 3.0, but often their appearance has much to be desired.

With all the many browser versions past and present, it's extremely impractical to attempt full compatibility with every one of them. Statistically, only a very small percentage of web users still use the older 3.0 (or lower) browsers, so it's best to focus your development efforts on the ones used most frequently.

If a client really wants full compatibility with pre-4.0 browsers, it can be done, but it may be at the expense of more advanced features. Make sure your client is aware of the trade-offs in supporting older browsers.

Browser list

This is a typical browser test list in order of importance:

Windows

Internet Explorer 5.5 or higher*

Internet Explorer 5.0*

Netscape 6.0 or higher*

America Online 6.0 or higher*

Netscape 4.xx*

. . . .

Internet Explorer 4.0

America Online 5.0

America Online 4.0

Opera 5.0

You really must test in this browser.

Mac

Internet Explorer 5.0 or higher*

Netscape 4.xx*

America Online 5.0 or higher*

Netscape 6.0 or higher*

. . . .

Internet Explorer 4.5

America Online 4.0

Opera 5.0

Omniweb 4.0 (OS X only)

iCab

Linux

Netscape 4.0

Netscape 6.0

Opera 5.0

Prioritize

Obviously time and budget are factors here, so start with the most current browser versions and work down as time allows. Your client may have statistical data on which browsers their clients use and if so, you'll want to pay extra attention to that list.

Don't assume that if you test on one platform that the site will look the same on another! For example, Netscape on Windows will display pages quite differently than its Macintosh counterpart. Despite the fact they are both called Netscape, they are essentially two different applications and will interpret and display HTML differently.

Using CSS and a little finesse, it's possible to make your pages look mostly the same on any modern browser, but you have to be willing to invest time and effort.

This is the OmniWeb browser in Mac OS X.

This is the iCab browser in Mac OS X.

This is the Opera browser in Windows ME.

Prepare the client

It's important to get your client onboard early with the whole site testing concept. After all, the time spent on it comes out of their overall budget and they should be able to understand and appreciate what they're paying for.

Sometimes it's hard for a client to understand why the site just doesn't work correctly in the first place and they may initially view any programming bugs as a sign of incompetence on the developer's part. In a case like this, you'll need to educate your client about the nature of web design and browsers. They need to understand that programming bugs are an inevitable part of site development and are not a problem unless they go unfixed.

Due to the many variables in browsers and computer platforms, it's impossible to develop a site that never has any errors or bugs. Even commercially released software has its share of bugs and problems. There's always something that pops up unexpectedly and needs to be fixed or adjusted.

To maintain your client's confidence, let them know what to expect before starting production. If they are *expecting* to find a few errors here and there, they will have no real reason to panic when something doesn't work at first. They will know that it's all part of the process and realize that any bugs will be fixed in due course.

Before the client sees it . . .

We recommend that you do the first round of testing internally before you show the site to the client—they could get spooked if they see the pages before you've had a chance to fix the initial problems. After you've completed your internal testing, you should definitely let the client take a look and play around with the site. Have them write down their questions and notes on any bugs they find.

Can't have too much

There's really no such thing as too much testing before a site launches. It's extremely important to get things right before the general public has a look. Ultimately, it is they who will do the most extensive testing on the site through typical everyday use. It's a good idea to include a link somewhere on the site that lets end users report any problems. If the site isn't working the way it's supposed to, you'll want to know right away. Even without a reporting system, trust us—users will write anyway and tell you exactly what's wrong.

Web Site Work is Never Done

This is one of the biggest differences between designing for print and the web: in print, you know when you're done.

Even if you've only built one web site before you bought this book, you surely learned that a web site is never truly finished. That's the great thing about the World Wide Web and that's the frustrating thing about the World Wide Web. We're all very understanding when we see a brochure that has outdated information in it—the new version is probably "in production" and will be printed real soon now.

But a web site that needs updating creates the impression that something is wrong with the company. A common-sense approach is to design a site so that only specific sections require updating, such as a "What's New" section or "Current News."

Maintenance of a site should include regular registration with search engines, as well as marketing the site both online and through traditional media. Amazingly, clients often have nice web sites and forget to include the web address in their print ads. It may be a new digital world, but traditional media is still as powerful and influential as ever.

Thought you were finished, huh?

The site may be built and launched, but your job is not yet done—a web site is never really complete. It needs to be promoted and maintained to realize its full potential and reach its target audience. But these things don't happen by themselves. Like the rest of development, you need to follow a plan to get it done correctly.

Site promotion

Promotion doesn't get into full swing until after your site launches, but you'll need to start planning for it early in the process. It's important to get listed in all the mainstream search engines, the appropriate specialty searches, and you'll want to build the site in a way that can be easily catalogued.

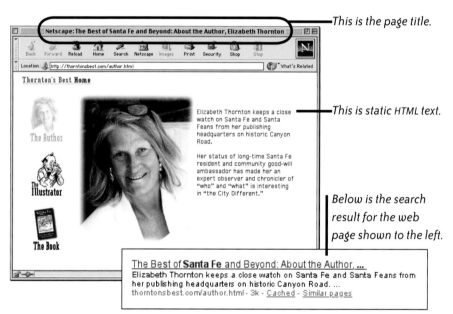

This is the page title.

This is static HTML text.

Below is the search result for the web page shown to the left.

*Most search engines are designed to pick up on keywords or phrases found within a site. Notice the search result for this web page (using Google) uses the **title** of the page as a header and link, and displays the first **HTML text** it comes across as a description in the result.*

In other words: be very conscious of the wording for your page title and the first words of HTML text on the page.

Meta tags

There are a number of possible meta tags, but the two most popular are "description" and "keywords." The information in these tags is for search engines only—it does not appear on the web page.

The **description tag** is a sentence that explains the focus of your web site. Not all, but many search engines will display this information on the results page. If it can't find a meta tag description, the search engine will usually display the first HTML text it comes across on your page, which might be a list of links (not very useful for the person looking for your page).

Searchable **keywords** can also be tucked away in the meta tag information on the HTML page; these keywords don't appear on the actual web page. A typical search engine searches every word on every page, not just the meta tags, so the best use of meta tag keywords is to describe the *content* on your page *in words that might not actually appear on the page.* For instance, you might have a site about Wolfgang Mozart, but the phrase "classical musician" might not actually be present in the HTML text; you can put "classical musician" in a meta tag so your page can still be found by those searching for that phrase. You might also want to put foreign translations of keywords in a meta tag so people in other countries who have an interest in your content can find you.

Meta tag keywords are not a magical solution for a content-less web site. For one thing, not all search engines look for them. And the ones that do are more concerned with the title and text on pages rather than meta tags because those are more indicative of what the site really has to offer, not the marketing stuff that many people put in the meta tag.

```
                         Url's Internet Cafe
  [tools]        Last Saved: 5/22/01 at 5:29:32 PM
                 Mac HD :Applications :BBEdit:Url's Internet Cafe

<html>
<head>

<META NAME="Description" CONTENT="Illustrator John Tollett teams with
computer book author Robin Williams to create an educational, humorous
site that sells unique, original gift items.">

<META NAME="Keywords" CONTENT="gifts, tshirt, tshirts, t-shirt, t-shirts,
mousepad, mousepads, coffee mugs, coffee, cups, denim shirts, humor,
Robin Williams, John Tollett, computer books, digital workshops, Url, Url
Ratz">

<title>Url's Internet Cafe</title>
```

The tags shown above are indicative of where they belong on your HTML page (between the <head> tag and the <title> tag). Some web authoring software will place the meta tag information in the correct spot for you, once you type the description and keywords into a dialog box.

1. Url's Internet Cafe
Illustrator John Tollett teams with computer book author Robin Williams
to create an educational, humorous site that sells unique, original gift...
URL: www.urlsinternetcafe.com/

Notice that the "description" sentence in the meta tag above is what appears in the search results shown here.

Build it in

Below are a few guidelines for designing pages optimized for search engines. These are things you should build directly into each site, so if your site is already complete, you might have to go back and add these.

Also, these guidelines refer to those search engines that send out automated "spiders," "crawlers," or "robots" that search through your pages and send data back to a huge index. If you have a thoroughly compelling reason to build your pages in such a way that they can't be indexed by search engines, you just have to accept the fact that the information on the pages won't be found automatically and you'll have to manually (and regularly) submit your site to the search tools and directories yourself.

- **DON'T use frames.** Search engines generally have trouble finding content within framed sites, so it's best to avoid them altogether.

- **DON'T build your entire site in Flash.** While very cool, Flash sites are not based on HTML and therefore can't be catalogued in search engines.

- **DO use static HTML text on the home page** that contains your top search terms (key words and phrases). A number of search engines find the first words in the first HTML text they come across on the web page, and use that as the description in the search results, so make sure those first words are descriptive of your site.

- **DO give every page a unique page title.** This is very important because it's a primary resource for search engines.

- **Avoid** any non alphabetic or numeric characters in the page title, especially those that are used in computer talk like code, path names, etc. Particularly don't use these:

  ? ! < > * / + - @ & = :

- In static HTML text on the page, do use the **main keyword phrase** that is in your title.

- **DO design clear, consistent navigational links** on every page. You never know from which page in your site a crawler will enter, and it follows the links out from that page.

- **DO make sure that each page contains meta tag information,** including a description (25 words or less) and keywords (up to 10) listed in order of importance.

Also keep in mind:

If a visitor has to **register** or fill out a **form** before proceeding to the next page, this effectively locks out not only the visitor, but also the searching web crawler—any pages beyond the registration page cannot be indexed by a search engine. If you want those pages indexed by a web crawler, make the registration optional.

Search engines cannot index **dynamic pages.** Any page generated on the fly is not accessible to the crawlers. The *content* on pages with a ? in the URL can be indexed, but the crawlers cannot follow any of the *links* out from that page. It is possible to code a workaround to allow dynamic pages to be catalogued, so ask your programmer before they begin their work.

Active Server Pages (.asp) with a ? in the address cannot be indexed.

Crawlers cannot search information provided by **Java applets** or in **XML coding.**

Images, MP3 files, other **audio files,** and **video** must be manually submitted to most search engines.

Text that is in **GIFs, JPEGs,** or other **graphic images** (except SVG images, see page 115) is not searchable. Provide ALT tags to identify graphics that you want to be indexed.

Information in the **higher levels of your directory** will be considered more important; many crawlers will not venture past the third or fourth level. That is, if you have content pages that are stored in a folder within a folder within a folder within a folder in your web site folder, they probably won't be found.

Crawlers follow **links on a main page** to find most of your pages. A central page with good navigation to the other pages makes it easier for the crawler to find your content.

AltaVista recommends that you have a full set of your content in a form that **blind people** can access with text readers. Anything that stops a blind person also stops a web crawler.

Submitting to search engines and directories

First of all, remember that **search engines,** such as AltaVista or Google, use automated crawlers to index pages, as described in the preceding information. **Directories** like Yahoo or the directories associated with search engines (Excite, for instance, has both) are created by humans. Directories will not find your site by themselves—you must submit your site to a human who reviews the site and deems it worthy (or not) to be in their collection.

It's not *difficult* to register a site with the major search engines and web directories—it just takes time and patience. You could do it yourself, but you may want to consider hiring a specialist for the job. The task of optimizing and registering a site with search engines has become a very specialized skill and there are companies and individuals who do this for a living. For the best results, you'll want to consider this option.

If the budget doesn't allow this as an option, you can do a minimal job yourself without too much trouble, and you can really learn the depths of it and do a great job with more trouble.

The simple thing is to go to each of your favorite search engines and directories, click the button that says something like "Submit your site" or "Add your URL," then follow the directions. For most search tools, submit the addresses of your top three or four pages and the automated system or the humans will find the rest.

The more difficult thing is to research every search engine and directory and find out exactly what each one is looking for, then follow each of their requirements. See the last page of this chapter for resources on learning more.

Whether you do it yourself or hire someone, make sure it is clear in your original contract with the client exactly who is responsible for submitting the site and how much it will cost. Clients typically assume this is just built into the budget.

Don't be fooled

You've probably seen services advertised that promise to register your site with 500 search engines. This means you'll pay to have your site registered with approximately 490 search engines you've never heard of. If *you've* never heard of them, neither has anyone else. Don't waste your client's money. It's better to register really well with the 10 best known search services than poorly with 500.

There are a huge number of specialty search services, however (there really are over 500 search engines). There are searches that specialize in just arts and crafts, or orchids, or sites dealing with ancient history, or travel, women, sports, government, water, etc. Find the two or three specialty search engines or directories that are appropriate for your client and register with those as well as the big ones. See **www.searchenginewatch.com** and **searchtools.com** for comprehensive lists of search engines.

155

Maintenance and updating

Who's going to do it?

The need to maintain and update is different from site to site. Some sites contain timeless content that rarely needs an update, while others require daily care and feeding. Regardless of their content, all web sites benefit from frequent attention. The users of the site will return more often if they can expect new material and a fresh look on a regular basis.

Once you accept that regular maintenance is necessary, then the question arises, "Who is going to do it?" The quick answer is, "The designer, of course, because she's the one person who is most qualified." While that may be true, there are always situations where the client will need to be able to make their own updates. Or you may feel most satisfied in designing and building the site, but bored to tears in maintaining it, so you *want* someone else to update it.

Aack, the client's going to update!

As the designer, you will need to be involved in devising a maintenance procedure so your client clearly understands how to do it, and so the integrity of your design is left intact. There are few things more disappointing in web design than seeing your once-beautiful web interface get messed up by a client who doesn't know what they're doing. Before that happens to your site, sit down with your client and create a maintenance plan that works for both of you.

If you are building a site that you know your client will be maintaining, from the very beginning you need to consider how easy or difficult it will be for them to make changes. Designs that use lots of layers or DHTML are much more likely to be compromised by your client's editing than simpler, straightforward HTML. Discuss it with your client and let them know the tradeoffs involved. Let them make the choice between a simpler, easier-to-maintain design, or one that's more sophisticated, but harder to update.

Who's going to teach them?

In our opinion, it's impractical to think you can teach your client HTML and web development in a short amount of time. Unless that's something you want to do and they are willing to pay for lessons, it's a far better plan to instruct them on a need-to-know basis. Most clients have neither the interest nor the time to become web developers, they just want to be able to change their own text as needed.

If you've developed a **content management system** (CMS, see page 109) for them, it will be easy for them to update almost anything on their site whenever they want and they won't be able to tamper with your design.

No CMS?

Clients not fortunate enough to have their own CMS will need more attention and should be pointed in the right direction. Start off by recommending a web-authoring application for them. The best choice is for them to purchase the same application you use. That way you'll be able to help them when they call with questions. With all the great programs available now, there's no reason that your clients should edit web pages directly in HTML—there's just too much chance for error and confusion.

The clients, using their new authoring program, should learn how to open a file, read comment tags (see below), make changes, save it, test it, and then upload it to the server. Anything more is probably too much. Avoid getting sidetracked by trying to teach them JavaScript or explaining the finer points of database programming. If they need something more complicated to be done, they should contract with you.

Comment tags

One thing you *can* do in the HTML code is add **comments,** which are tags that do not appear on the web page, nor do search engines index them. They are simply notes to the client to help them in the updating and maintenance process. Simply type any note you want between `<!-` *and* `->`.   For instance:

```
<!- GET OUT OF THIS AREA. DON'T TOUCH ANYTHING HERE.->

<!- You can edit any of the text you see in this line.->
```

Get it in writing

Most clients are smart enough to know their limits, but it's still a good idea to discuss how things will play out over time. If you have an ongoing relationship with a client, get together and determine the types of site changes they will make and kinds of tasks that are best left to you. It's usually wise for a client to only make text changes to existing pages and for the designer to handle major navigational or structural changes. You also will want to discuss the possibility of future additions and enhancements to the site. It's important that your client knows they can rely on you to advise them on how to make their site even better in the future.

Resources

The specific details about what search engines and directories look for when indexing your site, which is different for most every search tool, is constantly changing as new technology is constantly introduced. If you are going to submit your sites to search engines and directories yourself, you need to keep up with what they're doing. The best resource is the web itself, and the best resource on the web is:

SearchEngineWatch.com

This is a fabulous site with indepth information about everything relevant to search tools. It's run by **Danny Sullivan** who originally created the online guide, "A Webmaster's Guide To Search Engines," that was so valuable. Now there is an amazing amount of free stuff on this site, including a free newsletter, submission tips, articles, and much more. For very serious users there is a subscription option that really digs up the dirt.

Also **search the web** for more information—there are thousands of pages with great (and not-so-great) information on each aspect of this process.

If you want to learn how to *use* search engines more efficiently, get the book, **Search Engines for the World Wide Web: Visual QuickStart Guide,** by Alfred and Emily Glossbrenner.

Section Three: 3 Idea Source

A medley of Information

No matter what you are there for, being on the web is an experience, and designers are the ones who determine what it is like.

—*Thomas Hine*
The New York Times

Slicing and Dicing

One way to start a page layout is to create an HTML table and then proceed to drop GIFs, JPEGs, and text into individual table cells in an arrangement that is as pleasing as possible. It's not very flexible, but it's good enough for some people.

Keep that technique in mind, in case you suddenly lose interest in creative satisfaction. If you're reading this, you've probably set your web-design bar a little higher than that, and you're ready to slice and dice.

Not so long ago if someone had told us that our future careers were going to involve slicing and dicing, we would have been very concerned. As it turns out, slicing is one of our favorite things because:

- It dramatically transforms web design limitations into design possibilities.

- Slicing enables more efficient HTML page design by enabling you to selectively optimize every designated area of a layout.

- The creative potential of using rollovers and image swaps is enhanced by the increased design flexibility that slicing provides.

- The ability to design more freely and experimentally adds a lot more fun to a project.

Avoid the HTML box

Even though technical programming issues can affect design decisions, we emphasize the importance of designing visually rather than approaching web design totally from a programming perspective. Visual design tools such as Adobe Photoshop, Photoshop Elements, Jasc Paint Shop Pro, or Macromedia Fireworks allow you to experiment with layouts that are imaginative and visually eye-catching. Creating a beautiful layout is a good start, but converting the design to an efficiently functioning web page can be complex and nightmarish—albeit less so if you know what the potential problems are.

If you choose to design and produce a web site by hand-coding the HTML, creating tables, placing graphics into painstakingly planned table cells, etc., your layouts will be ordinary and your deadlines will be in jeopardy. Even if you know how, why spend hours hand-coding a complex HTML page when it can be done in a few seconds, and more accurately, with easy-to-use software? The time you save by not having to go through this process *once* will pay for the software.

The web grows up

In this detailed reconstruction of a sample web page, it would be easier to show you a more simplistic design, but that would give you the impression that all page designs are non-problematical. So here's an example of a web page layout we created in Photoshop in which we went out of our way to create a design that would force the HTML text to wrap around a couple of images (a book cover and the author's photo) to prevent the layout from having what we call an "HTML box" look, or a "first generation" look. We describe the first web page layouts that appeared on the Internet as being stuck in the "HTML box" because they were extremely limited in design possibilities: these early designs usually consisted of a headline, followed by text, then a rectangular photo, then more text, usually all centered. Many of these web pages had elements, such as photos or logos, falling in unpredictable positions on the page—depending upon browser type and window size—because most designers didn't know how to take advantage of the table code to help constrain the positions of text and graphics.

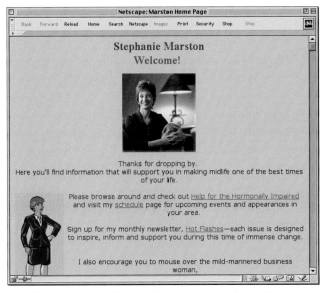

This "first generation" simple layout treats each graphic as a free-floating element on the page, with nothing to control the width of the text or the structure of the page other than the arbitrary width of the browser window. (It also uses the standard, default, gray background and default blue links.)

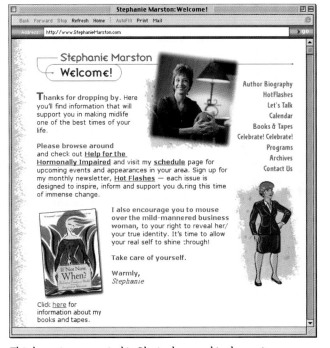

This layout was created in Photoshop and is shown in a Photoshop window. The browser interface is on a Photoshop layer to simulate what the page will look like in a browser. We designed this layout with an understanding of the table structure we would later impose on it.

The table box

One way to control the position of elements in a layout is to place the elements into the cells of a table. Placing page elements into a table helps to control the layout, but this technique can still result in a boxy, modular look that's visually unexciting.

Placing page elements into the cells of an HTML table provides more design potential. Also, the presentation of the page in different browsers is more predictable.

Stacking graphics on top of each other in one cell, such as the navigation buttons and illustration at the upper-right, can create problems under certain conditions, such as when adding HTML text below the navigation images, which might stretch the table cell's depth and cause the navigation images to spread apart.

Instead, place (nest) the navigation slices in their own, separate table so they're held together snugly into one unit; *then* place (nest) that table within an existing cell in the main table, as shown on the opposite page.

This is the same page shown to the left, but we've turned on the table borders so you can see exactly what we did. This simple table holds elements in place (although not as reliably as would a more complex table).

The table un-boxed

The table box technique works, but if you take it a step further, it works much better.

Rather than limit your imagination to placing complete elements into the cells of a table, take advantage of the ability to cut images into pieces, even cut right through the middle of photos if necessary. Then place the individual pieces into separate cells of an HTML table where they will be "glued" back together seamlessly, like a puzzle.

Using this "slicing and dicing" technique, you can also create empty (or partially empty) table cells so that later you can type HTML text in these empty cells.

The design flexibility offered by this slicing technique enables you to design more efficient, interesting, and fluid layouts, as you'll see in the following examples.

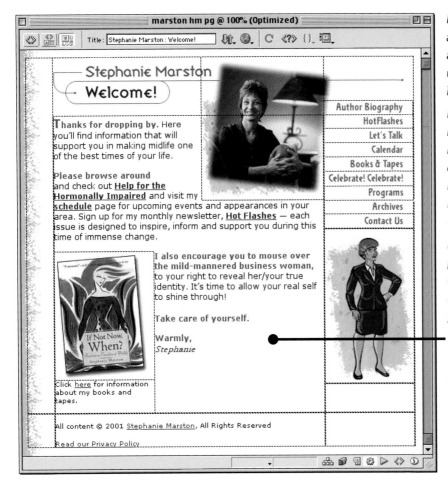

Here is our layout in Dreamweaver after it was sliced and placed into an HTML table. You can see the various cells of the table that are holding the graphics and text.

Notice the top photo is actually cut into five pieces: the top and bottom main pieces, and the small slivers of color that fall into the right navigation column. Each piece is contained in a separate cell.

The graphic headline with the rules is also cut into three pieces, each piece sitting in a different cell (the second and third pieces are included as part of the photographic image).

The center section that holds the HTML text is actually a number of individual cells merged into one rectangle. Later, we'll drop in the nested tables that you see in the top-right and bottom-left of this rectangle, and the HTML text will wrap-around them, as you see in our layout here.

How we constructed this page

The overall process

After several design variations, this approved layout was ready for final production. In Photoshop, we dragged guidelines onto the file where we planned to slice it apart, as shown to the right (the body copy is for comp purposes only and will be eliminated later and replaced with HTML text).

We opened the layout in our image optimization software (Adobe ImageReady, in this case). In seconds, ImageReady used our guides and sliced apart the layout, created a web page, built an HTML table that contained a table cell for each slice, and dropped the graphics directly into the appropriate cells. Wow.

In Photoshop, we dragged guidelines to the designated areas that we wanted to slice into separate graphics. These same guides will determine the shape and number of cells in the HTML table that ImageReady will automatically create.

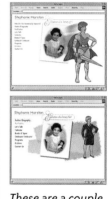

These are a couple of the many design variations we went through before deciding to work with the one shown to the left.

Balancing download speed and image quality

Our slicing plan revolved around two main goals:

Our first goal: Create an empty cell in the table into which we could later place HTML text that would flow around a couple of images. That's slightly more challenging than it sounds because a table cell cannot have an irregular shape such as the shape we want the text to flow through—table cells are always rectangular. We will address that problem (pages 172–174), but for now we proceeded to look carefully at our second goal.

Our second goal: Optimize the balance of download speed and image quality. We noticed that several of the images would be best suited as JPEG files and others would look better and be smaller in file size as GIF files. To this end, we would need to create unique slices so the software could save each image in the different file formats necessary for making the graphics look their best, yet download quickly.

To make the slicing and image optimization processes easy, we first opened the Photoshop layout file in Adobe ImageReady, a software tool for optimizing images for the web: from Photoshop's File menu, we slid down to "Jump to" and out to "Adobe ImageReady."

We wanted these two files as JPEGs.

We wanted this image, the navigation bar above it, and the headline graphic to be GIFs.

At this point in the slice planning, it's not only important to make file format decisions, but also to decide which areas need to be unique slices so when we start optimizing the images, each image will be its own separate table cell.

ImageReady works as a standalone product, even though it is automatically installed with the newest versions of Photoshop.

Slicing it up

We could have performed the slicing from within Photoshop, but we prefer ImageReady for several reasons, including the "Create Slices from Guides" feature and the ease of combining several slices into one. Since Photoshop keeps adding additional web features to its new releases, the differences between Photoshop and ImageReady may become less noticeable over time.

From ImageReady's Slices menu, we selected "Create Slices from Guides." As a result, our layout was sliced everywhere a guideline appeared.

In this example, creating slices from our guidelines created more pieces than we needed. We combined several groups of contiguous slices into one to create the larger slice shown below. (To do this, Shift-click on separate slices to select multiple pieces; from the Slices menu, choose "Combine Slices.")

We also used the "Combine Slices" feature to combine all the navigation slices into one single piece; later we'll place a nested table containing all the separate navigation slices (see pages 177–179) into that single cell space, but for now we used the navigation slice as a placeholder.

Notice that we combined many smaller slices of the large text area into one large slice, even though our comp layout showed other images within that square space. Our plan was to add those images later, as elements placed in nested tables. For now, this large slice would act as a placeholder until we inserted real HTML text into the table.

Back to optimizing the graphics

Now that we have the layout sliced up, we're ready to optimize each piece, as we mentioned two pages ago, using the
"Optimize" palette, shown below.

- We designated the slices that are flat color (the cartoon
  illustration, the type graphics, and the decorative ruled
  lines) as GIF files with a limited color palette.
- We designated the photographic images (the portrait and
  the book cover) as JPEGs with fairly low quality settings.

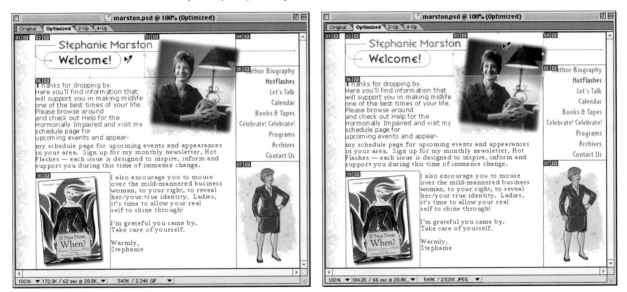

*With the Slice Selection tool, we selected
each individual slice and adjusted their
optimization settings in the "Optimize" palette.*

We returned to the ImageReady document to opitimize and save the bottom-half of the portrait and the book cover image as extra slices. Later we'll place these into nested tables, and we'll place those nested tables into the main table cell that contains our HTML text.

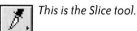 *This is the Slice tool.*

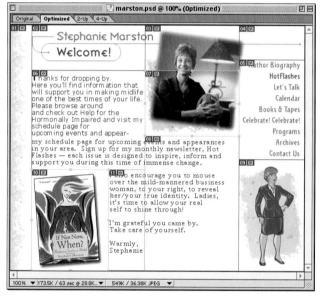

We used the Slice tool to drag new slice selections around the bottom-half of the author photo and around the book cover.

We used the Select Slice tool to select the bottom-half of the author's photo slice, then optimized it in the JPEG format using the "Optimize" palette.

From the File menu we selected "Save Optimized As… ." In this dialog box, we chose the "Images Only" and "Selected Slices" options. By doing this, we're saving only the JPEG image instead of having ImageReady create an HTML table or code.

We repeated this procedure for the book cover image slice. Once we had optimized all slices, we were almost ready to build the HTML table.

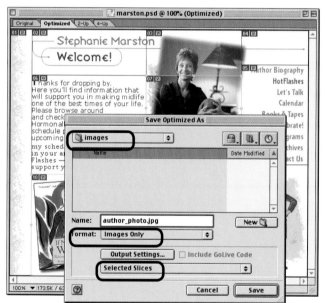 *This is the Select Slice tool.*

We saved these two JPEGs into a new "images" folder that we created. Later, when we slice and save the entire layout, we'll save all the other optimized images into this folder also.

The HTML text

Up until this point, the body copy did not present a problem because it was a graphic created on a Photoshop layer just for layout visualization. The challenge now was how to make the real HTML text flow through the layout as we planned.

If this were a simpler design, the text could just flow into a rectangular-shaped table cell and web-design-life would be easy. We could even have the text wrap around some random images, as we did on some of the site's interior pages, without any problems. But no-o-o, we chose to be difficult.

In this interior page of the same web site, the text is simply flowing around graphics that are placed on the page.

The alignment properties of the various photo images have been set to "left" or "right," forcing the images to the left and right margins, which makes the text wrap around the images.

This is the easier way to do things.

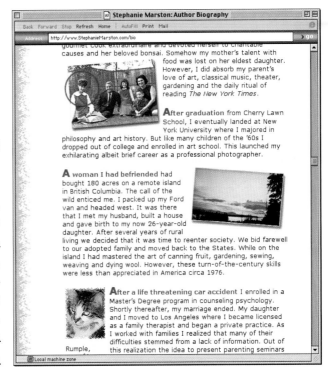

Who wants the easy way out

Our layout called for something more imaginative than the simple text wrap shown on the previous page. We wanted the text to begin underneath one image (the "Welcome" headline), wrap around the bottom-half of another image (the author's photo), and continue down the page to wrap around the book cover image.

The yellow-orange color block in this layout, shown in Photoshop, shows the polygonal shape that we wanted our text to flow through. Unfortunately, a table cell with a shape like this is impossible to create in HTML.

This image shows the only shape possible for an HTML table cell: a rectangle.

The solution was to slice through the middle of the author's photograph and place that photo segment into a separate, one-cell table.

We nested that one-cell table into the main cell that contains the HTML text (upper-right).

The book cover and its caption we will place into their own two-cell table.

We'll also place (nest) that small table with the book cover and caption into the main cell (lower-left).

Use spacers to hold cell shapes

Some cells were intended to be empty cells, allowing the page background texture and color to show through. However, if a cell is completely empty, you run the risk that its size will change when text and graphics are placed into other cells. To solve this potential problem, most web authoring programs have a feature that places a "spacer" file in a cell.

A spacer is a transparent, one-pixel by one-pixel GIF that has been stretched to the dimensions of the table cell; this allows background images or page background colors to show through as it holds the table cell to its intended shape. If you later need to place something into a cell that contains a spacer, just delete it (or change the dimensions of the spacer). If you want the cell to remain "empty" and clear so you can see the background color, leave the spacer there forever.

In ImageReady, we used the Select Slice tool (circled, below), to select Slice #1 (the first cell on the left). In the "Slice" palette, from the "Type" menu, we selected "No Image," which placed a spacer in the selected cell.

We then used the Select Slice tool to select the large cell that will hold the HTML text. In the "Slice" palette, from the "Type" menu, we selected "Image." Later we'll throw away this image and replace it with HTML text, but for now it serves as a placeholder.

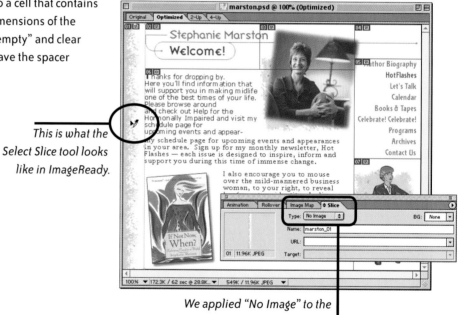

This is what the Select Slice tool looks like in ImageReady.

We applied "No Image" to the selected slice (the cell along the far-left edge).

Let's get ready to build

Finally, with all our planning and optimizing complete, we're ready to build the actual HTML page. We're initially going to let ImageReady put the page together for us.

From the File menu, we selected "Save Optimized As…." Using the settings shown, ImageReady created an HTML table, cut the image into slices, optimized each slice according to our settings, placed each slice in the appropriate table cell, created an HTML page containing the table, and created an "Images" folder that stores all the newly created, individual image slices. Not bad for a few seconds of work.

Here's the web page that ImageReady put together for us, as seen in a browser. The text area at this point is still a graphic slice rather than HTML text. The book cover and the bottom of the author photo are still part of the text-area graphics.

And at the moment, the navigation area is still a single graphic slice instead of individual slices; later, they will be separate graphics each linked to other pages, and they'll have rollover behaviors attached.

Finishing touches

A few details remain to finish up the page. In Dreamweaver, we opened the HTML file that ImageReady just created. The text on the page is not HTML text, but a graphic of our layout which was placed in the table cell. Since we need to type text into that space, we deleted the graphic so the table cell would be empty, ready for us to type.

We typed the body copy into the text cell as HTML text, emphasized key words and phrases with color and bold formating, and created links to interior pages. We placed the JPEG image

of the bottom-half of the author photograph into a one-cell table; then we nested (inserted) that small table into the upper-right corner of the cell that contains the HTML text. We designated the large cell's vertical alignment property as "Top." The alignment setting of the nested table containing the photo fragment is "Right."

We placed the bookcover image and caption in a one-column, two-row table, then inserted that small table into a line of the text and assigned it an alignment property of "Left."

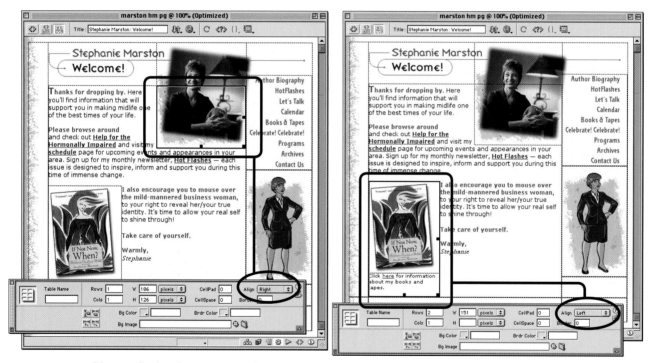

We were not able to make the photo segment align properly with the rest of the photo until we placed the segments into a nested table.

We created a two-row table for the book cover: one cell is for the cover, plus the caption has its own cell. We placed this small table into the text and gave it an alignment property of "Left" so the text would wrap around it.

The trouble with tables

Up until this point, the navigation area on the right side of this web page was filled with a static GIF file that ImageReady had created during the "Save Optimized As…" operation. We didn't separate this section into individual slices at the same time as the rest of the page because we've learned from experience that the navigation pieces will be easier to control if they reside in their own table, which will be nested inside a cell of the main table. When we've built our new navigation table, we'll delete the static GIF file and nest the new navigation table into that cell.

An unpleasant characteristic of tables that you'll discover sooner or later is that they can be undependable rascals. When you've spent hours perfecting a layout, it's quite unsettling to see your web site on a different computer and realize that your layout has been stretched out of recognition.

Individual users can change their font to display default HTML text at various sizes, and this can stretch neighboring text cells. These unexpectedly larger cells in turn can cause surprising layout revisions as the stretched cells spread your sliced graphics apart. You can usually avoid this by building groups of elements (such as all the navigation slices) into their own tables, then nesting those tables within cells of larger tables. (See another technique for solving stretching problems on page 174.)

Slicing the navigation buttons

To finalize the navigation element of our page, we planned to slice the navigation image into individual pieces. Then we'll build a table just for the navigation slices. We'll nest that small table into the appropriate cell of the main table.

Our original thought was to use the navigation that we create for this home page on all interior pages. But later we made some design decisions that slightly affected that plan: as we designed the home page, we moved the tilted author's photograph to the right, slightly into the horizontal space of the top two navigation buttons. Since this intrusion into the navigation space helped to free the design from a boxy, modular look, we decided to let the intruding photo edge be part of the top two navigation slices.

But as a result of that intrusion on the home page, for interior pages we need to create new, clean versions of the top two navigation buttons that do *not* have traces of the tilted photo in them. The rest of the button slices will be unchanged from the home page version. These two new navigation slices are so small (approximately .5k or less) that adding a couple of new files to the overall site download is inconsequential to the page weight (it's just more work for us).

In our original Photoshop file, we drew guidelines where we wanted to slice the navigation area into separate files. We cropped away everything except the navigation area, then from the File menu, we slid down to "Jump to" and chose "Adobe ImageReady."

We proceeded to create the main navigation slices and the HTML table for the navigation which would be nested into the table cell created for the navigation slices.

We planned to have the plain words of the navigation turn into a button when moused over, as in the "Celebrate! Celebrate!" button shown below, right. See more about rollovers, mouse overs, and image swaps in Chapter 16.

First we sliced and saved the file with all layers turned on for the "Normal" state.

- From the Slices menu in ImageReady, we chose "Create Slices from Guides." We then optimized each slice as a GIF file with a very limited color palette to minimize the file sizes.
- From the File menu, we chose "Save Optimized As…."
- In the "Save Optimized As" dialog box, we selected "HTML and Images" from the Format menu. We also selected the "All Slices" option, as shown below.
- We clicked "Save." ImageReady created the HTML code and all the GIF images needed for the "Normal" version of the navigation buttons.

This is the "Normal" button state.

These are the buttons we created for the "Over" state. The width of the widest button (Celebrate! Celebrate!) was used as a guide for the maximum size of the navigation slices.

This is the rollover effect; that is, when the mouse rolls over a link, the image changes (swaps) to a new button shape.

Note: *Sometimes we just need to revise a single button or graphic. In that case, we first select the appropriate slice, then choose "Images Only" from the Format menu, instead of "HTML and Images." We choose "Selected Slices" instead of "All Slices."*

Back at the HTML page

After ImageReady created the HTML page for the navigation, we opened that page in Dreamweaver, copied the table, and pasted that table into the navigation cell of our main page in Dreamweaver, replacing the static GIF image of the navigation buttons.

Dreamweaver had created an "Images" folder for the navigation image slices. We moved the graphics from that folder and put them into a different "Images" folder, the one that Dreamweaver had previously created for the home page.

In Dreamweaver, we created links for each of the navigation slices.

Back to the navigation buttons

We then returned to Photoshop, to the original navigation source file. We turned on all the layers that represented what the slices look like in a rollover state, and repeated the slicing procedure ("Save Optimized As…") to create rollover versions of all the navigation slices.

This is the Photoshop file with all layers turned on that contain a rollover version of a navigation button.

In the "Save Optimized As…" dialog box, we chose "Images Only" from the Format menu since we had already created a table for these navigation buttons; these new images were copied to our main Images folder and will be used later for "rollover" behaviors. See Chapter 17 for more on rollovers and image swaps.

Really, we're getting close now

We have two final steps to take.

1. In Dreamweaver, we added the background image that creates the texture on the left, plus the subtle, overall background hybrid color (see pages 210–214 for details about hybrid color).

This is the final HTML table as seen in the web authoring program, showing three nested tables: the navigation table; the book cover and caption table; and the one-cell table that holds the bottom half of the author's photo.

This is the background image we used in this site. It repeats itself down the page, creating the border on the left edge. (The image is actually much wider than you see here.)

2. We turned the cartoon into a rollover by assigning an "Image Swap" behavior that activates when a user rolls their mouse over it.

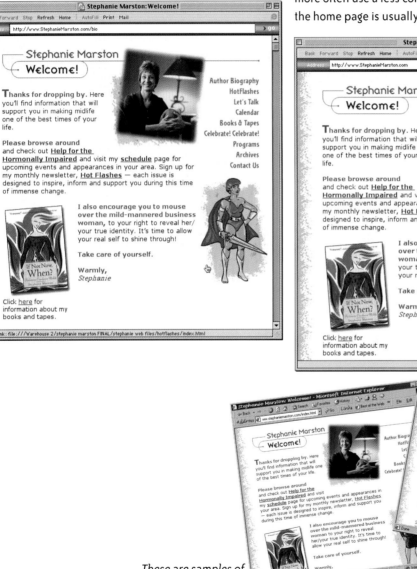

That's all, folks!

The result of all this slicing and dicing is an attractive layout that breaks through the common design limitations of ordinary table cell layouts. Interior pages that need to change more often use a less complex design, but setting a tone on the home page is usually worth some extra effort.

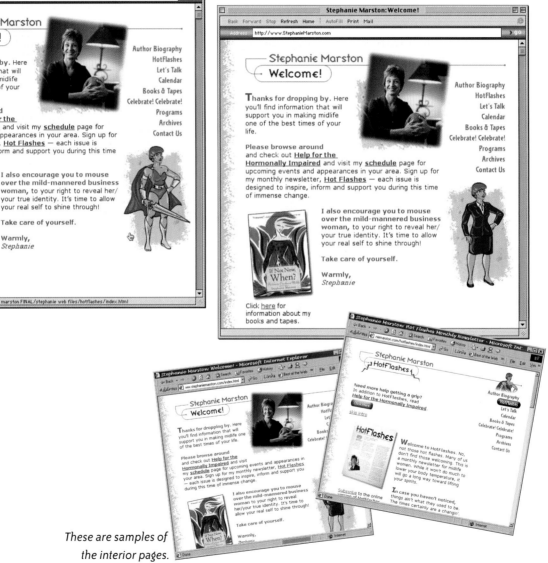

These are samples of the interior pages.

A few quick examples

Knowledge is power

Because cell stretching is such a frustrating problem, as we whined about on page 177, you should be aware of the potential problem so you can plan ahead to avoid it. So here are a few more examples of how we sliced a layout apart to build an efficiently constructed page, made of GIFs, JPEGs, and HTML text, and worked through the challenge of table resizing.

Above is the same example, but we changed the HTML page background color to yellow to better show you where the cells of the table are being stretched. (The graphic files have white backgrounds which ordinarily would blend into the white background of the page, as on the left.)

You can see the navigation buttons on the left side of the web page are being forced apart; it should be a solid black bar down the side. When we first created this page, everything was okay; later when we made HTML text revisions, the table stretching problem occurred.

As we discussed earlier, if the visitor to your site enlarges the text in their browser, it can force cells to expand. To protect the navigation buttons from the stretching effect created by other table cells, we placed all the navigation elements in their own private table. Then we nested that small, private table into a cell of the main table.

In the example below, we changed the page background color and assigned a value of 6 pixels to the navigation table border specifically to show you the nested table on the web page. Now when the main table cells stretch, it doesn't affect our nested table.

The nested table protects the navigation elements from the influence of other table cells when those other table cells are stretched larger to accommodate more content.

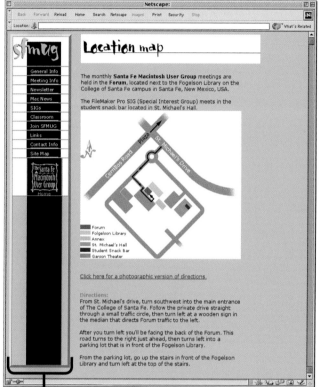

This is a nested table.

The bottom cell of the nested table is filled with black. The height of the black cell is determined by how many Returns we've typed into it. When we create pages that are longer than the existing black bar, we type more Returns in the bottom black cell to extend it as much as necessary.

Unnested problem

In this example, the navigation on the left is being stretched apart and it's affecting the appearance of the edge of the main text block, in addition to adding unwanted space between navigation slices.

Nested solution

Below, we avoided the stretching-table problem by placing the navigation in its own table and nesting that table in the appropriate cell of a larger table. Now our problem cells are held together by their own table, nested within the cell of a larger table.

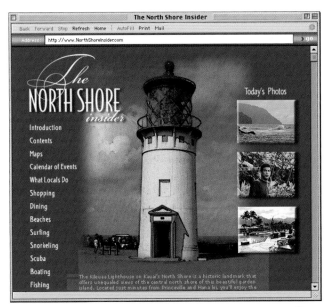

We created the original table for this layout by automatically slicing the entire layout image. The process created a separate slice for each navigation element (left-hand side), but made the slices susceptible to stretching apart, as you can see.

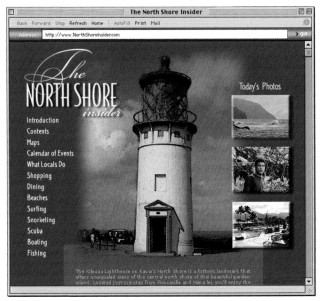

We merged the navigation cells into one cell so we could place (nest) a complete table in it. The nested table contained individual cells for each navigation element. You can see how they stay tucked together neatly.

Alternatives to ImageReady

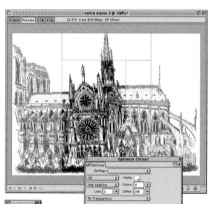

In **Macromedia Fireworks,** use the Tools palette's Slice tool to draw slices. Select the slices with the Pointer tool and optimize them in the Fireworks "Optimize" palette.

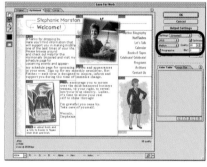

In **Photoshop's "Save for Web…"** feature, as shown above, the optimization controls and interface are very similar to ImageReady's (except Photoshop cannot combine slices). If you have a version of Photoshop with this feature, you'll find it as a command in the File menu.

If you have an earlier version of Photoshop that does not include the "Save for Web" feature, you can always do it by hand. Step-by-step directions are in our other book, *The Non-Designer's Web Book.*

To slice and optimize in **Paint Shop Pro:** from the File menu, choose "Export," then "Image Slicer." You'll get the "Image Slicer" dialog box, shown above.

Use the Grid tool to divide the image into equal pieces, or the Line tool to create uneven slices. Use the Pointer tool to select individual slices to optimize.

Something about Backgrounds

13

Do you like backgrounds on a web page? If you answered "no" then you're mistaken—every web page has a background, even if it's white. Our answer to that question would be, "Yes, unless the background is distracting or interferes with the readability of the page."

A background that you don't notice is a good background, but it's not the only good background. Most of what we say in this chapter could be considered common sense because as a designer, you're accustomed to thinking in terms of legibility, clear communication, contrast, etc. But for some strange reason, the ease of creating flamboyant backgrounds on a page seems to be so seductive that many web builders are often tempted into bad design behavior, almost as if they're in the middle of a mid-design crisis. With a touch of good judgment, you can avoid the heartbreak of bad background design.

Dazzle vs. readable

Which do you choose?

Creating a web page that has dazzle can be a good thing ... unless that dazzle is being supplied by a page background that's irritating the holy pixels out of everyone (everyone except the designer who obviously gives dazzle a higher priority than communication). If you need dazzle, it should come from the page content, not the page background.

Backgrounds can be created in a variety of attitudes. Some are so subtle you don't realize they're there at all. Others are more obvious, ranging from beautiful to interesting. And then there's the "Hideous" category, covering the gamut from distracting to unbelievably ugly.

Your background attitude not only affects the readability of your web pages, it is a testimonial to your sense of design awareness and experience—or lack of the same. Even if you're not an experienced designer, you can easily avoid that "Hideous" category by observing a few guidelines for effective communication.

Simplicity

As a general rule and guide, **simplicity** is a very powerful communication technique. As it applies to web page backgrounds, simplicity can make a page more readable, legible, and inviting. There are exceptions to every rule, and someday we're probably going to design a web site with a complicated background. But normally we prefer unobtrusive, low profile backgrounds—readers never complain that the background of a page is too simple or that a page is too easy to read.

The fact that hideous backgrounds are easy to make is not a good enough reason to use one.

(It always amazes us that everyone else can see how distracting and ineffective an obnoxious background is—everyone except the designer of that page. How does that happen?)

Visual impact

Visual impact is a good thing when it's focused on the *content* of the page. It's not such a good thing when it's focused on the *background image* and competes with the page content. **A background works best when it's not trying to be the foreground.** Use background color, texture, or images to enhance the presentation of your page content, not as visual competition to the page content.

A background image can serve to aid in the visual organization of a layout, and it is a simple way to create a layered look by placing text or other images on top of a background image.

Exercise self-control

There are various ways to use backgrounds. Each of the examples in this chapter is slightly different *visually,* but each one is the same *technically:* a GIF or JPEG file that the web browser repeats (tiles) across a page. Tiled background images can be used to create the impression of a pattern design, or a texture, or to create a design emphasis on only one side of a page.

Between the powerful digital tools and the stock images that are available to designers, there's not much to keep one from going background-crazy except for self-control and good judgment. Almost any image can be tiled and made into a background, but we prefer simple backgrounds that assist readability and legibility.

Smaller is not always better

Theoretically, a repeating background image loads so fast that the page background appears instantly. This is usually true, but keep in mind that if you make your background image *too small,* the background may load slower than if it were a larger file, particularly on all the slower machines in the world.

The GIF file shown to the right is 2 pixels x 4 pixels, which resulted in a file size of 3.8 bytes. The designer logically reasoned that such a small file would be lightning fast to load. But because the file had to load so many times to fill the browser window, the background actually took longer to completely fill the window than a larger file (shown below-right) would have.

This tiny graphic, 2 pixels by 4 pixels, creates the pattern shown to the right.

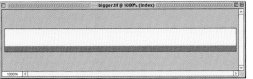

Contrast

We use a white background more often than any other because it's the easiest, most familiar reading environment for our readers. When we don't use white, our usual choice is a light pastel color that still provides dramatic contrast with black (or very dark) type (and if we can't find the right pastel, we build our own as a hybrid color; see pages 210–215). Aim for maximum contrast between the background and the page content.

As shown on the following pages, sometimes we **reverse** the color scheme to make the page background black (or a very dark color) and the type white (or some other light color). This technique is very dramatic—it's also very tiresome and boring if used on every page in the site. For maximum visual impact, use reversed text sparingly, such as on a home page, an intro page, or a special page.

If a page with a dark background contains content that a reader may want to print, they have two problems: If their defaults are set to print the background, you won't make friends when your web pages take a week's supply of toner to print out. And if a visitor's defaults are set to ignore the background when

printing, the white type won't show up on their printed page. Either way, it's annoying.

As the designer, you have two options. Get rid of the dark background, or create a separate, printable page and provide the visitor a prominent link to the printable version.

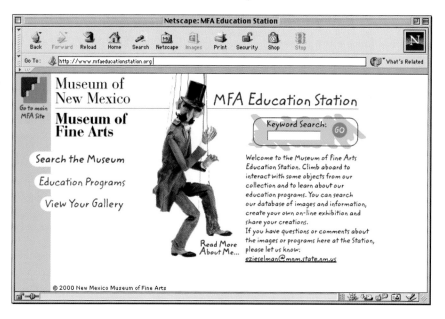

This entry page, which had minimal text and no reason to print, was designed with a black background for visual impact and for contrast with the animated *GIF* of the burning typewriter. Once you're in the site, you never see this page again—its purpose is just to create an attitude before entering.

The entry page shown to the left leads to this intro page, above, whose background is a dark gray color. For this page we wanted the dramatic look of a dark color, a color that could visually relate to the entry page, but not black (the conference colors are black and white). Using gray allowed us to use both black and white text. But notice we didn't use the default gray that's common in undesigned web pages.

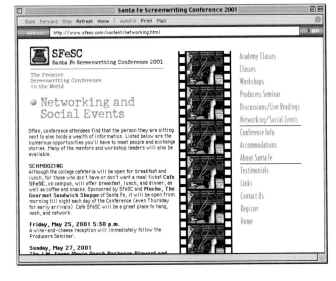

All of the interior content pages, which contain a lot of text and which might be printed, use white backgrounds to make the pages more readable and printable.

Although we let go of the dark pages in the interior of the site, we maintained the black, white, gray, and gold color theme, plus a very consistent pattern of headlines, text, and navigation.

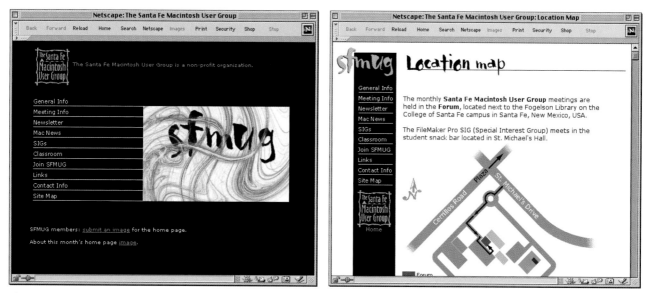

The Santa Fe Mac User Group home page uses a black background, then switches to a reader-friendly and printer-friendly white for all interior pages. There's really no reason anyone would want to print this home page, and there's no lengthy text to read.

We pulled in the black bar and gold color on interior pages to create a consistent look throughout the site.

Every interior page creates a
strong, consistent identity.

Look around

You already know through common sense that the most readable background is white or very light. But be conscious whenever you find a web site that really feels professional and sophisticated to you—notice its background. We guarantee it doesn't have a color or pattern that makes it the slightest bit difficult to read. Use this "clean" technique to make even smaller or personal sites look sophisticated.

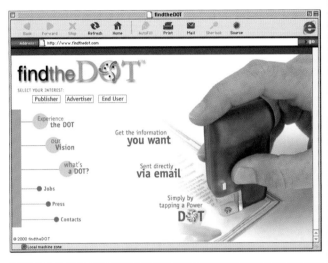

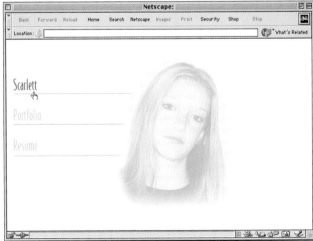

The ForzaTech site for our 18-year-old Turkish exchange student is one that he will change and adapt as he and his econometric work changes and grows.

Can you imagine how a busy, patterned background on any of the sites shown here would change a visitor's impression instantly? If you're not a great designer, go for clean. It always works.

Background edges

Background edges create the illusion that a separate graphic is running down the left edge of the page, adding decoration, color, or visual organization (perhaps all of the above), to the site design. Actually, the left edge of the design is just part of a horizontal background image that repeats as many times as necessary to fill the page window. Background images such as this can be complex and rich in appearance and still load quickly. By keeping the complex and decorative elements to the left side (or top) of the design, the main content area can remain clean and clear so you can create very readable text.

A background image with a strong (but simple) left edge element is often used to visually separate left-side navigation from the rest of the page by placing the navigation graphics in the left-most cell of a table. This has become so common that it is now a familiar sight to visitors, which means they don't have to figure out what to do when they get to your site (conventions on web pages are good; they help visitors find their way around this amorphous mass).

Background edges are effective as long as the content area remains subtle enough to enhance readability, not harm it. No matter how interesting a background may be, clear communication is more important than decoration. If you or your client likes decorative backgrounds, this left-edge solution works better than covering the entire page with a texture or pattern.

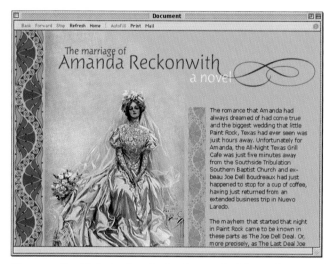

The repeating Victorian border background adds a richness and atmosphere to this page. A smaller, muted version of the same border creates a framing effect around the image and an old-fashioned decorative touch to the text block. To build this small border, we stacked duplicate GIF images in their own table cell.

NOTE: *This is an ideal image in which to use the weighted optimization technique for compressing image files (see pages 54–55).*

This is the graphic that tiles, or repeats, down the page.

An old-time example

To create a background for a site with an old-fashioned flavor, we found a stock image of a floral pattern. In this example, we want to make a background that only appears as a border along the left edge of the pages.

To do this we need to make a long, thin, horizontal graphic that will repeat, or tile, down the page. Because the tile is very wide, you only see the left edge of it once. If the file was not so wide, the floral pattern would show in the browser more than once, as shown on the next page.

The resulting appearance on the page is the left-edge border. In reality, if you had a huge monitor you could open the window wide enough and see another column of the image.

First we cropped a vertical slice from the stock background that we found.

Using a beige color picked up from the image, we added a small gradient of color to the top and bottom of the image. Next, we added a very small black gradient to the right edge of the image to give some dimension to the right edge.

We added 1200 pixels of width to the canvas size of the file and filled all but the floral pattern portion with a beige hybrid color (see pages 210–215). The 1200-pixel width is designed to hide the tiling effect from view in the browser. If the background image is a single, flat color, the GIF format can compress an extremely wide file down to a very small size.

We optimized the file as a GIF with a limited color palette of 16 colors. This palette was too limited to accurately render all the colors of the original, but it helped to make the file size very small, and we discovered that the limited color palette gave the image the look of old-fashioned, silk-screened wallpaper. So even at 1200 pixels wide, this file compressed to slightly over 10K.

When the graphic file is tiled by the browser as a background, the tiled images create an attractive border for the page.

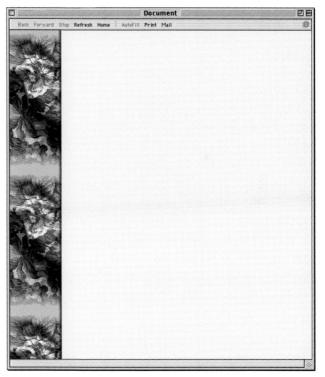

This simple technique adds visual interest to a page without getting in the way of any other content.

Tips for making horizontal background tiles

When you design a horizontally formatted background image, make the width of the background image larger than the largest browser window will be. A common large monitor size is 1024 pixels wide. Using this measurement as a maximum browser size, make the background graphic slightly wider, say 1100 pixels, so the tiling of the background image won't be noticeable in the browser window.

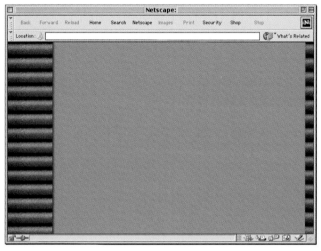

This background image is not wide enough to hide its tiling effect as a background image in a browser, as you can see in the window below.

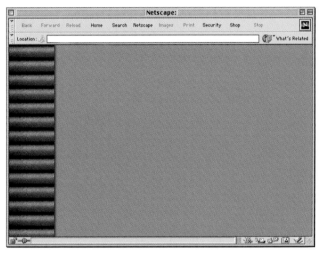

As the tile image repeats in the background, the left side of the background image is visible in the right side of the window.

*By making the background file **wider** (as shown below) than the browser window can realistically be opened, the tiling effect is hidden.*

Vertically formatted background tiles

It is just as easy to create a border across the top of a page as it is to create one down the side, as shown on the previous pages.

A vertically formatted background should be sized according to how deep the page is expected to fall. If the page is totally viewable in one non-scrolling window, a height of 800 or 900 pixels should be sufficient for the height dimension of the background file (considering that a common large monitor size is 1024 pixels x 768 pixels). If the page is a long scrolling page, the height may be drastically larger, even up to 10,000 pixels. If the background image is simple and optimized properly, the file can still compress to a reasonable download size, but there are, of course, many times when the extreme length of a page will make this approach impractical.

Generally speaking, we don't use long scrolling pages, so this technique works well.

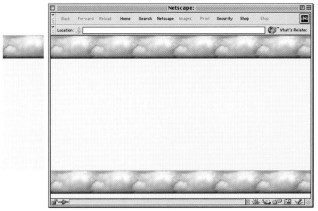

The height of this vertically formatted background file is not large enough to hide the tiling effect as the image repeats across the page—the top of the background image is seen repeating in the bottom portion of the window.

By making the background file's height dimension greater than the anticipated web page length, you can hide the tiling effect of the background image.

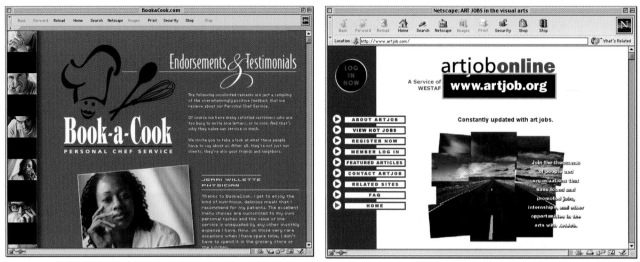

A simple, two-color background image looks richer with a table cell that contains small JPEGs positioned over the darker area to the left of the background pattern. The overall dark value of the background creates a dramatic contrast with the headlines and content.

A horizontal background image can create a strong visual division between the navigation and content areas.

Web pages present a horizontal appearance, rather than a vertical one like most things we read. A left-edge image can be used to contain the content area in a smaller space, resulting in shorter, more readable line lengths for body copy.

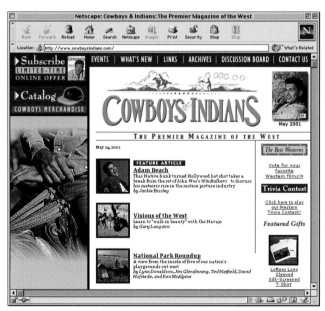

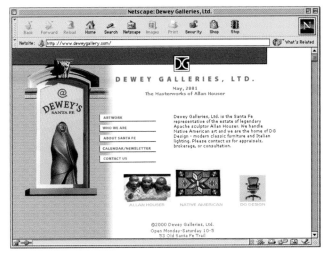

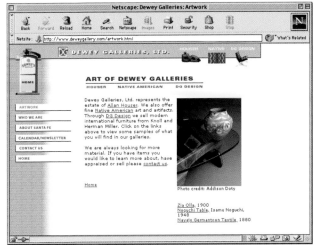

These two pages are examples of a subtle design variation in the background image between the home page and the interior pages of the site.

The personality and identity of the site are unaffected by the variations. The smaller left-edge image provides more room for content on the interior pages.

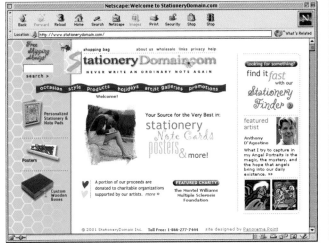

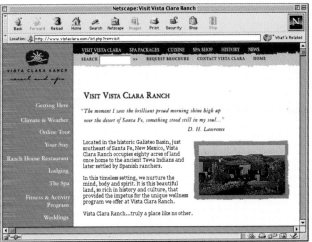

Textured and patterned backgrounds work very well when the texture doesn't extend all the way across the page.

These two sites take advantage of the beauty and richness of textures and patterns without affecting the readability of the main content on the page.

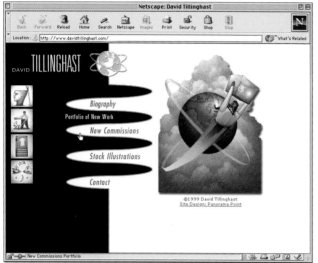

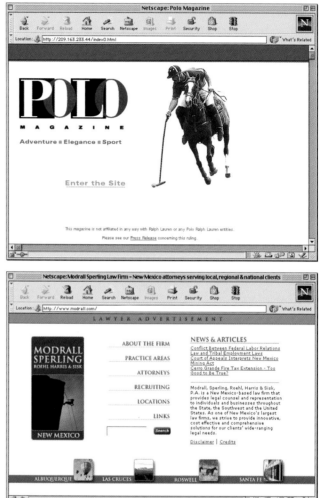

You can create unique effects by placing graphics precisely on top of background edges. The unusual shapes and strong contrast make the design inviting and memorable. Although the technique of placing buttons on the left-edge area is a tried-and-true convention, a creative designer can always do something fresh and exciting with the concept, yet still communicate clearly.

Contact

This is one of the graphic buttons used in the page above. We placed a gray border around the edge so you could see its actual shape.

The two pages above both use vertically formatted background images, as shown on page 195, to create a bar of color across the top. In the bottom example, the text "Lawyer Advertisement" is a graphic positioned at the top-center.

Large-image backgrounds

This background technique goes against our usual recommendations and guidelines that we have concerning backgrounds: be subtle, stay small, don't be too noticeable, keep a low profile. However, large-image backgrounds can be an effective exception to these guidelines. Used with good design judgment, they can help create visually interesting, dramatic layouts.

Page designs that contain a lot of text or other content don't work as well with large-image backgrounds; you need to design the page content so the background image remains uncluttered enough to be recognizable. If it's a struggle to identify the background image, it's a struggling design.

Large single-graphic backgrounds incorporate the challenge of both vertical and horizontal backgrounds: make the width and height dimensions large enough to hide the tiling effect in a browser window. This can result in a file that is very slow to load if you're not careful.

This type of background image works best as a flat-color GIF file with a very limited color palette. That's because the GIF format is excellent at compressing very large areas of flat color into very small files.

A low-contrast typographic treatment makes a dramatic backdrop for this page. The type used in the background is aliased to help reduce the file size. The strong vertical shapes of this font and the low contrast make the aliasing jaggies less evident.

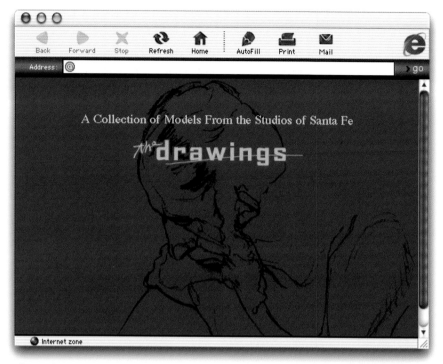

This web page was successful for three main reasons:

- The large image was designed to be highly compressible, which enabled a fast download in spite of its size.

- The dark background color and the even darker drawing contrasted strongly with the other elements on the page, which made a readable, visually pleasing layout.

- The simplicity of the page layout enhanced the visual impact of the drawing and the legibility of the text and headline.

Use good design judgment in deciding how the content of the entire page relates to the background image. Realize that text placed on top of an image is difficult to read. Use contrast to create separation between the background image and other content on the page. And look for opportunities to use this technique. Working with large-image backgrounds can generate fresh new ideas and unique, interesting layouts.

The power of simplicity

The image shown directly below, with its extended background, measured 1600 x 1200 pixels. The original file was 7.32 megabytes, but the GIF file weighed in at 9.7K. One reason the image compressed so efficiently was simplicity: the image has no shading or shadows, just flat type and large expanses of flat color.

If we look at the background image in Photoshop's "Save for Web" 4-Up window, shown below, we can see the efficiency of GIF compression on flat-color image files like this one. The original file (shown in the upper-left quadrant) was 7.32 megabytes. Using GIF compression, the file size changed to 9.7K (upper-right quadrant).

By comparison, a JPEG compression that yielded a comparable size (15K) resulted in completely unacceptable quality (lower-left quadrant). To achieve comparable quality, the JPEG version had to be set to the highest quality setting, resulting in a file that was 94K (lower-right quadrant).

We used a logo background to decorate this otherwise bland page.

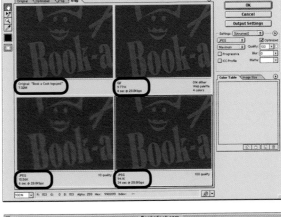

Good software can provide simultaneous previews of multiple optimization settings.

Using a background image allows us to create a multi-layered look just by placing text and other images on the page. By placing all other elements in a table, we can control where the page content falls in relation to the background image.

A JPEG photo as a background image

The background image example below uses a photograph saved as a JPEG. We converted the photo from full-color to a colorized image which reduced the number of colors and the file size (fewer colors = better compression results). The subtle, colorized version also made a more pleasing, less obtrusive background.

Only a fraction of the background image is showing in the window. The pale yellow background stretches the file dimensions out to 1200 x 1000 pixels (to the right side and down, under the main image), making it very unlikely that anyone will see evidence of the background image tiling.

We opened the photo in ImageReady, set the JPEG quality setting to a medium setting of 35, and applied a slight blur to remove the image artifacts (lumps and bumps) that JPEG compression can cause, especially along edges. Blurring the image also helped to reduce its file size.

Even at 1200 x 1000 pixels, we were able to optimize this image to a file size of 15K.

In the ImageReady "Save For Web" dialog box, we can adjust the JPEG quality setting and see a live preview of the compression results.

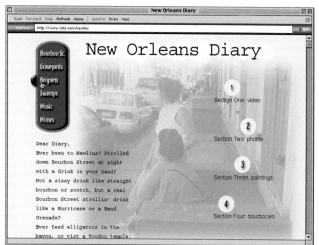

Using the photograph as a background image allowed us to place images, text, and navigation elements in a table on top of the photo to achieve a layered look. The muted color of the photograph adds visual interest and a lot of contrast with the other elements on the page.

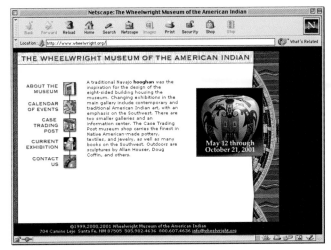

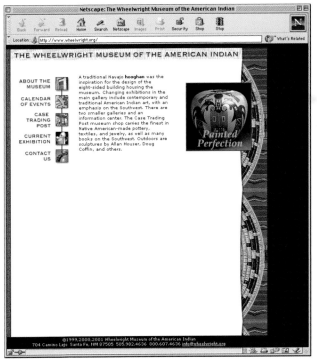

The Wheelwright Museum site uses a background that contains a repeating Native American art image at the right-hand side. The burgundy strip at the bottom (and to the right, if you open up the window, as we did above) is actually the background color within the frameset that adjusts up or down depending on how deep the browser window is opened.

If you have a good reason to use frames (like in this case), it's nice to make them as transparent as possible to the end user.

This window appears the first time someone visits StationeryDomain.com. It's activated by a JavaScript command that sizes the browser window to exactly fit the content.

The honeycomb pattern is a non-repeating background graphic.

Background patterns

Background patterns are tiled images that repeat endlessly to fill the background of a web page. We categorize background patterns into two types:

- Images that fit together seamlessly to create the impression of a single image or a background texture which we'll call a **texture background.**

- Images that float in their own space, creating a decorative background of multiple images, much like **wallpaper.**

Interestingly, background patterns like the second type are actually referred to as wallpaper. That's an excellent name because these kinds of background patterns make fabulous wallpaper; in fact, they make much better wallpaper than web page backgrounds. Even so, a lot of web designers have decided to wallpaper the web instead of their hallway.

Look around the web and visit some high-profile corporate web sites and notice how many of them use wallpaper for a background. None. That's a serious clue that wallpaper is for amateur designers, web hobbyists, and hallways. Wallpaper is very distracting when you're trying to read text on a web page. We've mentioned before that some web techniques can become tedious or boorish after several pages. Wallpaper can reach that level in one page.

We've used textured backgrounds before, although not often and usually at the insistence of a client. Because we're open-minded, we realize that someday, for some reason, we'll need to use a wallpaper background (we're really stretching our imagination now).

In either case, in this section we'll look at some tile pattern techniques and discuss how to make them as usable as possible.

There are many collections of stock images and patterns that are ideal for background image creation. However, very few of them can actually be used "as is." They almost always need some tweaking to make them usable, depending on what you plan to do with them.

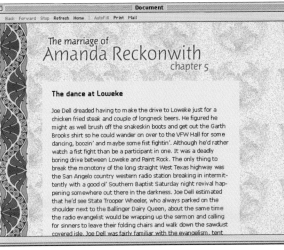

This is a sample of a background texture. Notice we put the text in a solid-colored table cell so it would be more readable.

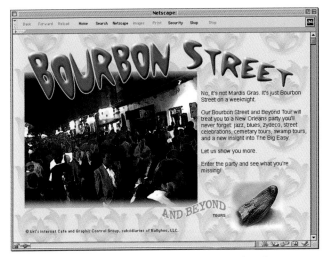

Wallpaper background is fun to use as long as there's not much text that needs to be read against it.

This alternate background image measured 1100 x 183 pixels and weighed only 17K. We were able to compress such a large file so efficiently by using Photoshop's weighted optimization feature (pages 54–55). We optimized the small left side of the graphic as a JPEG with a quality setting of 25. The rest of the image was optimized with a quality setting of 5.

Altering a background tile for clarity

Shown below is an interesting texture that could function as a tiled background—with a little work. There are two issues we had to address to make this pattern usable:

1. The **pattern** had to be altered so text could be read when placed on top of it.

2. The **edges** had to be altered so the tiling effect wouldn't create hard, unaligned edges.

To make the **pattern** acceptable for a background, we desaturated the image (in Photoshop: from the Image menu, choose "Adjust," then select "Desaturate"). We also lightened the image using the Levels dialog box (from the Image menu, choose "Adjust," then "Levels"); we adjusted the Output Levels slider.

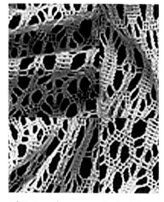

This is the original image from a stock image CD.

This is a close-up of what it would look like if we tiled this image without altering the edges. You can clearly see the distracting seams. What you really want is a "seamless" background.

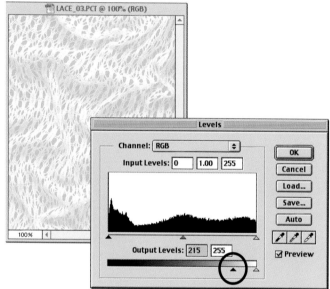

The lace image had to be adjusted so text would be readable when placed on top of the background. In Photoshop's "Levels" dialog box, we screened back (grayed out) the image using the "Output Levels" slider (slide to the right); this maintained the texture details that made the image recognizable as lace.

To alter the **edges** so that they will tile seamlessly, we used the Tile Maker filter. Some versions of Photoshop include this filter under the Filter menu, under "Other…," but current versions of Photoshop place the Tile Maker filter in ImageReady, which is automatically installed with newer versions of Photoshop.

We opened the lace file in ImageReady. From the Filter menu we chose "Other…," then selected "Tile Maker." We used the settings shown below and the Tile Maker filter altered the edges so that they would match seamlessly during the tiling process.

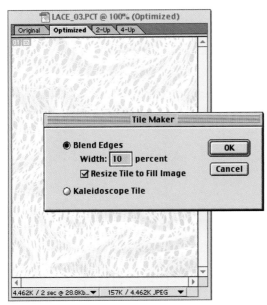

Photoshop's "Tile Maker" filter creates seamless edges so a collection of tiled images looks like one single image.

When the file is **tiled as a background image** in a browser, as shown below, the lace texture appears to be a single large image instead of many small ones.

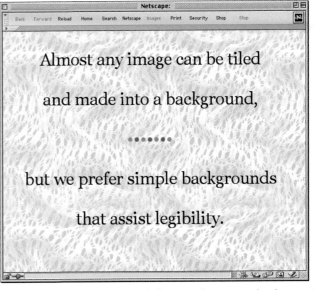

The page is readable even with the complex pattern background becaused we grayed back the image to create a significant amount of contrast between the text and the background.

Quick and easy texture

We do like backgrounds that add a subtle texture to a page. Tiled texture backgrounds, such as wood or marble, can be totally seamless, unobtrusive, and add richness to a site. You can create a beautifully textured background that won't distract your reader just by adding noise to a flat color.

To make the example below, we created a file in Photoshop and filled it with a pale yellow, browser-safe color. From the Filter menu, we chose "Noise," and from the submenu,

selected "Add Noise…." In the "Add Noise" dialog box, shown below-left, we set an amount and chose "Monochromatic" to limit the number of colors created by adding noise.

When we optimized the file as a JPEG, we applied a small amount of blur to make the background more subtle and easier to read against. Later we added the black and red striping to the left edge to add emphasis and contrast to the simple flush left layout.

background.psd @ 100% (Layer 0,RGB)

100%   Doc: 118K/118K

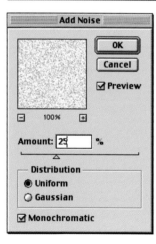

Add a small amount of noise to a file to instantly create a nice texture. This quick and easy technique can also add an interesting effect to a photograph or other sorts of graphics.

Add Noise

OK

Cancel

☑ Preview

100%

Amount: 25 %

Distribution
● Uniform
○ Gaussian

☑ Monochromatic

Netscape: Robin Williams . faq about my name

Back   Forward   Reload   Home   Search   Netscape   Images   Print   Security   Shop   Stop

faqs about my name, robin williams
actually, this is really an fta (frequently told answers)

no, i am not mrs. doubtfire.

no, i did not play mrs. doubtfire in the movie.

no, i am not **the** robin williams if you are referring to the hollywood actor (duh). i have longer legs.

yes, i am **the** robin williams if you are referring to computer/type/design books, articles, and public speaking.

no, i am not related to robin williams the actor.

no, robin williams the actor is not my brother.

yes, i was born robin williams. i think i am older than the actor, also, so i was named robin williams first.

no, i have never met robin williams the actor.

nor has he met me.

no, i do not want to call robin williams the actor and ask to do a fundraiser together.

yes, i get calls for robin williams the actor all the time.

no, i do not tell jokes. not intentionally.

This background image won't compress as efficiently as a solid color would, but the visual richness of the texture on the page is sometimes worth an extra kilobyte or two.

Wallpaper patterns

If you've created a fabulously beautiful, complex background image that must, for whatever reason, be used on a web page, subdue the image enough to make text readable over it.

One of the worst things that can happen to you as a designer is to become so enamored with an image that you become more concerned with showing off the image than with communicating the message on the page. Lapses in judgment like this make some web sites look amateurish, or even worse, completely unreadable.

For years we've tried to warm up to this type of wallpaper, a repeating-image background, but it's time to admit it just doesn't work. Wallpaper looks lovely on living room walls or on web pages when there's no text to read (very seldom).

If you have a great logo or important image that means a lot to you and to the attitude you want the site to convey, find some other (more effective) way to use it instead of as a wallpaper pattern. Try one large image, or display it as an individual graphic, or focus it on the entry page. More is not better.

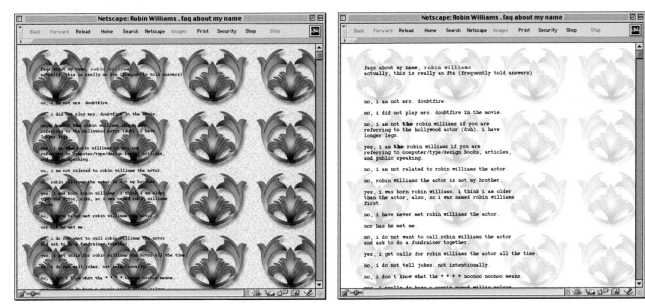

Hybrid-color backgrounds

The easiest background to use is a flat, web-safe color. Of the 216 web-safe colors, there are only a handful that we're ever tempted to use as a *dark* background, and when looking for a *light,* pastel background, the number of appealing color choices drops drastically. Many of the web-safe colors are just too garish and brassy.

Fortunately, you can create **hybrid colors.** These are color blends that are made of two or more web-safe colors. The hybrid color is actually a color swatch of a grid of pixels in which a pattern of two or more web-safe colors fills the grid. The grid is so small (usually 2 x 2 pixels) that your eyes can't separate the colors and so your brain mixes them together, creating a new color. But the *browser* sees each pixel in the swatch as a web-safe color.

To the left is how the hybrid color appears to your eyes. Above you see the actual combination of pixels that create the color.

Hybrid super-hero

The background color used on this site design is a hybrid color made of white and a web-safe light yellow. The hybrid color is paler than the lightest web-safe yellow. It's so light that it could almost go unnoticed, except when seen next to a solid white shape such as in the illustration.

The closeup below shows the hybrid color background, a pattern of pixels. At normal size our eyes mix the two colors, white and yellow, and create the *impression* of a new color. How easy it is to fool ourselves.

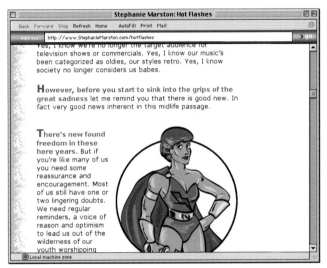

This hybrid color is much more attractive than the lightest colors offered in the web-safe color palette.

This close-up shows the pattern that's creating the pale yellow hybrid color.

There's a tool for every job

Photoshop has a tool to help you easily create and apply hybrid colors. Under the Filter menu, select "Other...," then choose "DitherBox™..." to access the DitherBox window, shown below.

Click on the RGB box (circled below) to access a color picker. In the color picker dialog box, choose a color that you want to duplicate in a hybrid color combination.

With your chosen color now showing in the RGB box, click the left-facing arrow to automatically create a hybrid color that simulates the original color as closely as possible using only web-safe colors.

This new color is added to the list on the left with a default name of "New Color." To rename the new color to something more descriptive, click the "Rename..." button.

To fill a selected Photoshop layer (or a specific selection on a layer) with the chosen hybrid color, click the "Fill" button.

Collections of hybrid colors remain in the DitherBox until manually deleted, making it easy to apply the hybrid colors not only to backgrounds, but also to illustrations, type graphics, or any visual element created for an entire web site.

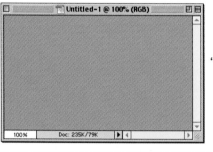

This file was filled with a new hybrid color that we named "buckskin."

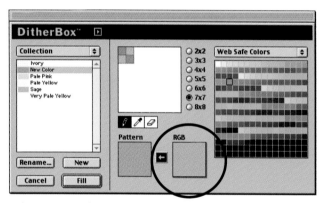

Select an RGB color, click the arrow, and you've created a hybrid color.

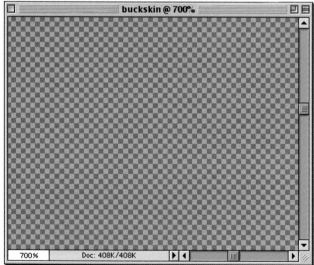

At this 700% enlargement you can clearly see the two separate web-safe colors that create the "buckskin" color.

In the case of hybrid colors, avoid contrast

Some colors can't be simulated very well with a hybrid color because the web-safe color palette is just too limited.

Web-safe colors that don't have much contrast, such as light yellow and white, or dark blue and dark purple, make good combinations for hybrid colors because the low contrast makes the pattern of the colors very hard to see; your eye is more likely to blend the two closely related colors together into one new color.

Colors that have a lot of contrast, such as light yellow and dark purple, don't work well because the pattern of colors becomes very easy to see; your eye can easily see the difference between the two even though each bit of color is so small.

Save your original files!

If you apply a hybrid color to a background, a layer, or any other element, **always keep a copy of the original layered image file.** You may need to resize the file or an element from the file. If so, you'll need to **resize the original, then reapply the hybrid color.** Otherwise the precise rendering of the tiny web-safe pixels will be destroyed in the resizing process. Keep this in mind as you create layouts, *making sure to put hybrid colors on a separate layer.* If you're applying the hybrid color to part of an illustration, keep a copy of the illustration *without* the hybrid color so later, if necessary, it can be resized and the hybrid color reapplied.

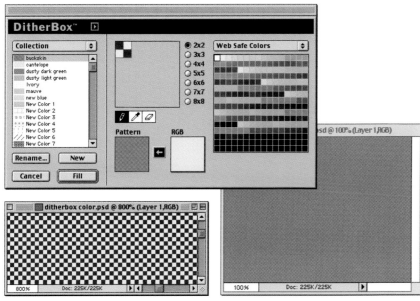

We used the Pencil tool to create the hybrid color using the 2 x 2 grid in the DitherBox palette. The strong contrasting colors result in a pattern effect rather than a smoothly blended hybrid color.

But, that said, you can carefully build simple yet interesting patterns in the DitherBox that can work as backgrounds, as described on the following pages.

Hybrid color is not just for backgrounds

In Photoshop, you can also apply a hybrid color to just the image on a layer instead of the entire layer. We checked the "Lock" checkbox at the top-left of the Layers palette to preserve the transparency of the "Bugs" layer background. When we clicked the Fill button in the DitherBox window, only the visible pixels were filled with the hybrid color, while the rest of the layer remained transparent.

Paint your own hybrid colors

You can create hybrid colors manually instead of letting the software automatically choose a color pattern for you: Select one of the grids provided (2 x 2, 3 x 3, etc.) and paint colors from the web-safe palette into the grid using the pencil tool. Keep in mind these are RGB colors printed in CMYK. To see how this really looks on a monitor, go to www.VirtualLastChapter.com.

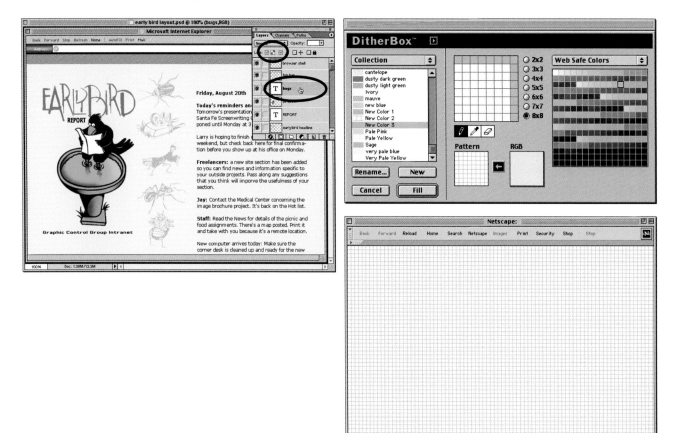

We created each of these background patterns by painting pixels in the DitherBox pixel grid, then we filled a Photoshop file with the newly created pixel pattern. We saved the files as GIFs and placed them in an HTML file as background images.

These examples show patterns made with a web-safe color combined with white, but you can, of course, combine any two web-safe colors.

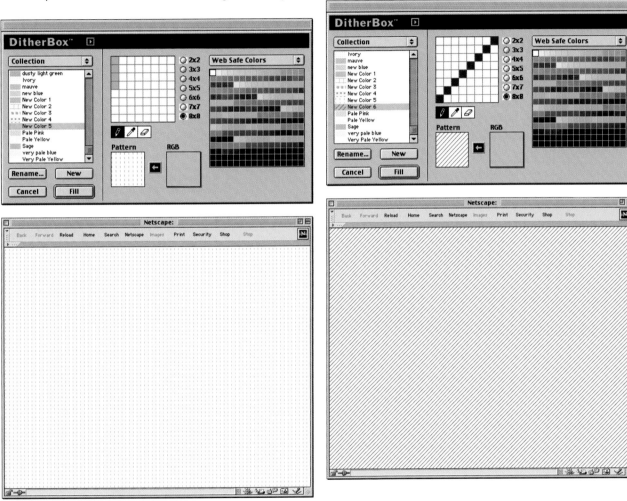

Create your own background textures

Amazing collections of stock images and textures can be found **online** in the form of freeware, shareware, and commercial retail products—check the web sites mentioned at the ends of Chapters 2 and 3, and do a search at Google (www.google.com, our favorite search tool at the moment) for something like "background graphics."

As you browse through some of the incredible collections that are available, don't be seduced into irresponsible design behavior by the beauty of a potential background image— most readers prefer readability and legibility over background dazzle.

Build your own collection of patterns and textures with which to create backgrounds. Use your scanner or your digital camera to input fabric, pages of handwriting, foreign paper and coin money, bus tokens, handmade papers, journal or ledger pages, leaves, dried flowers, rocks, handprints, movie stubs, crinkled paper, screen from a window, dirt, sheaves of wheat, rice, beans, paper towel, love letters, and on and on.

And of course you can always create unpredictable textures by simply opening any image and experimenting with combinations of various Photoshop filters.

14 Elegant Navigation

Web site structures can be complex and confusing. Even small, simple sites can be difficult to navigate without getting disoriented. In fact, finding your way around a well-organized, expertly designed web site can be a challenge if you're not familiar with the site.

As a web designer you need to accept a basic reality that we know is true from experience: Finding your way around a web site always seems a whole lot easier to the designer who created the site than it does to anyone else on the planet. Anything that's unfamiliar is confusing to some degree, so if we want other people to successfully "navigate" our site, we need to create a carefully planned "signage" system.

A good navigation system makes it easy to get *from* anywhere *to* anywhere else in the site, while giving you a perception of the overall content structure and where you are in relation to that structure at any given time.

This sounds like a tall order for a bunch of buttons. Ah, there's one of the main differences between an amateur who owns web software and a professional web designer: An amateur can use the software to create beautiful buttons and place them on a page. A professional web designer looks for elegant solutions to navigation design challenges: elegant solutions combine simplicity and refined visual presentation with clear communication and precise directions.

Navigation essentials

Plan the navigation

You shouldn't spend too much time on a site's navigation design until you've followed through with some of the planning aspects mentioned in Section II. Only after you and the client have a combined understanding of the realities, idiosyncrasies, and limitations of the project's content, functionality, and features can you confidently go forward with navigation design. Your chances of being totally off-base with your design are greatly reduced if your concept is based on a client-approved plan. This sounds logical enough, but it's a common hard-knocks lesson that many designers learn the hard way.

The navigation creates an attitude

Because it's on every page, the navigation design is usually the main contributor to the personality of the entire site. Navigation that is too flashy, too gaudy, or too large is also too much for most readers after several pages.

Try to approach navigation as a design solution of elegance. Elegance is defined in a dictionary as: simplicity, neatness, precision, dignified gracefulness, and restrained beauty of style. Elegance is good.

The goals for your navigation system

In addition to elegance, your system of navigation should have several other goals:

- Communicate clearly the major categories of content in a site
- Make it easy to get from any section of a site to any other section
- Provide a consistent look of familiarity throughout a site
- Create a unique site identity on every page

Active navigation

Although it's not essential, the navigation system you design has the potential to add a feeling of high-tech interactivity to a site by using rollovers, image swaps, or pop-up menus (see rollovers and image swaps in Chapter 16, and pop-up menus in Chapter 20).

Interactive navigation can be taken even further using Flash technology (see Chapter 23) to create large, complex, fast-loading, vector-based animation files.

But always remember: your purpose is not to dazzle, but to **communicate.** Many amateur designers (especially programmers turned "designers") mistake razzle-dazzle and high-end technology for sophistication. Without a design consciousness and a thoughtful site plan, the flashiest navigation buttons become mere junk.

Almost all of the navigation elements on this site use Flash. When you mouseover or click one of these links, the button "opens" as you see in the bottom example.

Image maps

An image map is a technique for turning specific areas of a larger image into a link. Web authoring programs provide tools for creating polygonal, circular, or rectangular shapes as clickable "hot spots." Creating an image map is an alternative to slicing a graphic (as discussed in Chapter 12), and is most useful when the clickable area needs to be an unusual shape instead of a rectangle. Learn more about image maps in *The Non-Designer's Web Book.*

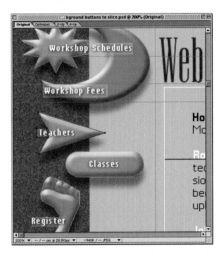

In this example, we used ImageReady's Image Map tool to draw irregular shapes around the various buttons and their text labels above. These shapes became the button hot spots. The Image Map palette allowed us to specify the URLs to which the hot spots will link.

Browse and learn

Repetition and continuity

An important aspect of navigation design is the sense of page continuity and site consistency that is created by the **repetition** of the same navigation system on every page. In web design this is commonly called **persistent navigation.** This repetition helps to reinforce the site's identity as it adds a sense of familiarity for the viewer. Unique page content would often make the different pages in a web site appear to be completely unrelated, except for the unifying visual affect of repeating the navigation signage system on every page. (We have had clients who think we are being lazy by creating persistent navigation elements, and request that every page be designed differently. We refuse, for the visitors' sakes.)

Navigation design should create an identity and add visual interest to each page of the site, in addition to providing an understanding of the structure and content of the site.

What you don't want to do is make the visitor figure out a new navigation system on every page they come across in your site. Even if the navigation is extremely simple, any variation in appearance or function can be disorienting, so be conservative and functional in design variations.

Learn from the good and bad examples

For an example of one of the clearest, cleanest navigation systems on the Internet, see www.adobe.com. Also check out www.apple.com. And www.sears.com does an incredibly clean job with their incredibly complex mix of information. At these sites, ask yourself:

- How long did it take to figure out how to navigate?
- As you go to different pages in the site, do you always know where you are?
- Is it clear how to get back to where you were to begin with?
- Can you see the overall structure of the site?

- Did you ever get to a page where you had to learn a new navigation system?
- Does every page have a unifying graphic identity?

Now go to www.kodak.com and ask yourself these same questions.

After you analyze the **ease** of the navigation, then ask yourself **how** the designer accomplished this (if it was done well).

- How is the information categorized?
- How is each category visually displayed so each separate category is clear to the user?
- What does color tell the user?
- How is color used to organize information?
- How does the designer tell the user where they are at every moment?

As you put into words how huge sites are organized and clarified for the user, it will become easier for you to incorporate those ideas into your own sites. Analyzing exactly *why* a site navigation is *confusing* is just as important—the more you put the problems into words, the less likely you are to create such problems yourself.

Unity with variety

You can maintain the consistency of the navigation even with some variation from page to page. For instance, you might establish an attitude on the home page, then switch to a similar—but not exact—version of the navigation for all of the interior pages. Often, the home page is more of an introduction to the site, allowing more design freedom than the content-packed interior pages that are more structured, making it easier to add or revise content.

The design flexibility of a navigation position between the home page and an interior page can be very useful as you design the home page for visual impact and interior pages for presenting content efficiently. The variation of navigation positioning can also add visual interest to a site (as long as it doesn't also add confusion).

Even when we allow some variation in the navigation on the home page and the interior pages, the overall look doesn't change. Fonts, color scheme, and verbage are usually the same, as you can see in these pages.

Interior pages are usually more frugal in allotting screen real estate to navigation than the home page or intro page. Interior page navigation needs to make room for content and cannot dominate the page as it can on an entry page.

Navigation styles

The nature of a site's content and its established identity is influential in determining design direction and what kind of visuals work best with the navigation. We like using visual tie-ins in designing navigation links, such as with the pottery theme in the example shown below. Navigation links that are more visually relevant than buttons can add a unique character to a site.

Navigation doesn't have to be represented by buttons or buttony objects. On smaller sites (as opposed to huge sites where it is too easy to confuse the visitor), you can use your imagination and keep your options open during the design phase of a project. The nature of the site will suggest ideas. Don't limit your ideas to just the most predictable solutions— or do use a predictable solution and put your own twist on it.

The use of pottery for buttons created a unique look and presented an image of the Southwest for this exclusive real estate development.

Text effects can transform type into navigation visuals as an alternative to the ubiquitous button approach.

Beveled and shaded buttons are used all the time because they are such strong visual clues. In this site we used the beveled button only for the rollover version. This adds visual interest and emphasis to the navigation without bogging the page down with a lot of "heavy" beveled, shaded graphics.

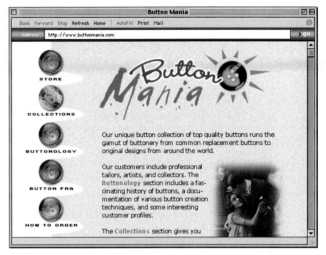

When appropriate for the site, experiment with playful design solutions, like these actual photographs of buttons used for the buttons.

The strong color-coding of this navigation helps visitors keep track of where they are. Although the color seems hard to miss in these two examples, many visitors won't notice it. But whether they consciously notice it or not, the color does

affect visitors' subconscious perceptions of where they are and where they've been, and will influence their level of comfort and familiarity with the site—even if they couldn't tell you it was because pages were organized by color.

Simplicity can be surprisingly effective

Simple type can make a pleasing and unobtrusive navigation
design. Stark simplicity is a valid design approach and it can
be used to achieve a sophisticated, elegant look.

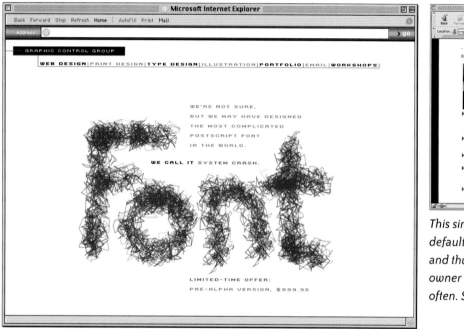

*This simple navigation uses the browser's
default monospaced font. (If it's so simple
and thus easy to update, you'd think the
owner of this site would update it more
often. Sheesh.)*

*Mini 7 Extended, a font from Web Page Design for Designers (www.wpdfd.com)
that's designed to be used in small and aliased form, made it possible to create
this stark, crisp navigation layout.*

[enlargement]

Sub-categorize your navigation

One important design decision is how much navigation should be visible on the main page, as well as on subsidiary pages. Large sites often have more main sections than can be shown effectively in a nav bar on each page. The most common HTML solution is to categorize all content into a small number of broad topics in the main navigation, with more detailed navigation provided on interior, lower-level pages.

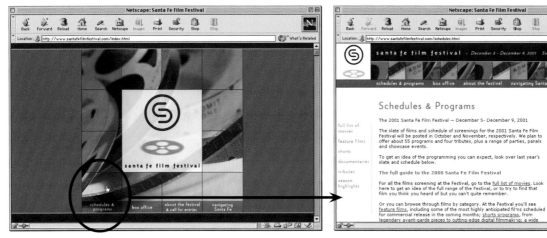

This home page has only four links, each a general category. The trick to having only a few categories is that each category must be clear enough so first-time visitors can find what they want easily.

Once you go to a link, there are of course more detailed options on each page that dig further into that topic.

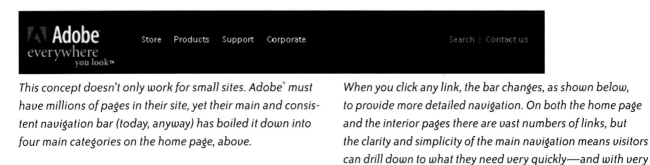

This concept doesn't only work for small sites. Adobe® must have millions of pages in their site, yet their main and consistent navigation bar (today, anyway) has boiled it down into four main categories on the home page, above.

When you click any link, the bar changes, as shown below, to provide more detailed navigation. On both the home page and the interior pages there are vast numbers of links, but the clarity and simplicity of the main navigation means visitors can drill down to what they need very quickly—and with very little frustration.

Be dynamic

One way to show a visitor the depth of the site from the home page is through pop-up menus (DHTML, see Chapter 20); when the user mouses over a link, it display submenus of other categories. This technique provides an excellent view of site content without taking up a lot of page real estate. It enables you to design an uncluttered page that contains a lot of information which remains hidden from view until a mouseover reveals the pop-up menus, as shown in the examples below. You can even create hierarchical pop-up menus.

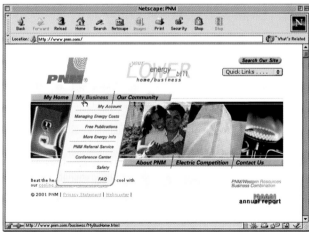

Previous, anyone?

Even a good navigation design can't anticipate every situation. For instance, sometimes you want a user to be able to go directly back to the "previous" page they were on, no matter where that page originated. That is, sometimes we create extraneous pages that don't reside in any of the existing main navigation categories. Visitors who aren't familiar with the site may not remember exactly what page or section led them to the current page, but they want to return there. They could, of course, hit their browser's "Back" button, but you might want to have a "previous" link on the page for them.

In this case, we use a simple JavaScript command that instructs the browser to return to the previously visited page. If your HTML authoring software does not provide the "previous" page link, you can manually enter the code below into your web page's HTML code.

```
<a href="javascript:history.go(-1);">
Previous Page</a>
```

The "Previous Page" link acts the same as the browser's "Back" button. It's a convenience for the user, not a necessity.

You are here

Always let visitors know exactly where they are in the site. One of the simplest solutions is to **provide a clue** in the navigation bar—change the link in an obvious way so visitors notice the one different link; they intuitively understand what it means. But to reinforce the message, make the navigation link that goes to this page **inactive** *on that page!* It's amazing how often we have (and we're sure you have also) clicked an active link only to discover it's a link to that very page we're looking at.

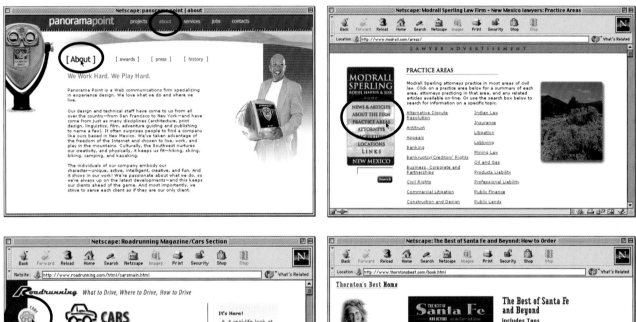

Each of these sites provides visual clues that tell the visitors where they are in the site.

You can also see, as shown by the arrows instead of browser hands on each of the links, that the links to these pages have been disabled.

Where to put it

Generally speaking, navigation can be positioned almost anywhere as long as it's easily accessible yet fairly unobtrusive: left edge, right edge, top of window, or bottom of window.

Positioning the navigation at the bottom of the window is least common and most often used when designing with frames because it's easy to create a bottom frame that is always visible (see Chapter 21 for information about frames).

No matter where the navigation is positioned on the page, it should fit completely into a standard browser window without having to scroll horizontally or vertically to see all the main navigation choices. That would be either 640 x 480 pixels, or 800 x 600 pixels, depending upon your information concerning the monitor capabilities of your target audience (see Chapter 4 about web site dimensions).

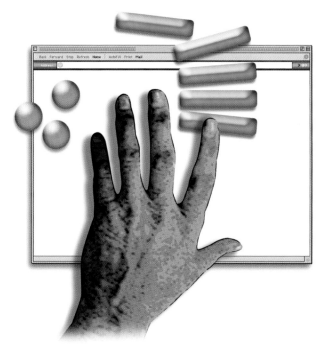

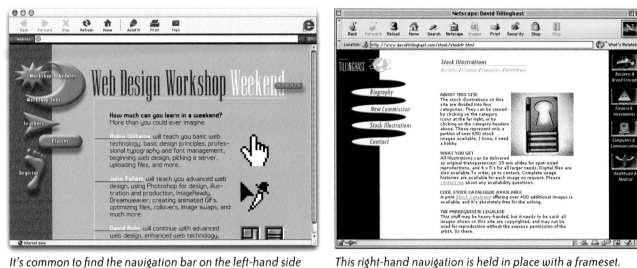

It's common to find the navigation bar on the left-hand side (or across the top). Don't feel like you're being unimaginative when following conventions—in this abstract, non-physical world of the web, conventions help to ground us. The less a visitor has to figure out simple things like navigation, the more pleasant their experience at your site will be.

This right-hand navigation is held in place with a frameset. You won't see the scroll bar separating the frames until you close up the window too small. This sort of layout can also be created with tables instead of frames.

Don't think you're stuck with one section of the page for links. This example shows a common solution: main navigation along the side, with more specific interior navigation along the top.

Bottom navigation isn't very common, but can be done. Just make sure you place it high enough that a visitor won't have to scroll to find it.

Don't forget to go Home

Don't forget to make a link back to the home page a part of the navigation design. Not only will visitors to your site be able to quickly re-orient themselves if they become lost, but sometimes people enter the site through an interior page instead of the home page, either because they were given that specific address, or because an Internet search resulted in finding that page.

You can add a "Home" button to the navigation element on all of the interior pages, but that may add clutter to your navigation that's unnecessary. A popular technique is to use a logo on every page as the home page link. Even though most people are accustomed to checking the logo for a link to the home page, you can reinforce the message and add interest to the page by assigning the logo a roll-over behavior that identifies the logo as a link back to the home page.

In this site, when a user's mouse rolls over the pen, the pen image changes and the word "Home" appears.

At Url's, we used the logo as a home button. But one of our employees complained that she couldn't figure out how to get home, so we made a VERY obvious mouseover image.

Creative

Below are several more examples of logos that take the visitor home, but with a little extra touch.

Web Design Workshop **The Virtual Last Chapter**

Web Design Workshop **The Virtual Last Chapter**

Mouse over any part of the title and the "W" changes to a visual clue that this link will take you home.

Mouse over the loop and you see the Home button.

Go directly home

Don't be misled into thinking you shouldn't clarify your Home button with the word "home." There are lots of clean typographic options for adding the actual word, and many of your visitors will be very grateful, especially if you have a site that brings in new web users.

Here are several examples of navigation that spell out the word "home" in addition to the logos that also link to home.

Plan to adapt

Navigation design should reflect a site's organizational structure and its content. Navigation's main function is to make moving around a site easy. In addition, the graphic appearance of the navigation should add to the site's visual appeal and enhance the identity and personality of the site. The navigation should present to the audience at least the top level of the site's structure, and it should enable you to move easily from any section of the site to any other section.

Planning is the key. A site's navigation design requires careful planning before you start designing. It's frustrating to spend hours creating a navigation scheme only to realize that some important topics were overlooked and everything must be redone. If the size and shape of the navigation changes due to poor planning, it can affect any design work you've already done on page layout. Plan ahead and get client approval in writing at every stage of the development process. Changes are unavoidable, but sharing the responsibility for navigation decisions helps prevent a lot of unnecessary redesign.

If you are working on a huge corporate site, accept the fact that your entire navigation system will have to grow and change as the site grows. A system that easily accommodates 300 pages might not accommodate 4,000 so easily, so don't try to make one idea fit forever.

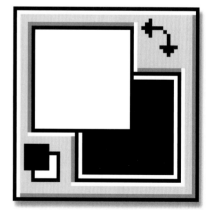

Button Button

15

Visually, buttons are like backgrounds; they can be simple or complex, utilitarian or fun, beautiful or ugly, dazzling or distracting, or some combination thereof. And, as with backgrounds, they give an immediate impression of the site and the quality of its content.

At some point in your web design career you'll have a good reason to create beautifully complex buttons, but most of the time, simpler and more elegant buttons (understated beauty) will aid communication and keep you out of design trouble.

In addition to some guidelines and suggestions, we also address the particular challenge of making it possible to read that small type that appears on buttons.

Button basics

Control yourself

With today's software capabilities, most bad button problems are a result of bad button judgment. A single click in Photoshop can change any shape into a fabulous-looking button, but it's up to the designer to use some restraint in determining the shape and size, complexity, and placement.

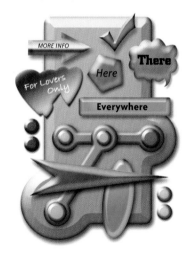

Bigger is not better

Even fairly simple buttons can be beautiful, especially to a designer. It's easy for a designer to forget that most people regard buttons as a way to access information, not as works of art. Don't force your appreciation of button beauty on the rest of world by showcasing buttons in an oversized presentation.

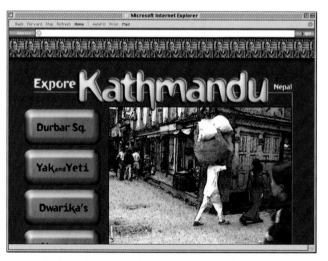

Generally, huge buttons indicate an amateur designer, and they usually give an unsophisticated look to a site.

Repetition

Be consistent with the appearance of buttons. Even if there's some variation in buttons throughout a site, make sure that your web project doesn't look like a portfolio of possible button effects. A uniform, consistent visual presentation helps to create and reinforce a site identity.

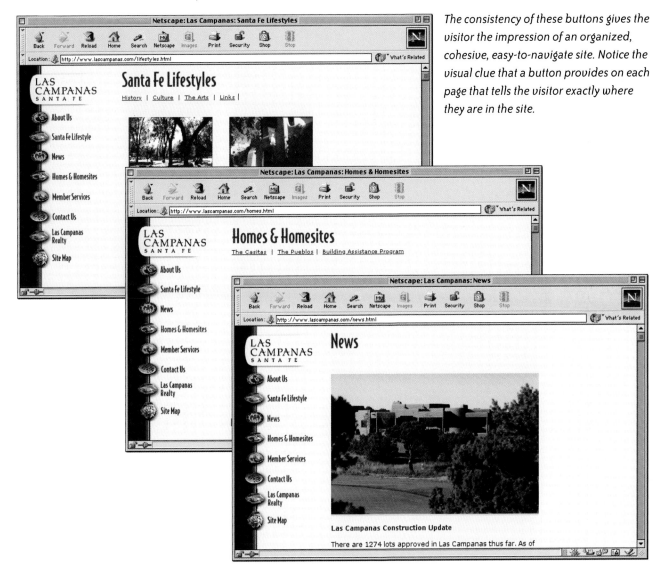

The consistency of these buttons gives the visitor the impression of an organized, cohesive, easy-to-navigate site. Notice the visual clue that a button provides on each page that tells the visitor exactly where they are in the site.

Clean up those edges

Buttons that are GIF or PNG files can be created with transparent backgrounds. This is useful when your web page has a textured or patterned background that you want to show through the background of the button image.

If the button has an anti-aliased edge, make sure the anti-aliasing is colored with a color that blends into the web page's background. If you don't take this step, your button will have a white fringe around it. It won't be noticeable on a white background, but any other background will cause the

button (or any graphic in similar circumstances) to appear to have a trashy edge. This effect is unattractive and looks unprofessional.

The trashy fringe (also known as "goobers") appears because, as a default, white is mixed into the anti-aliased edge of the image. To avoid this, Photoshop lets you choose a "Matte" color that's compatible with the page background color (as shown on the opposite page). This matte color replaces the default white in the anti-aliasing process.

This is the original GIF image. We put a border around the rectangular shape just so you could see where the edges are and what part of the image is transparent.

The transparent background of the GIF image allows the background of the web page to show through.

As you can see in this enlargement, a white fringe appears around the image because the GIF was not anti-aliased with a color that blends with the web page background.

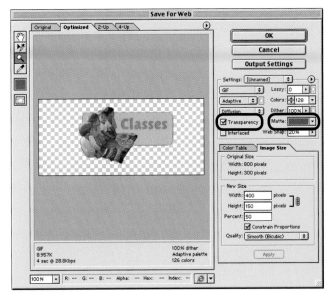

In the "Save for Web" dialog box, we chose a brown for the matte color and selected the "Transparency" option.

The brown matte allows the image to float over the background image without a trace of white artifacts.

This closeup view against a white background shows the brown matte around the GIF image.

Readable type on buttons

Aliasing and anti-aliasing

Navigation buttons are often small so you can accommodate all the categories and section links that need to be represented on the page. Making buttons small is not a problem, but making the **text** on the buttons small enough to fit on the buttons yet still readable can be challenging.

Most text that we use in graphic images is anti-aliased so the type will look smooth.

SERVICES

*The text on this button is anti-aliased so it appears fairly smooth **on the screen** at this size.*

This is the same button as above, enlarged so you can see the anti-aliasing effect up close.

The anti-aliasing (blurring) of edges that makes the curved edges of text look smooth instead of jaggy greatly increases the number of colors in the original image. The increased number of colors limits your ability to reduce the optimized file size. In many cases this is not a major concern—as long as the text is readable, the file may be reasonably small enough, even with the included extra colors created by anti-aliasing.

anti-aliased
aliased

You can see how many extra shades of color were added to the file (both above and to the left) to anti-alias the characters. This makes type at small sizes look very blurry.

Sometimes anti-aliasing makes text worse

On very small type, such as you may need on some navigation buttons, **anti-aliasing can be detrimental** to the point of being unreadable. When the main stroke of a font is just a pixel or two wide, the anti-aliasing blurs the entire letterform instead of just the edges. The result is a blurry, semi-transparent word that's hard to read.

There are several solutions. Any good image editing application gives you an option of setting aliased or anti-aliased type. In Photoshop, there are several alias/anti-alias type options to choose from; None, Crisp, Strong, and Smooth.

- **None:** No anti-aliasing effects are applied.
- **Crisp:** Makes the type edges appear sharper; the letterforms are not as heavy.
- **Strong:** Increases the density of the anti-aliasing and the letterforms look bolder.
- **Smooth:** Works best on normal-sized or large text. Using this option for very small type usually makes the type too blurry.

None:

She fell into an enigma.

Crisp:

She fell into an enigma.

Strong:

She fell into an enigma.

Smooth:

She fell into an enigma.

At small sizes, say from 6- to 10-point, Verdana looks much better on the screen when it's aliased (top) then it does when anti-aliased (bottom.)

This sampler shows Verdana at various sizes with varying levels of anti-aliasing applied. Obviously, the aliased type is easier to read.

The bottom section shows several fonts that were designed specifically for screen resolution at small sizes. See page 243.

Double the layers, double the effect

If any of the options shown on the previous page give you close to the results you want—but not quite—try this: apply the anti-alias option you want to the desired text layer, then duplicate that same layer.

The two layers will double the effect of the anti-alias operation. Turning one of the layers on and off will show you how much of an effect the layer-doubling techique is having on the text.

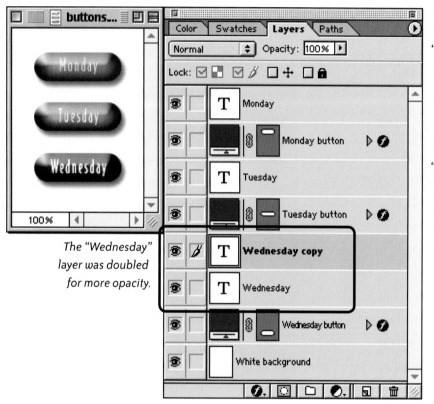

The "Wednesday" layer was doubled for more opacity.

The small text on the top button was anti-aliased in Photoshop using the "Crisp" option, which resulted in semi-transparent type that was hard to read.

The text on the middle button was anti-alised using the "Strong" option. The results were only slightly better.

The bottom button text was set with "Strong" anti-aliasing, plus a duplicate layer in the "Layers" palette. The duplicate layer resulted in double the opacity of the semi-transparent pixels and also made the type look stronger.

Some fonts are more readable when aliased

As you know, your monitor displays tiny "squares" called "pixels." Images on the screen, including letterforms, have to fit into these pixels. If you enlarge a color image, you can see the pixels and the individual colors in each pixel. When you look at the same image from farther away, or when the image is smaller, the colors blend together into your mind to form the single image. This is great for photographs and certain types of illustrations.

But letterforms have a lot of hard edges. And most fonts are not designed to fit into the low number of pixels on a monitor, but are designed for the small dots per inch of print. Thus most type, when it is sized small, has a hard time fitting into the pixels of a computer monitor. And when you anti-alias small type, it gets blurry and even less legible.

So the point is this: for small type on a web page, sometimes (depending on the font) the best choice is to set it as "aliased text"; that is, don't anti-alias it at all, but let each character fit into the pixels as solid colors.

To the right you see examples of anti-aliased text as well as aliased. Clearly, the most legible small type is the aliased version. But—*most fonts won't display accurately or attractively as aliased fonts because they weren't designed to fit within the pixel grid for optimal screen display.* As we mentioned above, most typefaces are designed for print.

See the following pages for more information on which typefaces look fabulous when aliased at small sizes.

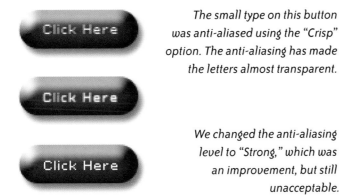

The small type on this button was anti-aliased using the "Crisp" option. The anti-aliasing has made the letters almost transparent.

We changed the anti-aliasing level to "Strong," which was an improvement, but still unacceptable.

Here we set the anti-aliasing level to "None," which created a strong, sharp, readable word (which looks better on a monitor than on a printed page).

Choose your font for aliasing

If you use a Macintosh for creating web pages, you have a number of fonts built into your system that are designed specifically for screen resolution. These fonts look clean and readable as aliased text on the screen, especially at "standard" sizes (typically, 9, 10, 12, 18, 24). Try them for your very small type in any graphic. They also look great in HTML text (see Chapter 18).

Geneva
Georgia
Monaco
New York
Trebuchet
Verdana

These fonts are on every **Mac,** *and several of them are also on* **Windows** *machines (Georgia, Trebuchet, Verdana). These were set at 12 point; notice how cleanly they fit into the shapes.*

By contrast, the font examples were below were set at 12 point also. These are designed for high-resolution printing, not for low-resolution monitors. Don't use them as small type on buttons!

Berkeley Oldstyle
Times Helvetica

Fonts specifically for small type on the web!

There are several companies that have created incredibly great and extremely affordable typefaces specifically for small yet readable and legible type on web pages. Thank goodness. Check out these two sites. And notice how clean the letterforms are, even at the small sizes you see here on the page.

Atomic Media (www.atomicmedia.net) offers fonts that come in Type 1 PostScript format for Mac or Windows. Their fonts have PostScript outlines for print design as well, plus they are especially made for Macromedia Flash files so they won't blur or fill like others do.

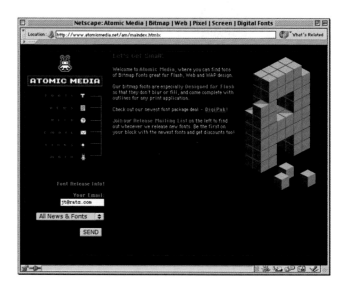

Web Page Design for Designers (wpdfd.com) has developed TrueType fonts for Mac and PC that are intended for interface design, either for web page navigational elements or for application interfaces. They are designed to be converted to pixel-accurate GIF images for use with buttons, nav bars or for small amounts of text of a single type size. They can also be used very successfully with programs such as Macromedia Flash and Director, and database solutions like FileMaker Pro.

In addition to the fonts, this site also has a lot of great information for web designers.

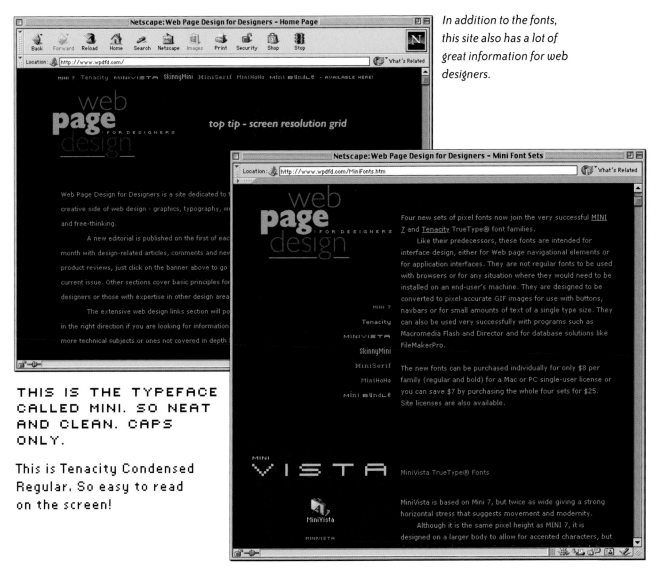

Combining aliasing and anti-aliasing

The page shown below uses a large headline font that is anti-aliased, combined with smaller, aliased type for the subhead text and for button text. Aliasing the subhead text made the graphic file much smaller. We didn't need much text here, but even a fairly large amount of aliased text can be saved as a small GIF file.

We created a rollover behavior so that mousing over a button swaps the button image with a melted version.

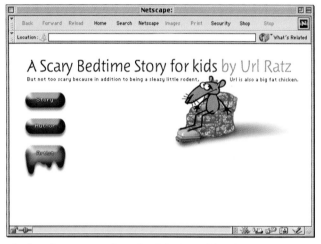

The headline is anti-aliased, while the subhead and button text are aliased.

The closeup shown below illustrates the difference between the anti-aliased headline text and the aliased subhead and button text.

Because the top half of the button is a light color, we added a drop shadow directly behind the aliased type, using Photoshop's "Layer Style" palette. The shadow serves as an outline around the white type. The original effect wasn't quite strong enough, so we duplicated each text layer (as explained on page 240. The double stack of layers increased the density of the shadow effect. One duplicate layer wasn't enough for the "Artist" button, so we duplicated the layer four times before we were satisfied with the contrast between the text and the button.

You can clearly see the anti-aliasing in the large headline. Up close and in print, it looks furry, but when seen from farther away on the monitor, the type appears smooth.

You can also clearly see how neatly the small type (aliased) fits into the pixels.

Button creativity

While simple communication and navigation are the main goals of a button, don't let that limit your design imagination. Nicely rendered, simple buttons are nice, but other less obvious approaches can also work. Some projects may allow you to consider using symbols, photographic images, illustrations, or aliased text as buttons without trying to simulate an official "button" appearance. Web users are pretty well conditioned to click on any lineup of small objects.

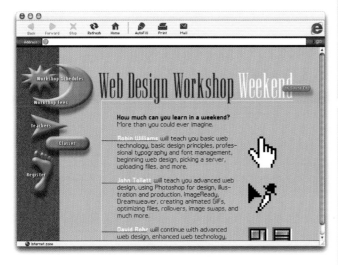

Photoshop Styles palette

There are lots of horrendously ugly things you can do with the Photoshop Styles palette. But if you use a little imagination, you can take potentially dreadful effects and use them to make unique—yet useful and effective—buttons.

We created these rubber-retro-high-tech navigation buttons in Photoshop using the Styles palettes.

The slider channel, described below.

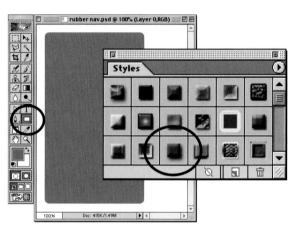

We drew a flat shape, then added bevels, highlights, and shadows by clicking an icon in the Styles palette.

We created the slider channels with a round-cornered rectangle. We applied "up" and "down" inner bevel effects to duplicate copies of this shape to create the result shown by the top channel.

The middle channel shows a shape with the "up" inner bevel applied, and the bottom channel shows the "down" inner bevel applied.

Stacking these two effects on top of each other produed the top channel.

The small rubber traction bumps are circular shapes with a bevel style applied.

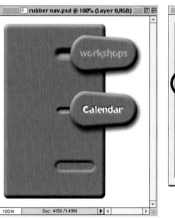

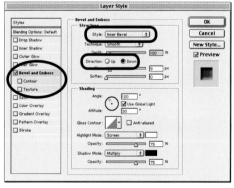

Rollovers and Image Swaps

Rollovers add interest and emphasis to navigation. They also contribute to the interactive feel of a site. Rollovers and image swaps are not limited to navigation graphics—they can be used anywhere to create visual interest, grab attention, emphasize, amuse, or to provide visual clues, such as indicating when a button has been clicked, or to pop up messages when an object is moused over. These techniques are a simple way to make web pages richer and more inviting.

Simple as the final effect may be, some very designer-intimidating JavaScript code is required to make rollovers and image swaps work. Fortunately, the creators of today's most popular HTML editing programs have designed the software to write the code for us as we click a few buttons (we love it when that happens). Now, instead of spending hours (or days) trying to make a rollover work, we do it in a minute or less and can spend more time on the design instead of the technology.

Rollovers

We use the terms "mouseover," "rollover" and "swap image," in various ways and often interchangeably. If you use any of the more sophisticated web authoring applications a lot, you'll get used to using the terms.

A **mouseover** is the act of moving a mouse over a specific area of a web page. "OnMouseOver" is a term used by JavaScript to describe an event that calls for an action, such as a "Swap Image behavior." Web designers usually consider a **mouseover** and a **rollover** to be the same thing.

But other than rolling a mouse over an area of a web page, the term **rollover** describes a variety of events that can occur when a particular mouse action takes place. An example of a rollover is when a navigation button changes appearance as the result of a mouse action, such as rolling the mouse over a button, pressing down on the mouse or clicking the mouse while over a button, and moving the mouse off of the nav button. Each change in appearance of the navigation button is referred to as a different "state."

A **swap image** behavior instructs a browser to replace one image for another (or "swap" them). For instance, in the example below, a mouseover action instructs the browser to swap the existing image with another designated image, and in this case it's the same illustration with an additional cartoon.

Mousing over this image of Kiki, a 1920s Parisian celebrity, displays the adoring rat.

Button states

By default, every button has at least one "state," or way of being, called **Normal.** The Normal state is what a button looks like when it first appears on a page in a web browser, and before anyone mouses over it. The most common nav button states are Normal, Over, Down, Click, and Out.

- **Over state:** the button's appearance when the mouse is rolled over it.
- **Down state:** the button's appearance when the mouse is held down.
- **Click state:** the button's appearance when the mouse is clicked.
- **Out state:** the button's appearance when the mouse is moved off of the image.

You can program buttons to incorporate any or all of these states. As the designer, you can determine the appearance of a button during any state. Most often, we prefer using only the Over and Down states because that is enough to give the page an interactive feel, and we've experienced problems with some browsers showing all the states accurately.

Software such as Adobe ImageReady or Macromedia Fireworks can automatically create rollovers. Or perhaps more accurately put, the software can generate the JavaScript code that makes rollovers work if you create a separate image for each rollover state. Some clipart libraries offer button collections that include "up" and "down" versions of the same button. The examples below were created quickly using Photoshop's "Styles" palette.

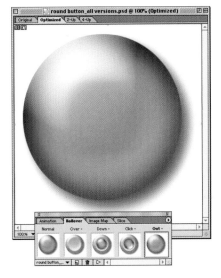

*A typical **Normal** button state. The **Out** state is usually, but not necessarily, the same as the Normal state, returning the appearance of a button to its pre-mouseover state.*

*The **Over** state reflects a change in a button's appearance, provides visual reinforcement that the button is active, and adds a feeling of interactivity to a page.*

*The **Down** and **Click** states can add more visual effects to the page.*

Rollovers inspire creativity

We almost always use rollovers in some fashion when we design navigation. But rollovers aren't always buttons. Some of our favorite techniques for adding interest to a page involve using rollovers in ways other than for navigation buttons. In the following example we used Adobe ImageReady to create rollovers for a web page.

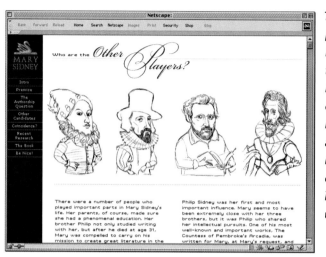

This is the original page layout, shown in Photoshop, with the "fake" browser interface layer turned on. Each illustration is on a separate layer, and variations of each illustration are on other layers so we can hide or show them when necessary.

The basic page already existed, so we focused on the new content by cropping the layout and opening it in ImageReady.

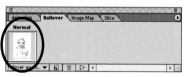

We used the Slice tool to slice the layout into five slices that would isolate the illustrations. To turn slice #04 into a rollover, we selected it with the Select Slice tool. The selection placed a thumbnail of slice #04 in the "Rollover" palette, designated as the "Normal" state.

 Slice tool    Select Slice tool

To add another state, we clicked the "New Rollover State" icon (circled, above) at the bottom of the "Rollover" palette. A duplicate of the "Normal" thumbnail was placed in the Rollover palette, designated as the "Over" state.

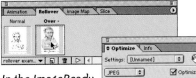

In the ImageReady "Layers" palette, we **turned off** the existing image and **turned on** the layer containing the image we had prepared for the "Over" state. The new image was displayed in the selected slice area, and a thumbnail of the newly activated layer replaced the existing "Over" thumbnail. This was the time also to optimize the new image using the "Optimize" palette.

Again we clicked the "New Rollover State" icon and a duplicate of the current thumbnail was displayed with a designation of "Down." We activated the layers that we needed for the "Down" state and optimized the new image in the "Optimize" palette.

We repeated this procedure two more times—once for the "Click" state and once for the "Out" state. We chose to have the "Click" state identical to the "Down" state, and we made the "Out" state the same image as the "Normal" state. This ensures that when a mouse moves off the image, the image appears unchanged.

That completed our rollover work for that slice. We followed the same procedures for each of the other illustration slices.

When we finished preparing the rollovers for the other slices, we went to the File menu and chose "Save Optimized As…."

In the "Save Optimized As" dialog box, we chose "Format: HTML and Images" so that ImageReady would do all the HTML, JavaScript, and image work for us.

We chose "All Slices" since we needed to create a table that included the entire layout.

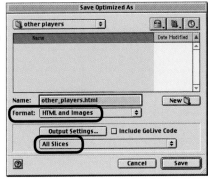

—continued

Rollover wrapup

To test the HTML file created by ImageReady (as shown on the previous pages), we opened it in several different browsers. The illustrations below show how the file tested in the "Normal," "Over," and "Click" states in Netscape. The "Out" state looked just like the "Normal" state.

After we were satisfied that the file was working properly, we opened the HTML file in Dreamweaver (we could have used GoLive or another HTML authoring program), selected the table, and pasted it into our existing HTML page shell (which we had also opened in Dreamweaver.)

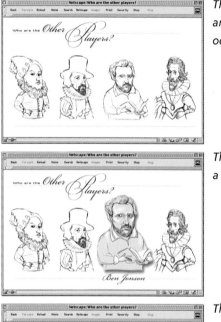

The page before any mouse action occurred.

The page during a mouseover.

The page during a mouse click.

This is the HTML table created by ImageReady, as seen in Dreamweaver. We put a temporary, one-pixel border around the cells to show the different slices.

This is how a mouseover-and-click looked on the final page after the new table was pasted into the existing page shell.

A slicing side thought:

Regarding the rollover example displayed on the previous pages: We were tempted to add more slices to this layout, which we would designate as "No Image" slices (see page 174). The top slice is larger than usual, so it made sense that we could turn some of that white space into empty cells rather than a white GIF file that had to download. This sounded reasonable, but GIF compression is so efficient in compressing large flat areas of color that we would have saved less than half a kilobyte, and the table would be more complex than necessary.

Cells 02, 04, and 06 are "empty," or filled with transparent GIFs.

Sometimes we put hidden rollovers on a page just for fun, which is not always appropriate for all sites. That's why we like Url's site—anything goes. Almost. It's great to be your own client.

Mouse over the image and it changes to show Url in his usual pathetic situation. If it's important for viewers to know there's an image swap on the page, add a line of text that informs them.

Often a rollover is used simply for fun. In this example, the door only opens if the visitor happens to run their mouse over the image. Of course, if it's really important that visitors see the rollover, don't hide it away where they will only find it by accident.

John created most of the illustrations in this site in Corel Painter, an image editing program whose digital painting tools simulate natural media tools, such as watercolor and chalk.

Url opens the door for you.

Image swaps

We call the following examples **image swaps.** Not because they look or act any differently than rollovers, but because we used Dreamweaver's "Behaviors-Actions" palette to assign an action called "Swap Image."

Technically, instead of the Dreamweaver "Behaviors-Actions" palette, we could have used the ImageReady "Rollover" palette and assigned "Normal," "Over," and "Out" states to selected slices in the examples. Designers tend to favor one technique over another based simply on familiarity with specific software.

We use rollovers and image swaps not only for navigation but also to add visual interest to a page, or even just to have fun—whenever that may be appropriate. As you browse the web, notice how other designers have implemented their rollover ideas; being conscious of how others have used this technique creatively will spark new ideas for your own projects.

Here are a few more examples of how we've used the rollover technique in various sites.

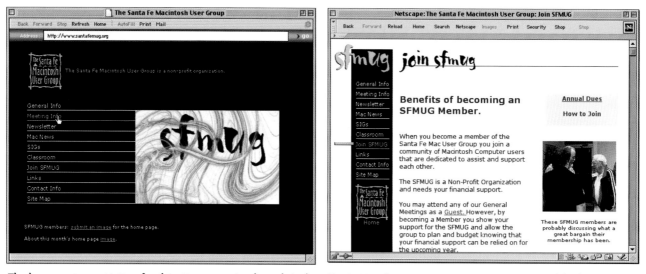

The home page navigation for this site uses a simple and stark design approach. The small Verdana navigation text is aliased so it will look crisp and clear at that size. Even though the navigation looks like HTML text, it has been saved as a GIF image. A mouseover swaps the GIF image with one in which the type has been colorized, creating a "turned on" look.

Navigation for interior pages use a variation of the home page design. Mousing over the navigation bar not only highlights the type, but a horizontal bar also points to the selection.

This is another rollover example that swaps an image other than the one being rolled over. Mousing over a number image at the bottom of the page swaps the large display image above the numbers.

This page works exactly the same as the images shown on the opposite page (bottom), except we used thumbnail photos to activate the "Swap Image" behavior.

Mousing over a thumbnail changes the large image.

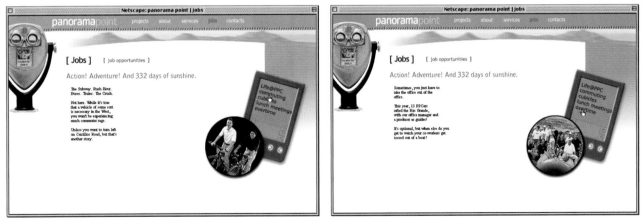

This is an example of a double-image swap: mousing over the list in the PDA not only changes the image in the circle, but also changes the text blurb on the left.

Slicing the swap

In this swap image example (a parody page from UrlsInternetCafe.com), the browser is instructed to swap images *other* than the image being moused over. The text to the right of the illustration is a graphic, not HTML text. The key words in the text have been made to look like links, but they're actually graphic slices with "Swap Image" behaviors.

The layout has been sliced and placed into the cells of a table. The slices were planned so that certain words of the text (graphic slices) could be designated as "Swap Image" links, instructing selected areas of the illustration to be replaced by some other image.

- Mousing over the slice containing the word "advice" instructs the browser to swap the existing image in another cell (the "Dr. Urlaa" cell) with a new image ("Go do the Rat thing").

- Mousing over the word "judge" turns the "doctor's" face into a scowl by swapping out the eyes and mouth image slices.

- Mousing over the word "past" replaces the torso image slice, revealing Dr. Urlaa's shady past.

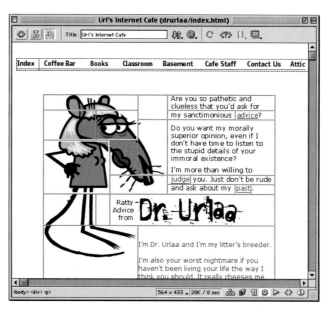

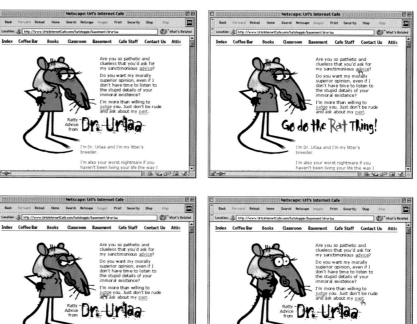

Site Index and Searches

A **site index** page adds to the ease of navigation and presents a site's content within a familiar and friendly context— an outline. Well-designed sites can still be confusing to a visitor, even to the designer who created them. A text outline of all the sections and pages brings both the site content and the site structure into clear focus without visual distractions or the disorientation of jumping blindly from page to page.

Search features, such as the text fields in which you enter a keyword you want to find, are valuable on large sites, especially those that offer lots of information or products, have an unwieldly number of pages that even an index couldn't clarify, or use dynamic pages that are created on the fly.

Site index or site map

In Chapter 7 we talked about **site maps** for the *designer and client* that are part of the planning process. The term also refers to the page in a web site that is for the *visitor* so they can see the contents of a site at a glance, which is why it's also called a **site index.** This page is often used as a supplementary navigation tool.

These pages show several examples, but most site index pages are simply a list of every page in the site, neatly organized and showing the basic hierarchy. They let the user find the page they're looking for without having to dig down through each section. (Years ago, designers tried to get very creative with these, but as sites got larger and more complex, they boiled down to simple, functional pages.)

DHTML menus, as discussed in Chapter 20, have helped alleviate the problem of finding certain pages in sites, but a site index is still a thoughtful feature. Not only does it make it easy for visitors to find a page, but it also gives them a clue as to how large the site is and how much is left unexplored.

Obviously, for huge sites, a site index page would be overwhelming, which is why a *good* huge site always has a search feature, as shown on the following pages. And for sites that use dynamic content where the page is created on the fly, a site map like this can't show every page anyway.

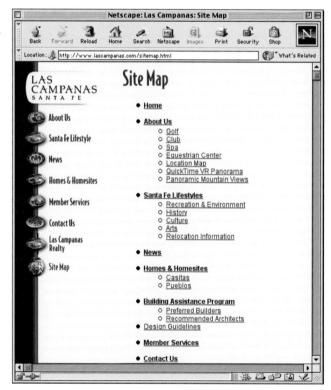

Placing the site's usual navigation on the site map provides design continuity and site identity to this all-text page, in addition to adding navigation options and just making the page more pleasant.

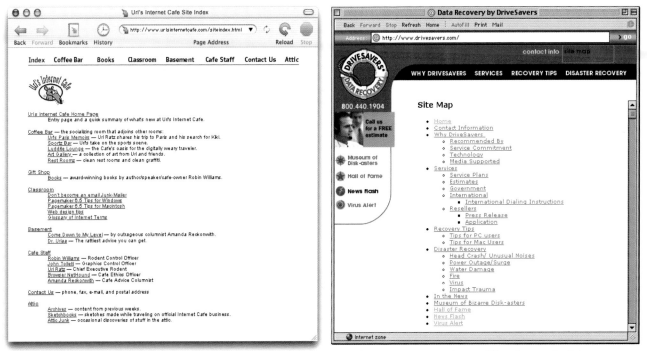

Without the navigation bars, the two site index pages shown here would look almost identical. But even the simple navigation above creates a site personality.

Site indexes that consist of simple HTML hypertext links are fast to load, easy for a visitor to search, and the links to every page of the site make it easy for the search engine crawlers (see Chapter 11) to find every page.

Complex navigation graphics will load instantly if the viewer has already visited other pages in the site and the navigation graphics are already downloaded to the viewer's computer.

Add a search function

On large sites, the first thing many visitors look for is a search box. No matter how thoughtfully you've designed the navigation, some users would still rather try their luck by typing exactly what they're looking for instead of browsing through pages of unfamiliar links. Most sites can benefit by offering a search function and these days it's so easy to create there's no reason to leave it out.

Commercial or custom searching software?

You have two choices for adding a search function to a site. You can use one of several services that will take care of it for you, or you can have your programmer take the time to code a custom search function. The path you choose depends on the number of pages to be indexed, your budget, and the level of searchability needed.

Free or low-cost commercial solution

Simple sites with straight HTML code and no database functionality are good candidates to take advantage of the free or low-cost search solutions available through several services over the web. Companies like Atomz or PicoSearch (see page 264 for web addresses) provide different levels of searching power, with the low-end being free and the more advanced options offered for a monthly fee.

These web-based services work their magic by initially "crawling" all the pages and directories in your site, cataloging every single word found in the text, title, or ALT tags (except for the HTML tags); they save the resulting information to an index file hosted on *their* search server. When a visitor makes a search query from *your* site, the query references the index file on the *search server* and returns a hit list with links to the relevant pages.

You can tell the service how frequently you want the index file to be updated (daily, weekly, monthly) depending upon how often you make changes to the site.

Custom solutions

The commercial web search services work great for regular static HTML pages, but sites that contain a combination of e-commerce, dynamic pages, or database functionality will likely need a custom solution. A database, for example, can't be indexed in the same way text on a straight HTML page would be.

If you need to provide searching for multiple content types within the same interface, you'll be looking to your programmer for some answers. He or she will be charged with the task of knitting together several different search technologies into a single interface.

Dynamic pages created on the fly can also be searchable, but your programmer will need to do a few tricks with page titles and URLs to make this happen correctly.

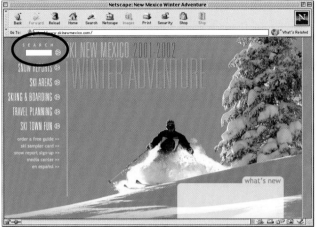

When you include a search feature in your site, it's best to make it available on every page. Don't force the visitor to go looking for it.

The search box appears in the same position on interior pages in this site. This also shows you a typical page of search results.

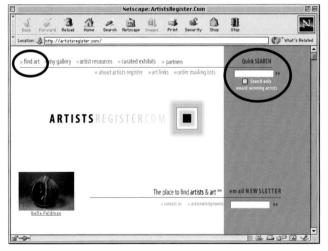

On the home page, a visitor can perform a "quick search" by simply typing in a word and hitting Return or Enter. Or they can click the "find art" link and go to a page with a number of more specific search features.

From this page, a visitor can choose from a number of search options, including a "combination search."

Resources

Below are several resources for free or low-cost commercial solutions for adding a search feature to your web site.

Atomz
www.atomz.com

FreeFind
www.freefind.com

siteLevel
intra.whatuseek.com

MondoSearch
www.mondosearch.com

PicoSearch
www.picosearch.com

Searchbutton
www.searchbutton.com

SiteMiner
www.siteminer.com

Webinator
www.webinator.com

To get up-to-the minute search feature information, plus all the current links to everything in the world about everything on search tools, go to Danny Sullivan's site. In the section, "Search Engine Software for your Web Site," you'll find information about general issues, usability, reviews, and more.

SearchEngineWatch.com
searchenginewatch.com/resources/software.html

For an in-depth analysis of what to think about before installing a search feature on your site, plus links to all of the tools available to you, use SearchTools.com.

SearchTools.com

HTML Fonts

18

As a design medium, the web can be a designer's dream-come-true in many ways: virtually unlimited space, as much color as you could possibly want, music, animation, and interactivity. And for HTML text, a choice of Helvetica or Times. Bummer, huh?

If you've come from the world of print design where your typographic creativity may have set you apart from the competition, welcome to the world where the fonts you can use are only those of the lowest common denominator.

Lowest common denominator

You *can* design with any font you want, including any original font you may have created, *if* you convert it to a GIF file or a JPEG and place that text on the page as a graphic. But this is only practical for headlines or special effects; setting entire paragraphs in a graphic format may look lovely, but it creates problems when it comes time to update or fix typos. Search engines cannot index graphic text, and text-readers cannot read the graphic text to people with vision impairments.

It is possible to post a font on your site for downloading (*if* you own the license for doing so) and instruct the audience to install it in their system so they can see your design as you intended, but no one's going to spend the time to do that—they'll just skip your page.

That's why Helvetica/Arial and various versions of Times are ubiquitous on the web. Probably every computer in the English-speaking world and far beyond has those fonts installed on it.

When you designate a font to display HTML text, you actually have more choices than our sarcasm would lead you to believe. Following is a list of fonts that are available on almost all computers.

Cross-platform fonts

The fonts shown below have been installed on almost all Macs *and* Windows machines for the past several years and so will show up on most machines in the world.

Arial, *Italic,* **Bold,**
Bold Italic

Arial Black

Comic Sans, **Bold**

Courier New, *Italic,*
Bold, ***Bold Italic***

Georgia, *Italic,*
Bold, ***Bold Italic***

Impact

Times New Roman, *Italic,*
Bold, *Bold Italic*

Trebuchet, *Italic,*
Bold, *Bold Italic*

Verdana, *Italic,*
Bold, *Bold Italic*

Webdings:

Times and Helvetica

Notice "Times" and "Helvetica" are not in the list shown to the left.

Times and Helvetica have been installed on every Mac since the very early days, so web designers often specify one or the other of these for web pages knowing that any Mac user will be able to see that specific font.

But these two fonts were not available on Macs until PostScript and PostScript printing was invented. Times and Helvetica are traditional typefaces that were specifically digitized to output on high-quality, high-resolution printers; they were not designed for the pixel-based computer screen environment. They were meant for print only!

The original Macintosh font **New York** is the bitmapped, screen resolution version of **Times,** and **Geneva** is the bitmapped, screen resolution version of **Helvetica** (and Monaco is the bitmapped, screen resolution version of Courier).

So we wish every web designer would stop specifying Times and Helvetica because they make the type on millions of Macintosh screens difficult to read.

If you plan to use HTML font tags that will override the users' defaults, please use Geneva for sans serif instead of Helvetica, and New York for serif instead of Times or Times New Roman. Thank you.

Preparation works much better than optimism. *John Tollett*	Preparation works much better than optimism. *John Tollett*	Preparation works much better than optimism. *John Tollett*
Arial	**Helvetica**	**Geneva**
Preparation works much better than optimism. *John Tollett*	Preparation works much better than optimism. *John Tollett*	Preparation works much better than optimism. *John Tollett*
Times New Roman	**Times**	**New York**

*These are examples of how the various fonts display on a Macintosh screen. (**Arial** is the Windows version of Helvetica, and **Times New Roman** is the Windows version of Times. Both are now installed on all Macs.)*

Screen fonts

Below is an example of how the cross-platform and city-named fonts appear on a Macintosh screen.

Now, we're not whining about how the type looks in Windows because in general type looks better in Windows; the PC monitors are typically 96 pixels per inch, while the Mac monitors are usually around 72 pixels per inch (this is changing). That fact, combined with the different ways the computers render the type sizes, means the font rendering is not such an issue in Windows. But on a Mac, a designer who forces a typeface on a web site can seriously impact a visitor's reading experience.

Geneva
Georgia
Monaco
New York
Trebuchet
Verdana

Berkeley Oldstyle
Times Helvetica

In the screenshot of these fonts on the screen, the first group creates characters that fit neatly into the pixels on the monitor. The second group is obviously designed for higher resolution—they snub this low-res lifestyle.

Customize the font tag

As you can tell by the list on the previous page, there are actually quite a number of fonts you can list in your HTML font tags that are common to both major platforms.

When specifying an HTML font, include a list of typefaces that are acceptable, separated by commas. The web browser will check the user's font list and apply the first one in the tag that it can find on the local computer. Always be sure to include the font names "serif" and "sans-serif" for Unix users.

```
<font face="Georgia, New York,
Times New Roman, serif">Mary,
Countess of Pembroke </font>
```

Web authoring software can apply the font tag automatically. The software typically provides you with several groups of font choices to choose from.

Adobe GoLive's Font Set Editor contains common font sets which you can edit, or you can create completely new sets.

Dreamweaver's editable font selection menu has several groups available for easy placement in your code.

You can edit the font groups to add or delete fonts on the list, which you should do because none of the automatic groupings is ideal. Here are the ideal generic groups:

sans serif: Verdana, Geneva, Arial, sans-serif

serif: Georgia, New York, Times New Roman, serif

monospaced: Monaco, Courier New

Using **Verdana** and **Georgia** as the first choices will help ensure that both Macs and PCs use the same font on your web pages. With **Geneva** and **New York** as second choices, you ensure that Mac users will have readable type even if they have older machines that don't have Verdana or Georgia loaded. **Arial** and **Times New Roman** (not Times) as third choice ensure that PCs will pick up a readable font if they don't have Verdana or Georgia (which is rare). There is never a reason (that we can think of) to include Times and Helvetica.

Another advantage to specifying Geneva and New York is that they appear larger on the screen. Since type appears smaller on Macintosh screens than it does on PCs, this can help even out the look of the page.

It won't hurt anything to call on fonts like Sand or Impact—most computers have these installed. If they're not installed, the worst that can happen is the text appears in the next font listed in your tag. The design of your page should never be *dependent* on the HTML text being a certain font and size because we guarantee it will rarely appear exactly as it does on your monitor.

You don't have to do this

Remember, you don't *have* to specify a particular font. You can leave out the font tag altogether and the worst that will happen is the users' defaults will appear, which are typically the typefaces and the sizes they like to read on web pages anyway.

Cascading style sheets

The best way to ensure that your HTML text maintains some degree of consistency across browsers and platforms is to use cascading style sheets. These are styles applied to HTML text at various levels (externally, internally, locally, globally) that help determine the appearance of the content.

You can set up style definitions, such as certain typefaces, sizes, weights, colors, etc., for specific type treatments such as headlines, another style for body copy, another style for captions, and so on. Then your code calls on that style throughout your web site and applies it to designated text. Not only does this help create a consistent look throughout a site, it also saves you many hours of time in building and maintaining the site because you don't have to define each individual instance of a particular style. For details, see Chapter 19.

Embedded fonts

The good news is that there is the potential to embed any font you want in a page design, and when users visit your page, a special font file is quickly and temporarily downloaded to their computers so they see your page in all its typographic glory. This concept is also call **dynamic fonts.**

The bad news is that, typical with anything Microsoft is involved in, there are competing font embedding standards and so you cannot embed fonts that *everyone* can view. Dang.

Netscape, in partnership with Bitstream, developed **TrueDoc;** Microsoft uses a technology called **WEFT** (**W**eb **E**mbedding **F**onts **T**ool). If you use WEFT, no one using Netscape will see your fonts. If you use TrueDoc, a larger percentage of users will see your fonts, but not those using Internet Explorer on a Mac, and IE users on Windows will have to download a small file called ActiveX before they can see the fonts (ActiveX is downloaded to your PC automatically if you go to truedoc.com).

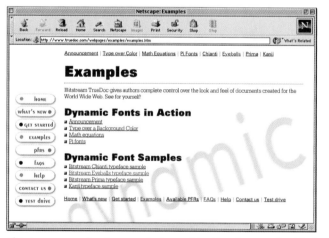

This is an example of a page that uses TrueDoc fonts embedded in the page. Support is built into Netscape so the fonts just appear on the page without the user having to do anything.

Creating and using the font files

With the font embedding authoring tool available from either vendor, you create a single font data file. This data file does not contain the entire font—just the characters that are actually used on your page or that you specify to include. The font data file is stored on your server, and you link to that file in your HTML code. You can use embedded fonts in your cascading style sheets.

Both technologies allow you to restrict the use of the font to a specific web site or directory.

When a visitor opens a page that contains embedded fonts, the browser automatically downloads the font data file to their computer, stores it in a temporary directory, and displays the characters on the page in that font.

Get the tools

You can download the authoring tools to build the font files. Microsoft's tool is called WEFT, the Web Embedding Fonts Tool; you can download it from **www.microsoft.com/typography** (look for WEFT).

You can download a number of dynamic fonts for free, ready to use on your web pages, as well as a free trial version of Bitstream's WebFont Wizard. Go to **www.truedoc.com.**

Lots more characters

Microsoft's WEFT technology (developed with Adobe and OpenType) and Bitstream's TrueDoc technology both take advantage of **Unicode.**

The standard text system on our computers has been ASCII, which only allows us 256 characters because it uses one byte per character (with eight bits per byte, you only get 256 possibilities). Unicode uses two bytes (sixteen bits), and so it's possible to create over 65,000 different characters in a font. This means it's possible to type and view languages that contain many more symbols than the average number in most European languages.

Below is an example from the TrueDoc site showing how Kanji appeared on the screen. The text you see is not a graphic—it's actually HTML text rendered in Kanji through TrueDoc.

This is an example of one of the possibilities of using dynamic fonts.

Resources

Below are several resources for you. Also see the type information in Chapter 15 on buttons, and in Chapter 19 on cascading style sheets.

Embedded fonts
Bitstream's TrueDoc
www.TrueDoc.com

Microsoft's WEFT
www.microsoft.com/typography
(look for WEFT)

Typography
The Non-Designer's Web Book
(discussion about readability, legibility, and how to make your text easier to read on a web page)

The Non-Designer's Design Book
(the second half of this book deals specifically with the problem of using more than one typeface on the page)

The Non-Designer's Type Book
(every person setting type in any way, shape, or form should read this book)

Cascading Style Sheets

19

Entire books have been written about cascading style sheets. In this one chapter about style sheets, our purpose is to give you an idea of what they are and why you'll love them, if you don't already.

Cascading basics

Style sheets are old friends

You may be familiar with the concept of style sheets from using them in other programs, such as word processing or desktop publishing applications. Style sheets in any program allow you to name and define whole sets of formatting so they can be applied easily and instantly to selections of text, or even to images in graphics applications. For instance, once you have set up a formatting definition (a style sheet) that typically includes a particular font, weight (bold, light, etc.), size, leading, color, spacing, indents, etc., you can apply that entire definition to selected text with the click of the mouse. Once text has that definition applied, you can change the style sheet definition and those changes are instantly applied to every piece of text that calls on that style sheet.

What exactly cascades?

Style sheets that you create for web design are called **cascading style sheets** (CSS). "Cascading" refers to how the style sheets are implemented. There are five different "levels" of styles, and each level can be overridden by the level above it; that is, the priority of the style cascades from one level to the next.

This is the order of cascading priority:

1. Default browser styles can be overridden by:

2. Imported styles which can be overridden by:

3. Linked styles which can be overridden by:

4. Embedded styles which can be overridden by:

5. Inline styles

The cascading style sheet system is advantageous to a designer because it provides the power to globally alter the style of an entire web site by changing an externally **imported style sheet** or by changing a single externally **linked style sheet.** The cascading system also has the flexibility to override any of those styles by applying an **embedded style** to a single document. Even that embedded style can be overridden by an **inline style,** which affects a single paragraph, sentence, or word. The flowing, or cascading, of priority from one style to another in succession gives CSS its name (and its power).

Not only can cascading style sheets be applied to selected text, standard HTML tags (such as the H1 headline tag or the <i> italics tag) can be redefined to show whatever formatting you choose.

Ay, there's the rub . . .

In this chapter we aim to give you a basic technical understanding of how style sheets work and, hopefully, an appreciation for how they can benefit you from the standpoints of design, production, and maintenance.

Some of the examples in this chapter might make it sound like you have to write CSS code to use cascading style sheets. Not so. We'll demonstrate our loyalty to software-generated code later in the chapter. We have, however, included just enough code to explain the basic syntax and structure of CSS.

CSS first appeared in 1996 and have been steadily gaining in popularity ever since. You may wonder, if they're so great, why have they taken so long to make it to prime time? Actually, they may be more prominent than you realize, since you wouldn't necessarily know at first glance if they're being used or not.

Beyond that, there are probably several reasons why CSS was a slow starter. Many designers who don't really like learning code have just recently realized that current HTML editing software enables you to easily create style sheets without knowing any CSS code. A lot of designers who had been hearing the term "cascading style sheets" for years weren't really sure what it was or why they should care.

But the biggest reason is not a shortcoming of designers at all. It's the fact that web browsers have been very spotty, inconsistent, and downright buggy about their support of official CSS standards and specifications. Different browsers have chosen to support (or display) different CSS specifications in different ways, often resulting in wildly unpredictable variations. This does not inspire confidence.

Improvements in the browser area have been taking place, but there's still a lot of work to be done by you-know-who and you-know-who-else (to not mention a few).

Test your style sheets in various browsers, as some styles will not look the same. In the example above-left, Netscape did not display the specified word spacing in the first sentence, nor the specified letter spacing in the bottom sentence. Hopefully, browser compliance will become more consistent and complete in the future. Until then, we ignore all but the most basic formatting attributes.

Advantages of CSS

While the current web browsers' inconsistent support of CSS complicates matters, there are still great advantages to using style sheets, at least in a limited manner. Hopefully, the full potential of style sheets will be implemented in future versions of browser software.

Smaller, faster pages

Web pages can get very code-heavy when a lot of text formating variations are necessary. Large tables, such as event calendars, can act extremely slow when each cell is burdened with various text formats such as bold or italic. With style sheets, all that extra code can be contained in an externally linked document, with the original HTML page pointing to it.

More production control

If you want to change font selection or other text formatting behavior in an entire web site, CSS enables you to change the entire site by changing a single style sheet document, rather than having to make code changes to every page in the site.

Web pages are being displayed in all sorts of ways: computer screens, printed out on home and office printers, PDAs (personal digital assistants, such as Palm or Handspring), and even wireless cell phones. CSS can be used to create separate style sheets that optimize web page content for each specific display device. This separation of content and structure is one of the biggest advantages of CSS.

More design control

While HTML gives you some design control over the appearance of a page, it seems very limited, especially if you've migrated over from the print world where design control is virtually unlimited. CSS removes some of the design limitations associated with HTML. Style sheets let you customize bullets for lists, and allow increased control of font sizes and leading, multiple levels of bold, style (italic and oblique), margin and indent control, and much more.

More type control

Type size controls in HTML offer only relative sizing (relative to the individual user's browser default settings), automatic leading (the space between lines of text), no flexibility in determining indents, and no control over letter spacing or word spacing. CSS gives an amazing amount of control over all of these things, and more.

Unlike HTML, with CSS you can specify the size of text in absolute sizes. The text size can be expressed as pt (points), in (inches), cm (centimeters), mm (millimeters), pc (picas), or px (pixels).

Using **points** as the unit of measurement yields good results when specifying absolute sizes (e.g., 12 point, 14 point).

Using **pixels** results in type that is similar in size across platforms and various browsers, but can be unpredictable in appearance when printing a page. The pixel option also disables browser font settings, which means a user cannot choose to enlarge the font size on their monitor, which has the potential to annoy a lot of people. (This option does still work with text-to-speech software, used by people with visual impairment.)

Much more

There are too many style attributes to cover completely in this chapter. We'll just mention that CSS also gives you control over font style, font weight (multiple levels of bold), text transform (small caps, all caps, all lowercase, capitalization), and text "decoration" (underline, overline, strike-thru, etc.). You could probably make a career out of mastering style sheets, but you can also get by with some good HTML editing software.

In this example, CSS enabled us to create open letter spacing (20 pixels) and an absolute font height of 36 pixels. The effect does not show in Dreamweaver 4 (left), but it does appear in a browser (below).

A quick peek at CSS syntax

```
H1 {color: purple }
```

Style sheets are made of **rules.** The code above is a CSS rule that instructs the browser that any text contained within <H1></H1> tags should be colored purple. Whether this code appears in the page's HTML code or in a separate style sheet depends upon whether you want to use an external style sheet (one that affects all pages in a web site) or an embedded style sheet (one that affects only the page in which it's embedded).

A CSS rule consists of a **selector** and a **declaration.**

The **selector** of a rule is the HTML tag that will be affected by the style being attached to it. In our example, H1 is the selector. Any HTML tag can be a selector, such as: **B** (bold text), **P** (paragraph content), **table** (table content), and so on.

The **declaration** of a rule is the code that defines what the style will be. In our example, the declaration is {color: purple}. The first part of the declaration (color:) is the *property*, and the second part of the declaration (purple) is the *value.* These are the basic elements that make up a CSS rule.

selector   declaration

```
H1 { color: purple }
```

property   value

Embedded style sheet

The page below uses an **embedded** style sheet. The CSS code comes before the <BODY> tag and looks like this:

```
<HTML>
<HEAD>

<STYLE TYPE="text/css">
<!--
H1 { color: purple; font-size: 46pt; font-family: georgia }
P { font-size: 19; font-family: courier }
-->
</STYLE>

<TITLE>Robin Williams Web Design Workshop:The Web Site</TITLE>
</HEAD>
<BODY>
<H1>Welcome to the Virtual Last Chapter</H1>
<P>You've read the book! Now see the examples in glorious RGB!</P>
</BODY>
</HTML>
```

The attribute <STYLE TYPE="text/css"> above tells older browsers without CSS support to ignore the style sheet code. The comment tags <!-- --> before and after the style sheet code prevents certain older browsers from really misbehaving and displaying the actual style sheet code.

Rather than creating an embedded style sheet, which would affect only the page in which it was embedded, we may want to use an external linked style sheet, which would affect all pages in the site. In that case, the code that appears on the web page would look like this:

```
<HTML>
<HEAD>

<LINK REL="stylesheet" HREF="workshop.css" TYPE="text/css">

<TITLE>Robin Williams Web Design Workshop:The Web Site</TITLE>
</HEAD>
<BODY>
<H1>Welcome to the Virtual Last Chapter</H1>
<P>You've read the book! Now see the examples in glorious RGB!</P>
</BODY>
</HTML>
```

This line of code instructs the browser to look for the style sheet named "workshop.css."

External style sheet

To create an external style sheet that used the same styles as the embedded style sheet, we created a separate text file named "workshop.css" (it can be named whatever is appropriate, but it must have the suffix .css), and uploaded it to the web site folder on the server. The **workshop.css** file would look like this:

```
H1 { color: purple; font-size: 46pt;
font-family: georgia }
P { font-size: 19; font-family: courier }
```

The single line of code on the web page (shown on the previous page: `<LINK REL="stylesheet" HREF="workshop.css" TYPE="text/css">`) can now instruct the browser to look for the **workshop.css** file for style instructions. Of course, any given style sheet can be more complex than this one, but the concept is the same.

Classes

For even more style versatility, the selector of a CSS style can have multiple style definitions (declarations), called *classes*. In our example, "P" could be given several style definitions to accommodate different layout possibilities and added to the CSS code. For instance, if we want all of the first paragraphs of a section to be green, the second paragraphs to be gray, and the third paragraphs to be red, we can write the class definitions like this:

```
P.first { color: green }
P.second { color: gray }
P.third { color: red }
```

You can name the class definitions ("first, second, third") whatever you prefer, but they must have periods in front of them to identify them as a class of the "P" selector.

Here is a web page that uses an external style sheet for most of its formatting. The page needs just one line of code that points to the cascading style sheet.

The text for the entire Santa Fe Opera site is formatted by cascading style sheets. This allows the text to look consistent from browser to browser.

Each page references a single external CSS file "4opera.css" as indicated in the HTML code above. By using a single external style sheet, site-wide text changes can be made in a matter of minutes.

The external style sheet code (right) is quite simple, with each separate style defined with a unique name and attributes.

```
<html>
<head>
    <title>Major Season Events</title>

<LINK rel="stylesheet" href="../4opera.css">

<script language="JavaScript">
<!--
//automatically call up the frameset
if (top == self) {
self.location.href = "int.html?2001.html";

function MM_preloadImages() { //v3.0
    var d=document; if(d.images){ if(!d.MM_p) d.MM_p=new Array();
    var i,j=d.MM_p.length,a=MM_preloadImages.arguments; for(i=0; i<a.length;
i++)
    if (a[i].indexOf("#")!=0){ d.MM_p[j]=new Image; d.MM_p[j++].src=a[i];}}
}

function MM_swapImgRestore() { //v3.0
    var i,x,a=document.MM_sr; for(i=0;a&&i<a.length&&(x=a[i])&&x.oSrc;i++)
x.src=x.oSrc;
}

function MM_findObj(n, d) { //v3.0
    var p,i,x;   if(!d) d=document; if((p=n.indexOf("?"))>0&&parent.frames.length)
{
        d=parent.frames[n.substring(p+1)].document; n=n.substring(0,p);}
    if(!(x=d[n])&&d.all) x=d.all[n]; for (i=0;!x&&i<d.forms.length;i++)
x=d.forms[i][n];
    for(i=0;!x&&d.layers&&i<d.layers.length;i++)
```

```
.usual {color: #000000;
font-family: Verdana, arial, helvetica;
font-size: 11px;
font-weight: normal;
text-decoration: none}

.bold {color: #000000;
font-family: Verdana, arial, helvetica;
font-size: 11px;
font-weight: bold;
text-decoration: none}

.header {color: #336699;
font-family: Verdana, arial, helvetica;
font-size: 11px;
font-weight: bold;
text-decoration: none}

.message {color: #CC0000;
font-family: Verdana, arial, helvetica;
font-size: 12px;
font-weight: normal;
text-decoration: none}

.popup {color: #ffffff;
font-family: Verdana, arial, helvetica;
font-size: 12px;
font-weight: normal;
text-decoration: none}

.required {color: #CC0000;
font-family: Verdana, arial, helvetica;
font-size: 11px;
font-weight: normal;
text-decoration: none}
```

Click-start your CSS

In the previous pages, we barely scratched the surface of the capabilities of CSS; our point is not to teach you how to write fluent CSS code, but to show you what it does and give you the gist of style sheets so you know whether you want to study it further.

In our offices, instead of trying to learn all the code necessary, we prefer to let our software write it for us. Even if you plan to learn CSS code, a good way to become familiar with style sheets is by using the style sheet features found in HTML editing software.

If you enjoy the challenge of coding, there are several books available that can teach you everything you want to know about cascading style sheets (go to the World Wide Web Consortium site, www.W3C.org, and look in the CSS section for books they recommend).

Creating style sheets in Dreamweaver

Dreamweaver enables you to create style sheets with your mouse.

To create a new style sheet, we opened a new HTML document and pasted text into it, with "Paragraph" formatting (the text was surrounded by the <P> </P>

tags). The floating "CSS Styles" panel usually contains a list of available style sheets that you've created.

The default of "none" is the only option available since we haven't created a new style yet. We clicked the "New Style" button at the bottom of the panel.

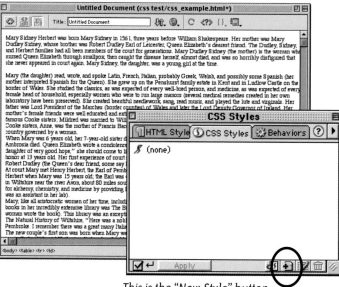

This is the "New Style" button.

To create an external style sheet, we entered a name in the "New Style" dialog box. From the "Type" options, we selected "Make Custom Style (class)" and from the "Define In" options we selected "New Style Sheet File," then clicked OK. (If you choose "This Document Only," it creates an **embedded** style sheet which applies only to the current page.)

After clicking OK, the "Save Style Sheet File As" dialog box opened and we saved this new style sheet as "largestyle.css." The name can be anything, but it must end with .css. We clicked "Save."

The "Style Definition" window opened and we selected the "Type" category and specified style attributes for some of the options in the right side of the window. Options that weren't important to our style plan were left blank. We clicked OK.

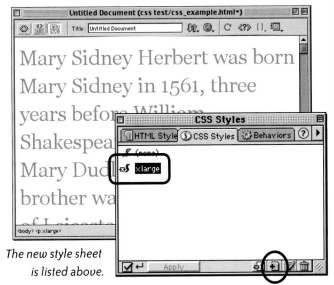

The panel list in "CSS Styles" now showed the new style sheet that we named "xlarge." We clicked that new style in the panel and the HTML text immediately reflected the style sheet specifications.

The new style sheet is listed above.

In Dreamweaver's Code Inspector we can see the link code that tells the browser where to look for style definitions.

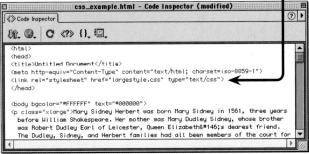

The style sheet that Dreamweaver created is nothing more than a text file that contains the following text:

```
.xlarge { font-family: Georgia, "Times
New Roman", Times, serif; font-size:
36pt; font-style: normal; line-height:
48pt; font-weight: normal; color:
#999999; background-color: #FFFFFF }
```

Embedded styles

Next we wanted to create a style that would display any HTML italic text (text surrounded by the <i> </i> tags) as 24 point Georgia italic and as a dark orange color. By choice, this would be an **embedded style** that affects only the current page.

We clicked the "New Style" button at the bottom of the CSS Styles panel (as shown on the previous page).

In the "New Style" window, in the "Tag" field, we chose the "i" tag (the HTML tag for italic). From the "Type" options, we chose "Redefine HTML Tag." From "Define In," we chose "This Document Only."

In the subsequent "Style Definition" dialog box, we set the various "Type" attributes, including font, size, line height (leading), color, etc., then clicked OK.

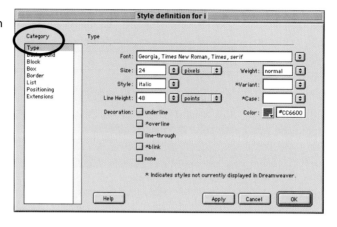

Back in Dreamweaver, we selected sections of text and used the keyboard shortcut to change it to italic. The selected text immediately reflected the new style definitions for "italics."

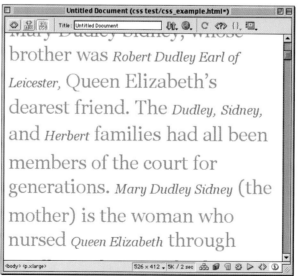

Dreamweaver's "Code Inspector" shows the original linked external style sheet, plus the new embedded style that affects only this page. Notice that Dreamweaver added the "Comment" tags before and after the embedded style definition to prevent older browsers from mistakenly displaying the style sheet code.

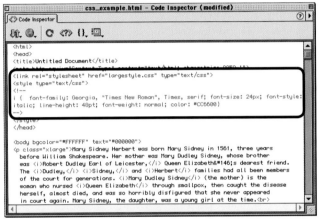

CSS provides more typographic design flexibility than previously possible. In the example below, we created another style sheet (named ".extreme") which specified the line height (leading) as a much smaller value than the font size to achieve an oversized, slightly overlapped effect.

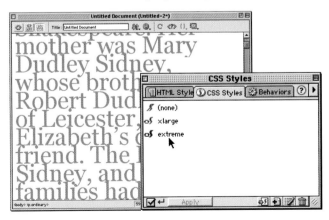

Creating style sheets in GoLive

You may prefer Adobe GoLive's powerful CSS features. The GoLive "Style Sheet" panels enable you to create internal and external style sheets, customized with the "CSS Selector Inspector." You just select the styles you want and let GoLive do the coding for you. You can easily create new HTML tag definitions and new CSS classes that give you unprecedented control over the design and maintainence of a site.

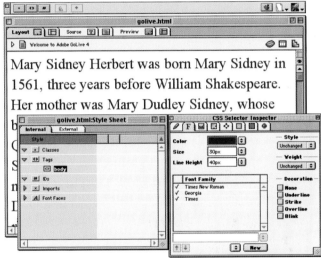

GoLive's "Style Sheet" palette gives access to internal and external style sheets. The "CSS Selector Inspector" makes it easy to customize style attributes.

Resources

For more information

An organization known as the World Wide Web Consortium is responsible for developing the official cascading style sheet specifications. Who are they? To quote the W3C home page, "The World Wide Web Consortium develops interoperable technologies (specifications, guidelines, software, and tools) to lead the Web to its full potential as a forum for information, commerce, communication, and collective understanding."

Visit **www.W3C.org** for an incredible amount of information about style sheets and almost anything else concerning web technology.

How do you choose?

It's a difficult choice: the combination of Macromedia Dreamweaver and Fireworks vs. the combination of Adobe GoLive, Photoshop, and ImageReady. The automated power and versatility of competing brands of software make it very hard to recommend one over the other. Especially when we like how certain features are handled in one product, and prefer the implementation of certain other features in another product. The decision of which software works best for you will probably be based on subjective preferences rather than technical superiority of one product over the other. You may even resort to using several (or all) of them, as we do, for specific tasks.

Training resource

A great resource for learning these programs is **Virtual Training Company** (www.vtco.com). You can use many of their training videos for GoLive CSS (in streaming QuickTime format) on Adobe's GoLive site for free.

Sign up with VTC's Online University for a low monthly fee and have access to their entire library of streaming QuickTime video instruction, covering a wide range of software applications. VTC also offers full-course training CDs in single or multi-user versions.

20 Dynamic Pages

Dynamic web pages don't just sit there waiting to be read—they exist to animate, make noise, interact, change, randomize, and otherwise call attention to themselves. Unlike their unchanging, static cousins, dynamic pages don't stay the same for very long—they're always doing something interesting to engage the web audience.

Appealing as dynamic features may be, the web designer needs to know when to draw the line and use them only as a means to further communicate the site's message.

What are dynamic pages?

The most exciting web sites are the ones that are kept fresh on a weekly, daily, or even hourly basis. The users of the site quickly become repeat customers because they know they can expect something new or different on their next visit.

A changing site like this can be considered **dynamic** because selected text, graphic elements, or even entire pages are frequently different from visit to visit. Dynamic pages often display moving elements or reveal additional information through interactivity. Sometimes they can also be easier to maintain than a static HTML page, but they are definitely trickier to set up—they require technologies with a little more kick than your average HTML.

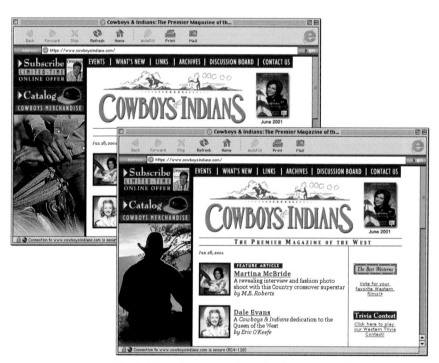

The left-hand photograph on this home page changes randomly each time the page is visited or refreshed. PHP provides the randomization function to keep the site looking fresh.

The limits of HTML

Everyone knows that HTML is the primary foundation for any web page. In fact, there's not a single web site out there that doesn't use it. HTML tells your web browser software how the elements on a page are supposed to be arranged, which graphics and colors to display, the size and font in which the text will appear, and it enables a single page to link with many others.

But HTML by itself only goes so far. Simple HTML alone isn't enough to create a truly dynamic site—it needs some help from some other clever scripting languages. These days, web designers can take advantage of technologies like JavaScript, DHTML, ASP, PHP, Perl, Flash, Generator, and many others that go far beyond what HTML was designed to do.

Static pages

Not all sites need to have dynamic features, of course. Many small web sites exist simply to display pages of unchanging information. A site of this kind can be considered **static** because it remains relatively the same over time. Since it doesn't change much, a static web site is usually a low mainte-nance project. It just sits there and does its job whether its owner is thinking about it or not. There's nothing wrong with having or creating a static site, but a long shelf-life doesn't necessarily make for the most interesting place to visit on the web.

This page is considered a static page. The site gets updated regularly as the author completes new books, but the site code contains only basic HTML.

Dynamic user experience

There are really two ways to characterize dynamic features in a web site. The first can be described as a **dynamic user experience,** in which elements on a page either move, reveal themselves through interaction, or change frequently. This is the type that web users get excited about and designers go crazy with. These dynamic features keep a site fresh and make for a lively user experience.

The second type of dynamic feature, **dynamic content control,** is described following this.

This very dynamic educational site allows the visitor to click on a segment of the mesa photograph and view a close-up of the petroglyphs on that section.

JavaScript enables a new window to open which contains an interactive Flash file.

Above is a page that contains movie clips. When a visitor clicks on the image, a QuickTime movie loads and plays.

Programming options

Page elements that comprise a dynamic user experience are usually dependent on JavaScript or Dynamic HTML (DHTML) to do their tricks, but PHP, ASP, or Flash can also play a role.

JavaScript is probably the most commonly used HTML supplement because it can bring so many useful features to a page. It powers button rollovers, detects browsers, preloads images, opens and sizes browser windows, displays alert messages, plays sounds, and the list goes on.

Most professional web editing programs will write certain kinds of JavaScripts for you, but there are also freeware or shareware scripts on the web that can probably perform any function imaginable.

If you're not the do-it-yourself type, you can always contract with a web programmer to get some JavaScript functionality into your pages.

A clever JavaScript allows this home page to cycle through and display images selected randomly from a database containing hundreds of art photographs—all as you watch in real time.

Dynamic HTML

Dynamic HTML is not really another separate scripting language, but the term is used to describe a combination of JavaScript, HTML, and cascading style sheets. Working together, these web technologies allow elements on a page to move, change through interactivity, or otherwise display dynamic behavior.

It's important to note that DHTML pages will only display correctly on 4.0 or higher browsers, so if backwards compatibility is an issue, you may want to consider other options.

A key feature that makes DHTML possible is that post-4.0 browsers support "layers" as defined by the <DIV> tag. Layers are independent modules that can contain regular HTML code, but can be superimposed over other parts of the page and be aligned with pixel-level accuracy. Combined with JavaScript, a layer can be made to move around the page, appear or disappear with interactivity, and perform other useful little tricks that straight HTML could never do alone.

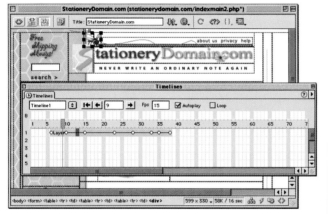

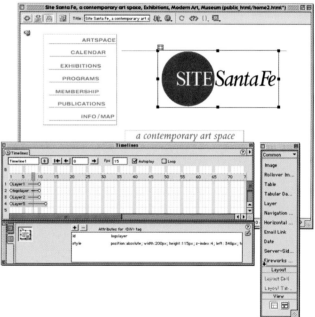

Each of these sites uses the DHTML features of layers and JavaScript to make graphics move around the page when the page first loads. Both are shown in their Dreamweaver editing environment.

Flash and the .swf file

The .swf file format, popularized by Macromedia Flash, is another way to bring download-efficient dynamic content onto a web page. It ties up motion, sound, and interactivity into a single web-ready package. In fact, there's so much to say about it that we've written a chapter just about motion graphics (see Chapter 23), and there are entire books written just about Flash.

Much of Flash's functionality parallels that of DHTML, but it accomplishes the task in a very different way. Flash is a more cohesive, often more predictable, way to deliver dynamic content, but it does require a special plug-in.

DHTML, on the other hand, displays automatically in 4.0 or higher browsers. Not that Flash content is difficult to include—Macromedia claims that 96 percent of the web audience is capable of viewing Flash-enabled pages.

This animated Christmas card included music and a number of small movie clips.

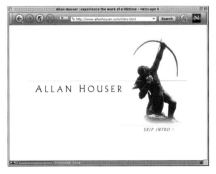

This animated introduction plays a movie and music. Flash is adept at animating both line (vector) and bitmap (raster) images, as shown in both of these examples.

Dynamic content control

The second way to characterize dynamic features in a web site is by **dynamic content control,** which is not at all apparent to the end users. In a site like this, portions of page content such as text and graphics are stored in a database or reference file and can be altered without directly editing the HTML in every page. This kind of functionality may be transparent to the average user, but is an enormous timesaver for the person or group charged with site maintenance.

Cowboys and Indians Calendar

Address: http://www.cowboysindians.com/admin/calenadmin.phtml?&calendar_id=71 **go**

Catalog Admin

Calendar

- new event
- show all events

Happenings

Links

Calendar Administration

Event Name: Barry Goldwater Photography [Search]

Start Date: March ⬍ 31 ⬍ 2001 ⬍

End Date: September ⬍ 30 ⬍ 2001 ⬍

City: Phoenix [Search]

State: AZ [Search]

Location:

Telephone: (602) 252-8840

Description:

Internet zone

current and upcoming events at Cowboys & Indi...

Address: http://www.cowboysindians.com/events/index.html **go**

CATALOG | SUBSCRIBE | EVENTS | WHAT'S NEW | LINKS | ARCHIVES | DISCUSSION | CONTACT US

COWBOYS INDIANS HOME

Events

June 23, 2001 - July 07, 2001
APHA World Show
Fort Worth, TX

March 31, 2001 - September 30, 2001
Barry Goldwater Photography Exhibit
Phoenix, AZ
(602) 252-8840

Internet zone

The simple web form above displays text stored in a database and administers the listings for this automated "Events Calendar." PHP allows each listing to appear on the actual web page before the event occurs and then makes it disappear for good after the date has passed.

PHP and ASP

PHP and ASP are both powerful, yet separate, scripting languages that can be embedded into HTML code; they enable pages to perform a variety of complex tasks. While they can perform operations that replace the functionality of Perl or other CGI scripts, they also allow portions of a web page to be treated as "includes." An include is a smaller external HTML file that is referenced by the main HTML page and can be updated dynamically.

Both PHP and ASP are referred to as "server-side" scripting languages, meaning that while they are embedded in the original HTML page on the host server, they are first interpreted by the server and then written back to the web browser as regular HTML.

By using includes, it's possible to create a single file that's used multiple times throughout a web site. For example, persistent site navigation is a great candidate for an include, allowing every page in the site to use the same HTML code for that part of the page. By making the navigation (or other persistent element) an include, you'll save yourself the time of going through every page of the site when you want to make a change.

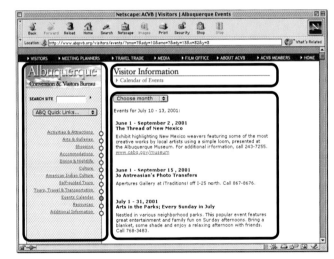

The interior pages of this site use PHP includes on several areas including the persistent navigation. When a single PHP include file is modified, the change displays automatically on every page in the site that references that file.

The circled areas on this page indicate an include within the overall page template.

Macromedia Generator

Macromedia Generator is a server-based technology that allows the client or site administrator to create customized, on-the-fly, Flash animations. Think of it as content management for Flash in that it allows content to be handled independently of the file structure.

Generator-enabled files could appear in the form of headlines, banner advertising, stock tickers, weather reports, or within an interactive Flash animation.

To use it in a site, your client must be willing to license the Generator server software from Macromedia. Assuming they'll spring for the software and to have a programmer configure it on the server, the web page part is relatively easy to set up.

The Macromedia Flash application has the ability to create Generator templates and can handle the implementation. As with the other kinds of content management, pages that use Generator aren't obvious to the end user—the real benefits of this technology are known only to the people updating the site behind the scenes.

Flash 5 allows you to build a Generator-savvy template that will enable the resulting Flash file to be dynamically updated from an external data source. Of course the template can't work alone—you need to tie it into the nearest Generator server to enable it to do its updating feats.

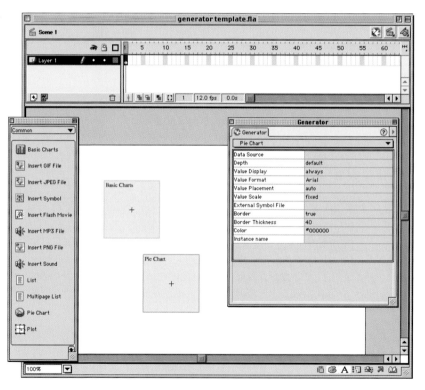

Content Management Systems

In Chapter 6 we described the function of a content management system (CMS) and how it can save time and effort with site maintenance. By establishing a system that separates the content from the structure of a page, text and graphic updates can be done by just about anyone who knows how to type (like a client, for instance)—no knowledge of HTML is required.

A site built with a CMS doesn't contain many individual HTML pages. Instead there are a few key HTML templates that call on the content files from a database as they are needed. Pages are rendered on-the-fly and text and images are automatically inserted into the appropriate areas of the template. Web sites with hundreds or thousands of pages can greatly benefit from a CMS, and the client can potentially save a good deal of money in maintenance costs.

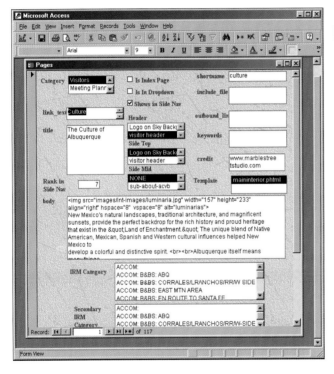

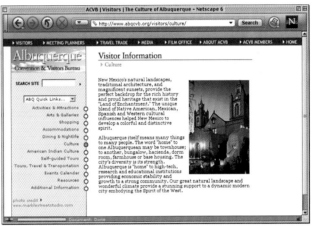

The text data that's shown in this Microsoft Access window (left) is dynamically linked to an HTML page (above) that will eventually display the text in its proper format when requested. Any changes made to data within the Access form will immediately be reflected in the corresponding web page.

Resources

Below are links where you can find more information about each of the dynamic page solutions.

DHTML

www.webreference.com/dhtml

www.dynamicdrive.com

Flash

Also see Chapter 23.

www.flash.com

www.flashkit.com

www.moock.org/webdesign/flash

JavaScript

Also see page 114.

www.javascript.com

javascript.internet.com

www.webreference.com/js

PHP

Also see page 113.

www.php.net

ASP

www.asp.net

Content Management

(commercial software)

Also see page 109.

www.vignette.com/

manila.userland.com/

www.atomz.com/services/
atomz_publish/index.htm

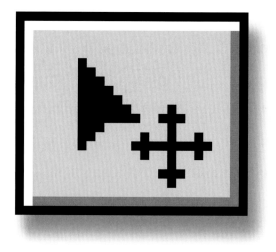

21 Frames

Some people love them. Some people hate them. We try to be nice when they're in the room, but otherwise we do our best to avoid them.

Frames offer solutions to a design challenge that eventually confronts every web designer: managing large amounts of content in a limited amount of visible screen real estate. Frames can help meet that challenge by displaying multiple web pages simultaneously in a browser. Depending upon the skill of the designer and the organization of the site architecture, the final results for the viewer may be good or bad.

Don't let our lack of frames-enthusiasm sway you from using them, but be aware that even in the best-case scenario, using frames is more problematical than not using frames.

Frame basics

What are frames?

Frames are used to subdivide a single web page into multiple HTML pages. This is a typical example that you've surely seen (or created): Along the left side are buttons. When you click a button, everything on the left side stays in place and only the content in the center changes. There might also be a frame across the top that holds the company information or perhaps an ad; as the content in the center changes, the company information or the ad stays in place.

The page structure

On a web page that uses frames, each of the different **frames** is actually a separate HTML page; all of the pages are held together by another HTML page called a **frameset.** The frameset page defines the number of frames on a page, the size and location of each frame, the source of the page that will be loaded into a frame, visibility of a frames border, and whether or not the frame will be scrollable.

The frameset page itself is not displayed by the browser—the frameset merely stores all this information and tells the browser *how* to display the different frames in relation to each other in the window.

Why frames?

Frames are often used to keep important page elements visible at all times, such as navigation buttons. Probably the most common (and annoying) use of frames is to keep advertising banners visible at all times. While there are superior navigation solutions available to designers, the technique of always-visible banner advertising will ensure the popularity of frames (at least among advertisers) for a long time.

And—it's pitifully obvious that some web builders use frames just because they know how.

This page has three separate frames. The top, horizontal frame spans the width of the page and holds the name and logo, the left frame contains the navigation, and the main frame displays the content.

First the bad news

Realizing that frames do have their place, we're still not inclined to give them much slack. Once you've implemented a frameset, or multiple framesets, the structure of your site automatically becomes more complex.

Maintenance issues

With multiple, individual web pages targeted at various frames in a frameset, maintenance becomes more complex, time consuming, and confusing. If you've passed the maintenance chores to someone else or to the client, the confusion can result in major problems with page content being displayed in the wrong places.

Ugliness issues

A scroll bar is intrusive enough when there's just one—the usual vertical scroll bar on the right side of the browser window. Most framed pages have multiple scroll bars that are just simply unattractive and distracting. They interfere with the overall design and damage the readability and visual appeal of the page.

Ugly or not, extra scroll bars may be useful in some instances as they can add to the ease of content accessibility.

In deciding whether to use frames or not, carefully consider the possible negative design consequences versus any possible navigation or content presentation advantages. Or, more simply put, is there a good reason to complicate the site?

Search engine issues

Registering a frames-based web site with search engines and making it accessible to robots and spiders is more difficult than with plain HTML pages. Most search engines and robots that catalog and index the pages of web sites will be able to identify the *frameset page* but *not the actual HTML content pages* that are linked to the frameset document. That is, content on a page that uses frames will not automatically show up in search engines.

Workaround solution: You can work around this situation by creating a **non-framed** web page that serves as a site index. The site index is an organizational outline of the entire site (see Chapter 17), where each item in the outline is a link to a page in the site. By registering the index page with search engines, the entire site, including each individual page, is made accessible to robots and search engines. And of course you can always manually submit the site to search engines and directories.

Printing issues

If visitors are going to want to print pages, frames can create problems. Few end users know they must click on the particular frame that they want printed *before* they choose to print; this means most people end up printing the navigation frame instead of the content frame, and they'll send you flaming email about the site.

Alternatives to frames

As you explore design solutions for effectively presenting content, you can usually find other options that offer better solutions than frames. Pop-up menus are less intrusive (no permanent scroll bars) and can be an attractive, temporary graphic element on the page. Pop-up menus can also accommodate many navigation links while temporarily occupying screen space. They can give an organizational overview of an entire section in a glance.

Dynamic content solutions like PHP (see page 113) provide the ease of frames by allowing portions of a page to reside in a single reference file.

By comparison, frames often look clunky and obtrusive. Some of us would even argue that frames make a page look technologically old-fashioned.

Good frame jobs

If you decide that frames are really the best solution to the particular design challenge of your web site, then here are a few guidelines for using them as effectively and attractively as possible.

No superfluous scroll bars

Use as few frames as necessary so that the distraction of unattractive scroll bars in the middle of the designed page is minimized. Inexperienced designers sometimes mistakenly think that the presence of extra, unnecessary frames adds interest to a page; in fact, they usually just add complexity and confusion while distracting from the visual appeal of the page.

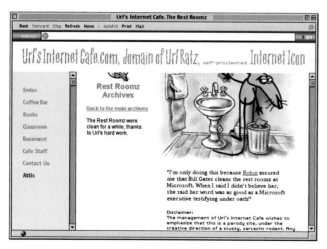

Turn scrolling off whenever possible so that the web page isn't cluttered with extra scroll bars. A well-designed web page can use the functionality of frames without making the use of frame technique visually obvious.

Avoid horizontal scrolling

Don't create a frame that requires horizontal scrolling. Everyone knows that vertical page scrolling is a web fact of life, but sideways scrolling is annoying and it adds even more scroll bar visual clutter to the page. Especially annoying is a navigation frame that requires scrolling sideways a quarter of an inch to see the entire frame content.

Don't scroll into the void

Create edges along the frames so a user doesn't see a page scrolling off into the void. This happens when the scrolling page is the same color as the frame it scrolls into, as shown to the left; as the page rolls up, the text and graphics just get cut off by invisible space because the user can see no edge to the frame. If the two framesets are two different colors (as shown on the opposite page), then the scrolling page appears to scroll *under* the top frame (or bottom frame), instead of just disappearing into nothingness.

It's visually disturbing to see content scroll up and get cut off for no apparent reason.

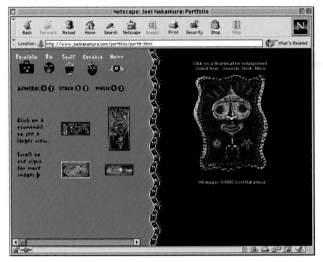

Other than making the site structure and maintenance more complex, we don't have any complaints about this kind of frame design: The navigation in the left frame stays visible as it determines what content is displayed in the large, scrollable, main frame on the right. The main content frame disappears under the top horizontal colored frame instead of into a void.

All rules, of course, can be broken by good designers. Here is an example of a frame scrolling sideways. The reason this particular page is successful is because the choice to scroll sideways was a **conscious** one, rather than an accident that appeared because the designer was sloppy or lazy.

In several of the other interior pages in this same web site, the scrolling frame was placed on the right-hand side so you still only see the one scroll bar that you're accustomed to seeing, not an additional one in the middle of the page.

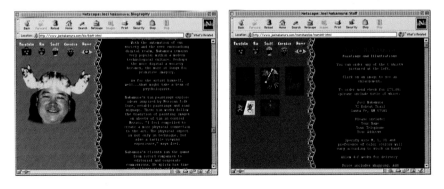

In this particular catalogue site, the client requested the use of frames. The home page, as shown above, has no frames, but the interior pages, as shown to the right, are constructed in framesets.

In this example, the column at the far right can scroll to show all the product categories in a section. Clicking on a category link in this frame will load a second frame to the left, displaying product photography and information.

In GoLive's Help section, which uses frames, the scroll bar has a perfectly good reason to be where it is—there are hundreds of items in that list, not simply six or seven. DHTML menus wouldn't be appropriate for this many items, either.

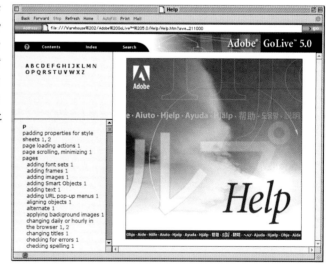

Bad frame jobs

These examples demonstrate some of the worst uses (and most common uses) of frames.

The top example shows the kind of frame design that gives frames a bad reputation. Too many scroll bars add clutter and confusion instead of making the navigation clearer.

In the bottom example, there's nothing about the layout that makes frames useful; there are no extensive navigation options that a user needs to scroll through, nor a banner ad that needs perpetual exposure.

In fact, the frames implemented here actually hurt the navigation rather than aid it: clicking on a thumbnail image along the top replaces the bottom frame content with an enlargement of the thumbnail, which replaces the navigation links, making them inaccessible. The page design has become a hodge-podge of scroll bars rather than a pleasing layout.

Creating frames

Creating frames used to be confusing. Current software makes them easier to implement, but unless you're familiar with the relationship between frames and framesets, you may create a mess and your frames won't work.

With software such as Dreamweaver and GoLive you can easily create an entire frameset by selecting a preset frames layout icon. You can place content into individual frames in the frameset, import existing HTML documents into any frame, or type directly into individual frames.

Any content or source file you put into a frame is saved as a separate HTML page. Each HTML page represented in the frameset designates a *target,* the name of the frame it will appear in.

So, a frameset layout that consists of three frames will actually need four HTML files to make it work: three HTML content pages that contain the content that is displayed in each of the three frames, and one HTML frameset page that describes the layout, position, size, and other attributes of the three frames, such as whether scroll bars are activated.

Creating frames in Dreamweaver

To create frames in Dreamweaver, click on the title of the "Objects" palette and from that drop-down menu, select "Frames."

The palette becomes a graphic menu of predefined frameset choices. Choosing one of the framesets automatically sets up all the frames and the frameset necessary to create the chosen layout.

Once you've chosen a predefined frameset, you can edit the frames in the document window by dragging the frame edges to adjust the width or depth to your liking.

You can enter content directly into a frame, or designate an existing HTML page as the source for that frame using the "Property Inspector" (shown on the following page).

The "Frames" panel, shown below, provides an easy way to select individual frames or an entire frameset, which is useful when you need to make a frame/frameset selection to save it.

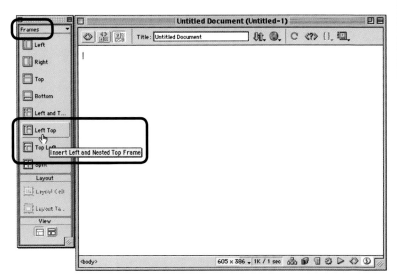

By selecting one of the predefined frameset icons,
we automated the process of creating a frameset.
In this example, the document window is still empty.

The "Property Inspector" makes it easy to define frame properties, such as name, frame source, scrolling and frame border options, and margin values.

Each frame and each frameset must be saved using a unique name. All links must include targets (the name of the frame in which the linked content will appear) so the linked content will appear in the correct frame.

After you've named the frames (or you can use the generic name assigned by Dreamweaver), you can choose the target in the "Target" pop-up menu in the "Property Inspector."

The HTML link code for a navigation button in the left frame of our example would look like this:

```
<a href="whenwhere.html"
target="rightframe">
```

This frameset code tells the browser to display the document "whenwhere.html" in the frame named "rightframe."

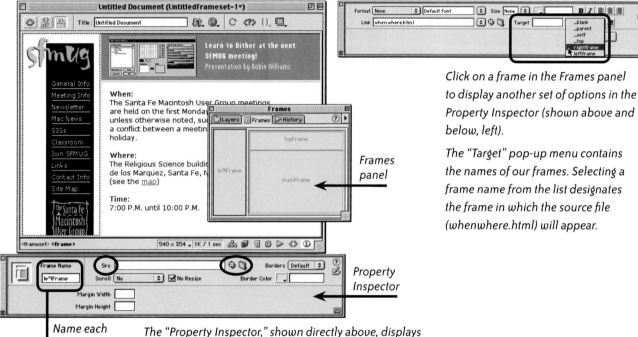

Click on a frame in the Frames panel to display another set of options in the Property Inspector (shown above and below, left).

The "Target" pop-up menu contains the names of our frames. Selecting a frame name from the list designates the frame in which the source file (whenwhere.html) will appear.

Frames panel

Property Inspector

Name each frame.

The "Property Inspector," shown directly above, displays different options depending on whether you click on a frame in the document window or in the Frames panel.

Click on a frame in the document window to set the source for a frame's content. Either type in a path name or click the folder icon and browse to an HTML file. The selected file will be placed inside the target frame.

Creating Frames in GoLive

Creating frames and adding content in Adobe GoLive is similar to the process in Dreamweaver.

At the top of the document window, select the "Frame Editor" tab (circled below).

From the Palette window, choose the "Frames" tab and select a predefined frame layout (also circled below).

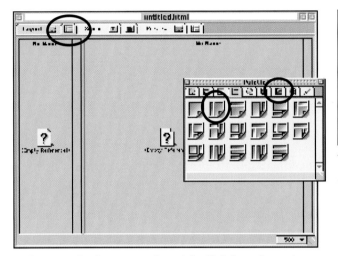

In the example above, we selected the "left frame" icon (top row, second icon) and dragged it onto the document window. The empty frames are displayed in the window.

To add the contents of a pre-designed HTML page, you can use the Point-and-Click button found in the "Frame Inspector," as shown below: click on the button and drag the pointer to the HTML file icon that you want to place in the frame. Or use the "Browse" button in the "Frame Inspector" to locate the desired file on your computer.

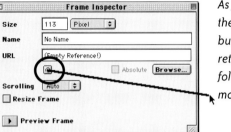

As you drag from the Point-and-Click button, you see a retractable line follow your mouse movement.

The "Browse…" button lets you navigate to the desired HTML source file, as you are accustomed to doing. **Or,** *with the Point-and-Click button (circled above), you can press that button down, drag to the file stored in your* **site folder,** *and let go.* **Or** *you can drag the file from the site folder directly to the frame.*

After setting an HTML source file, we can see the contents of that web page in the target frame by selecting the Frame Preview tab (circled).

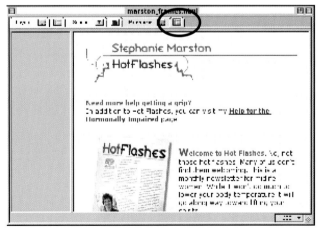

Be forewarned

The software automation of frames creation makes it easy to build frames in a web site. But give careful consideration to whether or not your site really *needs* frames before you implement them, as discussed on pages 300–301.

Frames can be problematical, and ultimately they will make the site structure and maintanance more complex and confusing, not only for the visitor but also for the person who maintains the site. It's not uncommon for smaller clients to take over the mainenance of a site once it's designed; the complexity of frames could be more than they bargained for.

Even some of our larger clients, who initially insisted on frames, reconsidered after the site was launched. Web design is complicated enough at its simplistic best. If your design plan includes more complexity (frames, Flash, e-commerce, database integration, etc.), make sure the complexity is justified by the site and client goals.

Finally, look around the World Wide Web. Visit the web sites of the best known corporations, hardware companies, and software developers whose sites are *designed* by professional designers (as opposed to being *built* by programmers). How many of them use frames? Very few, if any. If they do, the reason why they chose the frame option is probably obvious.

Animated GIFs

Animated GIF files are actually quite amazing. You can merge any number of different static images into one single file to create an animation effect. With GIF animation software you can determine the length of time that each image is displayed and how many times the sequence of images repeats. Adobe ImageReady, Adobe Photoshop, Macromedia Fireworks, and a host of other retail , shareware, and freeware products enable you to create animated GIFs quickly and easily.

Too much of a good thing

Animated GIFs are easy to make, they're usually trouble free, and they can add visual interest to a page. As with many aspects of web design, however, a little GIF animation goes a long way, and few things in life are more annoying than a little cartoon envelope flying in and out of a mailbox out of the corner of your eye while you're trying to read text on a page. Worse yet are the pages that have three or four of these non-stop GIFs.

Please...

Conservative use of animated GIFs can help create entertaining, attention-getting web pages. However, where GIFs are concerned, there's a very fine line between entertaining and annoying. Simplicity and subtlety are the key ingredients to using GIF animation successfully. Unlike Flash animation, which is capable of complex and lengthy visuals, GIF animations are simplistic,

repetitive, and monotonous in nature. When and where to use animated GIFs is a subjective judgment call, but there are a few common sense guidelines that we use to avoid looking like clueless amateur animators.

Please: Don't set the looping option to "Forever." Forever is a long time. Even ten seconds is a long time if you're actually trying to read content on the same page as the animated GIF. Set a reasonable limit to the number of times the animation loops. Remember that the readability of the page is being affected by all that motion.

Adding multiple GIF animations to a page looks unprofessional, even in this static version. All those rotating, waving, spinning, and folding motions make the web visit extremely unpleasant.

Now, we sometimes *do* use the "Forever" option if the animated GIF appears on an intro page that the visitor is going to skip right on through, or on a very simple page, or if the animation is extremely subdued.

Please: Don't use the same ubiquitous GIF animations that appear on so many other sites. If you're going to entertain us with animation, make it something that doesn't appear on ninety percent of all amateur sites. Envelopes flying in and out of a mailbox, pens writing letters which fold up and fly into an envelope, rotating globes, and rainbow-colored divider bars were pretty cool the first time we saw them—many years ago. Since then they've become one of the elements that makes a page look amateurish.

Please: Don't use GIF animations that have too many frames, making them large and slow to download. We seldom create animated GIFs that have more than three or four frames.

GIF animation software can "tween" between frames, a technique that automatically creates frames to fill in the animation sequence between two existing frames. Tweening can create an interesting dissolve transition effect, but the file size can balloon quickly with the extra frames. Let go of the idea of having smooth animation in an animated GIF file—smooth animation requires many frames, which translates into huge files.

Please: Don't place multiple GIF animations on a singe page—one animation is distracting enough. Using three or four rotating, spinning, flying, blinking images on a single page can take that page to the next level: from amateurish to nauseating.

That said . . .

In spite of its enormous potential to be distracting and annoying, there are still plenty of opportunities to make good use of GIF animation.

[Tip: To stop animations on a web page you visit, press Esc after the page has finished loading; in Netscape on a Mac, press Command Period.]

Dreamweaver's "Tween" feature creates a transition effect between two frames, automatically building the intermediate frames necessary. The Tween window allows you to set the number of new fames.

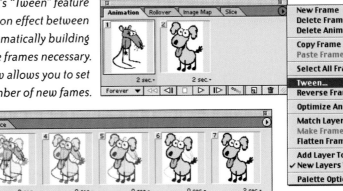

The "Animation" palette displays the new tweening frames, frames 2 through 6.

Add a dash of motion

Animation doesn't translate very well to a printed page, but we've included some examples of how we've incorporated GIF animation into some of our pages.

In case you're not familiar with how current software simplifies the creation of animated GIFs, we'll start with a how-to example. We're using Adobe ImageReady in this example, but there are a number of free or very inexpensive software packages that do the same thing: go to shareware.com and search for "gif animation."

Example of the process

As an entry page to a sketchbook section, we created a miniature sketchbook on the page. The left and right sides of the sketch book are different GIF files, and each one automatically cycles through three different sketches.

We scanned an empty spiral sketchbook and six different sketches. In Photoshop, we cut the spiral sketchbook in half, with each half placed on its own layer so we could create separate animated GIF files for the left and right sides. We also created a separate layer for each scanned sketch so we could turn each sketch on or off as needed.

We then opened the Photoshop file in ImageReady. The ImageReady preview below, shows a composite image of the layers containing the scan of a blank left page and one of the scanned sketches.

Using the "Optimized" palette, we optimized the image as a GIF, then clicked on the "Animation" tab in the tab array panel, as shown below. A thumbnail duplicate of the optimized image displayed as Frame 1.

To create a second animation frame, we clicked on the "New Frame" button at the bottom of the palette, which placed a duplicate of Frame 1 in the Frame 2 position of the animation palette. By turning off the active layer (sketch of the feet) and turning on a new layer (sketch of reclining figure), we designated the second frame of animation. We set the third frame in the same manner (clicked "New Frame," adjusted the layer visibility to show the desired sketch).

Next we selected the frame delay time and the looping (repeated plays of the animation) options. The looping options range from "Once" to "Forever," and you can specify any number of loops. We chose "Forever" from the pop-up menu in the the bottom-left corner of the Animation palette (circled, below).

We clicked on the small black triangle (circled, below) beneath each thumbnail and gave each frame of the animation a delay of 2 seconds: we chose "Other" from the pop-up menu and then entered the desired value in the "Set Frame Delay" dialog box that appeared.

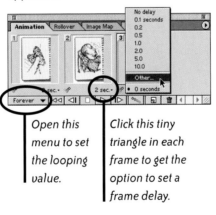

Open this menu to set the looping value.

Click this tiny triangle in each frame to get the option to set a frame delay.

We saved the file (from the File menu, choose "Save Optimized As…") which made the three separate frames into a single, animated GIF file. We followed the same procedure to create an animated GIF file for the right-hand side of the sketchbook image.

Using Dreamweaver, we created a table with one row and two columns, then placed each animated GIF in the appropriate table cell. In the example below, you can see the two animated GIFs placed in individual cells of a small, two-cell table.

New Frame button

Animating a logo

There are lots of other small ways to use simple animation for an extra touch. The client for the web site shown here asked for a flashing lightning bolt to add a small dose of visual interest to this HotFlashes Newsletter flag. The flag has been sliced, optimized, and placed in a table. This enabled us to create a very small slice that would be saved as an animated GIF. The HTML table shown in Dreamweaver (to the right) shows the separate slices that make up the table. The selected center slice is the animated GIF file.

The lightning bolt animation cycles through several frames in which the bolt alternates between "on" and "off." Setting slightly different time delays settings for each frame of animation created a more natural lightning effect.

We copied and pasted the final table into the text area of an existing page, after first ensuring that all image slices for the table had been copied to the images folder for that existing page.

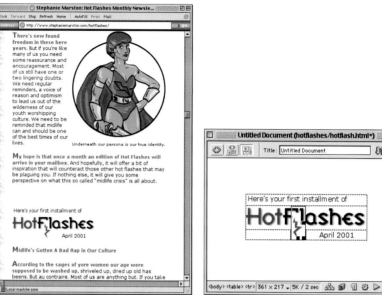

The small, flashing lightning bolt adds a touch of visual interest to a long, scrolling page of text.

By slicing the graphic we were able to make the animated part of the design extremely small.

316

Enhancing an illustration

A section of an author's book site features sample illustrations from the book. This brilliant illustration by Alban Butler inspired us to enhance it for the web with a subtle animation.

We sliced the image to create a fast and efficient animation. We turned on the table borders in this example so you can see how the image was sliced; only the middle slice needed to be processed as an animated GIF.

The slicing technique made the page much smaller and faster—rather than creating the entire large image as an animated GIF file, the only section that has to reload to animate is the small middle slice.

The humorous illustration first appears as originally created in the 1920s— a man studies his book.

The second frame of animation loads after a two-second delay. The man seems suddenly aware of something strange.

In the third frame, he looks nervously over his shoulder, then returns to his book study, frame #1.

Grab attention with subtlety

This screenwriting conference used a burning typewriter for their logo. Making the flames animate added interest to the intro page and created curiosity for the content inside.

Shown in Dreamweaver, you can see that image was sliced and placed in a table so that only a portion of the image would have to be animated, making the overall page download smaller and faster.

A combination of simplicity and subtlety can create a compelling page.

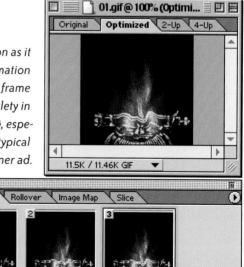

This is the three-frame animation as it appeared in ImageReady's Animation palette. The flames in each frame are very subtle variations. Subtlety in animation can be very pleasing, especially if you've ever seen a typical animated banner ad.

Animation optimization

ImageReady has a powerful feature that helps to reduce an animation's file size when you save the file by including only areas that have changed from frame to frame.

In the "Animation" palette (shown to the right), use the pop-out menu and choose "Optimize Animation…." You'll get the dialog box shown.

Check both boxes in the "Optimize Animation" dialog box to optimize the animation. The "Bounding Box" feature crops each frame to include only the area that changed from the previous frame. The "Redundant Pixel Removal" option makes transparent any pixel that is unchanged from the previous frame.

In the floating "Optimize" palette (shown to the right), make sure the "Transparency" option is selected.

In the "Animation" palette, make sure the frame disposal method is set to "Automatic" (Control-click [Mac] or Alt-click [PC] under the left corner of the thumbnail image to access the hidden "Disposal" pop-up menu.)

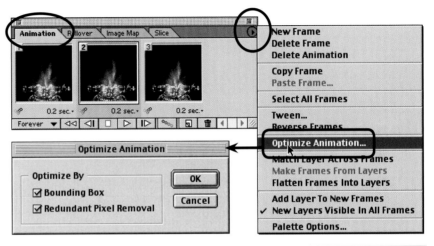

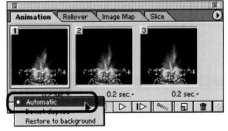

Add some fun to a page

The page below has a fairly large illustration in which the bar-tending rodent is wiping off the counter. An animation of this size would be larger than necessary, even with just two frames.

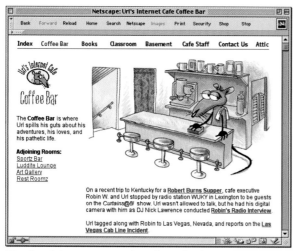

We sliced the image into five slices, had ImageReady optimize the slices and build the HTML table, then made the center slice (the smallest slice) a two-frame animation of the sponge moving back and forth.

We sliced the image so only a tiny section of it required animation (see Chapter 12 on slicing).

The dog cartoon below was sliced in Dreamweaver so we could animate the eyes, ears, and tail independently. Each animated GIF slice (slices 1, 2, and 4) used a different number of frames with different time delays to prevent the separate slices from looking synchronized.

The final page, below, shows no evidence that the image is actually five images held together by an HTML table.

Animated photographs

Most animated GIFs are cartoonish rather than photographic because those are the kinds of images that look best and compress best in the GIF format: images made of areas of flat web-safe colors with minimal shading and color gradation.

Even though photographic images look *best* in the JPEG format, you *can* save them as GIFs or use them in animated GIF files, as we did here. The limited GIF color palette usually compromises the quality of a photographic image—in the example directly below you can see the dithering technique the GIF format uses to simulate colors that are not in its color palette.

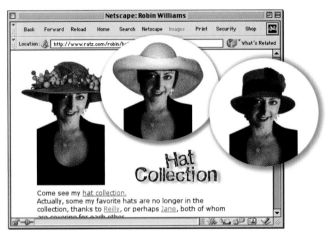

Robin's hat collection page features an animated GIF in which the hat she's wearing cycles through several different styles.

By slicing this image we're able to optimize the larger window as a JPEG for better quality, while using the GIF format only for the smaller animation slice.

Animation slice.

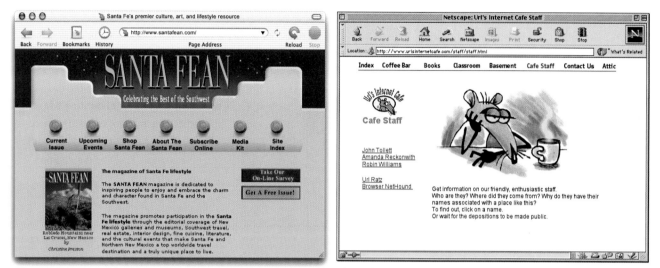

The animated twinkling stars on this page are so subtle that they almost look real. The understated effect gives the site a feeling of sophistication and elegance.

The only movement on this page is the steam coming from the coffee cup. The animation is just a small slice of the illustration.

Thanks to technology, Url cleans the restrooms 24 hours a day. As before, only a small slice of the illustration is animated—Url's left arm.

We use a lot of animated GIFs in this site because the site is primarily for entertainment. Even though we take a lot of liberties to have fun, we never put more than one GIF animation on a page and the animations are almost always three or four frames, at most.

GIF improv

We often decide to add an animated GIF to a page only after we've developed a design and had time to sit back and evaluate the overall effect of the layout. In this example, we were happy with the photo as it was, but it occurred to us that it would be fun to add a haunting effect to the tomb. The image was fairly large so we sliced it into pieces, making it necessary to animate only the small section containing the face.

This Layers palette demonstrates how we put every element on its own layer during the layout stage. The black circles indicate layers that have styles applied from Photoshop's Styles palette, such as beveled buttons and text, as well as the embossed face on the crypt. Some layers are experimental design ideas and not used in the final version.

Before we clean out the unused layers from our final source file, we save a copy of the layout with all layers intact in case we later want to retrieve something from an unused layer.

GIF weigh-in

The weight (the size in kilobytes) of an animated GIF file is determined by its width and height physical dimensions, the number of colors in the color palette, and the number of animation frames used to create the animation. To keep an animated GIF from becoming a large cumbersome file that slows down your page, be conservative in creating animations: use as few animation frames as possible; make width and height dimensions of animations reasonably small; and use limited color palettes to help reduce file size.

Also, use the slicing technique explained in Chapter 12 to minimize the area of an image that needs to be part of the animation. This will enable you to create an animation effect using fairly large images and still keep files in the smallest possible size.

These frames were created automatically with tweening.

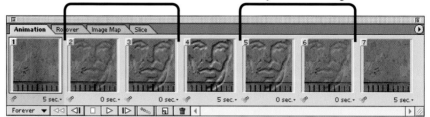

For this animated GIF, a small slice of the complete image shown on page 323, we used ImageReady's "tween" feature to automatically create the two intermediate steps between Frame 1 and Frame 4, and again to create intermediate Frames 5 and 6. More frames means smoother animation, but with a substantial addition of file size and download time. The final version of this six-frame animated GIF file weighed nearly 50K.

Our example shows seven frames because we needed to place a duplicate of Frame 1 in the palette after Frame 4 so we could instruct ImageReady to tween between Frame 4 and the next frame, automatically creating Frames 5 and 6 in the process. Frame 7 became unnecessary after the tweening process since we wanted to loop (repeat) the animation. We deleted Frame 7, which helped to make the animated GIF smaller.

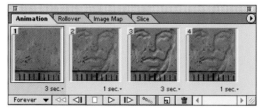

We decided to sacrifice smooth animation in favor of a smaller file and faster download. We deleted all but one intermediate step between the key frames (Frame 1 and Frame 3 above). The animation effect wasn't as smooth as before, but the file size was half of what it had been.

Motion Graphics

Motion graphics, popularized by **Macromedia Flash,** is one of most exciting web technologies around. Flash allows you to produce rich, interactive, and scalable vector-based animations that will download quickly into your web browser.

Flash, plus a handful of other programs, can export ".swf" files *(pronounced "swiff")* that can encapsulate vectors, bitmaps, sound, and video into a single cohesive format. It's possible to create entire Flash sites with fully animated layouts that transcend HTML entirely.

While Flash started the whole motion graphics trend, it's not the only application that can produce .swf files. Adobe recently jumped into the fray with **LiveMotion,** which can create .swf files that can be viewed and experienced in any Flash-enabled browser. Like Flash, LiveMotion is a complete authoring environment that lets you control timelines, add interactivity, play audio files, and many more amazing features. Its approach is different from the Flash application, but the resulting file format is just as compatible.

For smaller projects

Full-featured applications are great, but if you only need to create small files, there are several other programs besides Flash and LiveMotion that can export to the .swf format. Recent versions of Macromedia FreeHand, Macromedia Fireworks, and Adobe Illustrator can also save out to the .swf format.

Why use Flash?

A little Flash on a web site can add punch, sophistication, animation, and sound without adding much download time. A fully interactive, multi-layered Flash site can blow HTML completely out of the water.

In the past, animated GIFs were the most one could expect in the way of motion on a web page. But if not created properly, animated GIFs could be clunky, repetitive, and slow to download. These days, well-built Flash files have a smooth, high-tech feel while retaining extremely small file sizes.

Tired of angular looking table-based pages? Sick of the same eight fonts? A complete Flash web site will allow you to throw off the constrictions of HTML and design your layouts freely, embedding any fonts you like and placing (or moving) images into any position you like.

Make it interesting

DiscoverToys (discovertoys.com) is an imaginary toy store web site designed and produced by 415 Productions to demonstrate Macromedia products. It's an effective use of animation: just enough to grab your interest and facilitate navigation, but not so much as to cause confusion.

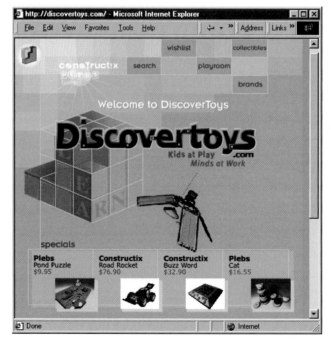

As with many animations reproduced on the printed page, you can't really tell what's going on unless you go to the site!

Flash can be sexy

The web site for DNAcommunications uses Flash extensively throughout the site. It's a great example of the sorts of things Flash can do and how quickly they can happen.

It's easier to get away with a Flash-intensive site if it's your own instead of a client's site. Although DNA's site is almost totally Flash, most of their corporate work involves utilizing Flash in smaller amounts on other sites.

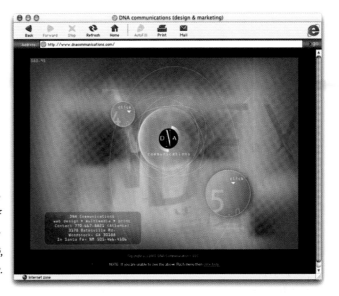

This is the DNAcommunications home page. Although there's a lot of animation, it's beautiful and subtle rather than obnoxious and overbearing, as many Flash-y sites can be.

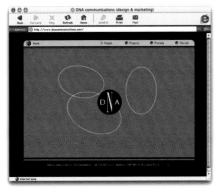

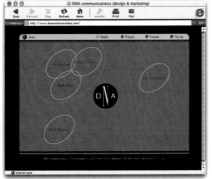

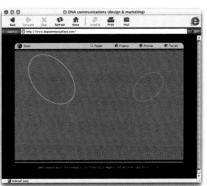

These four panels represent a few of the frames in the "People" section.

Click in the "DJ Teeslink" circle and it continues an animation to display DJ's bio and photo.

Flash enables this nearly full-screen animation to play smoothly and instantly, even on a slow modem connection.

Symbols

Flash makes good use of its resources and assets to keep file sizes small. You can create an image and make it a symbol, placing it into a library of symbols. Any time you reintroduce this symbol, you benefit from the fact that it is already loaded. Like a graphic logo used repeatedly on several pages of a web site, you don't add much to the download time by using it again. In Flash you can even edit "instances" (separate occurrences) of symbols, changing their properties while capitalizing on the benefit of a single download.

Here we put a snake on the stage by typing it in with the picture font Artifact. From the Modify menu, we chose "Break Apart" to turn it into an image, and then from the Insert menu, chose "Convert to Symbol," which brought up the dialog box shown below. As indicated in the dialog box, there are three kids of symbols in Flash: movie clips, buttons, and graphic symbols. We named our symbol "snake," selected "Graphic," and clicked OK.

The symbol immediately appeared in our "Library" panel, where we selected it and repeatedly dragged new instances onto the stage.

Then we used the "Effects" panel to give each instance a new color. With the "Scale" and "Rotate" buttons on the toolbar, we changed the dimensions and direction. We now have seven different versions of our snake, with the download time reflecting only one.

The "movie" itself has no animation and only one frame. Its actual dimensions are 453 x 238 pixels, but we set it to 100 percent width and 80 percent height.

Using symbols and scaling together created a .swf that is less than 1K (722 bytes, to be exact).

Symbols can be used in various ways, but the most powerful use of the symbol is as a movie clip, which enables you to have completely independent timelines nested inside each other. Full details of this technique are beyond the scope of this book, but Macromedia has a nice tutorial movie on symbol creation, available on its site. Go to **www.macromedia.com,** find the Flash section, and then look for the tutorials.

This is the original symbol.

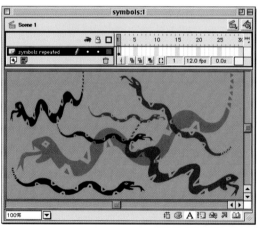

This example is not animated, but shows how an entire screen of graphics can be created using instances of a symbol, resulting in a file size less than 1K.

Scalabilty

Scalability is another feature of Flash files. You can use Flash as an image editing tool to create a vector graphic logo and give it a percentage size of 100 percent (100 percent of the screen size). It's nice to watch your 1K logo fill a 21" monitor instantly. Flash's real-time anti-aliasing can smooth the edges of the vector image (*rasterize* it) on the fly, making it look great no matter how it's resized.

You can also use this technique with full-blown Flash sites, filling the entire screen with your movie. When you combine percentage-based movies with framesets, you can fill one portion of your screen with a movie and maintain a static navigation section in the other frame. Macromedia uses this technique beautifully on their multi-frame home page.

Be sure to start with a movie that has a fast enough frame rate to transition well on the larger screens; otherwise you can end up with jerky motion and/or degraded bitmaps.

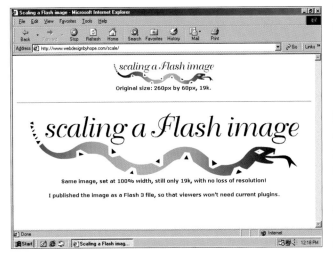

This example of scalability shows the original 5K movie on top, and the same movie scaled to 100 percent below. Grab the lower-right corner of the browser, resize the window, and the image shrinks and stretches cleanly with no loss of resolution (you may need to hit "Reload" or "Refresh"). Amazing.

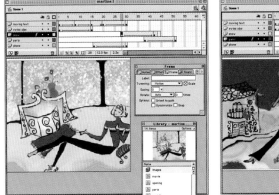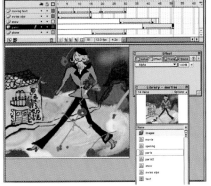

Even complex illustrations like the ones shown here scale beautifully when they're drawn completely in a vector format.

Create a Flash animation

Here is a condensed description of how we created the scalable Flash file shown on the previous pages.

We started by asking three questions:

1. **What size is our movie?**
   We wanted a small file which we would scale up later using percentages.

2. **What do we want to happen?**
   We wanted a gradient animating back and forth on a snake's body, plus some text.

3. **How long should it take?**
   It should loop indefinitely, with a single back-and-forth animation lasting two seconds.

In Flash we made a new file and sized it 260 pixels wide by 60 pixels high. We created two separate layers and named them "Static Images" and "Animated Gradient."

In the "Static Images" layer, we typed "scaling a Flash file" with the Text tool. We used the "Scale" button on the toolbar to scale the text to fit the upper portion of our stage.

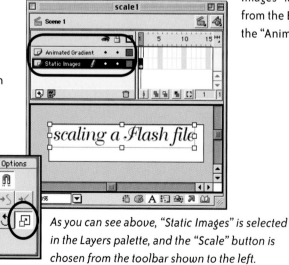

As you can see above, "Static Images" is selected in the Layers palette, and the "Scale" button is chosen from the toolbar shown to the left.

We got the snake from the picture font Artifact One and scaled it to fit the lower portion of our stage.

We wanted the animated gradient to apply only to the snake's main body, not to any of its decorative symbols. So from the Modify menu, we chose "Break Apart," then used the Arrow tool to click on the body to select it. We cut the selected snake body from the "Static Images" layer and chose "Paste in Place" from the Edit menu to put the snake into the "Animated Gradient" layer.

To execute the fill, we chose a green-to-black radial gradient at the bottom of the "Fill Color" palette and clicked on the head of the snake with the Paint Bucket tool. The snake's body was now gradated from green at the head to black at the tail.

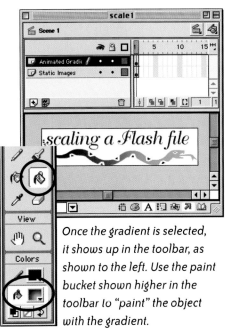

Once the gradient is selected, it shows up in the toolbar, as shown to the left. Use the paint bucket shown higher in the toolbar to "paint" the object with the gradient.

To move the green glow to the tail of the snake in a period of one second, we needed to move one second down the timeline. The default frames-per-second setting in Flash is 12, which was fine for this movie.

We selected Frame 12 on the timeline, then hit F6 to create a new keyframe.

We clicked on the tail of the snake with the Paint Bucket tool. Now the green glow was on the tail, gradating to black at the head.

To make the animation, we dragged our pointer on the timeline to select the gray frames between the beginning and Frame 12, as shown below.

The shaded frames between the starting and ending states are selected in preparation for a "tween."

From the Window menu, we chose "Panels," then "Frame."

In the Frame palette, we chose "Shape" from the "Tweening" menu. The first half of our animation was done.

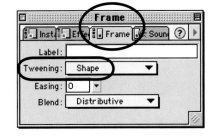

Now we needed to add 12 more frames with the gradient moving in the *opposite* direction to close the loop. After selecting the 12 frames on our animation layer in the timeline, we held the Option/Alt key and dragged them over to the right, down 12 frames, ending at Frame 24. We reversed the direction of these frames: from the Modify menu, we chose "Frames," then "Reverse."

We want the objects on the "static images" layer to remain visible for the full two seconds. Easy. We clicked on the first frame of that layer and hit F5 to create a new frame that inherited the images on the first frame. We dragged that frame out to Frame 24, the end of our movie.

We tested our movie by hitting Enter and voilà—the gradient moved from side to side continually, and it filled the screen at only 5K!

331

Getting it into HTML

Flash works seamlessly with Dreamweaver, so we often use these programs together, although it is certainly no problem to add Flash to any of the other high-quality web authoring applications, such as GoLive.

In this example, we inserted a Flash movie into a table on a home page.

First we created the movie and "published" it into the correct folder in our web hierarchy: When you **save** a Flash file, you are saving an original **.fla** file *(pronounced "flah")*. When you choose "Publish" from the File menu, by default Flash generates an HTML file and a .swf *(pronounced "swiff")* movie file, placing them both in the same folder as the .fla file.

This movie was built in Flash and published to the appropriate folder in the web hierarchy. The animation displays zeros and ones transforming into the designer's logo.

Saving a Flash movie generates a layered .fla file. To create your .swf file, the file you will place on a web page, choose "Publish" from the File menu, which by default produces an HTML file as well and puts all the files in the same folder.

Here are the three files created by default when you save and publish a movie.

The WYSIWYG way

You can use the HTML file generated by Flash as a starting point for building your web page. In this particular case, since we planned to embed the movie into an existing web page, we used Dreamweaver's interface instead.

We created the home page table in Fireworks with multiple-event rollovers, leaving an empty cell at the top of the page for the Flash animation.

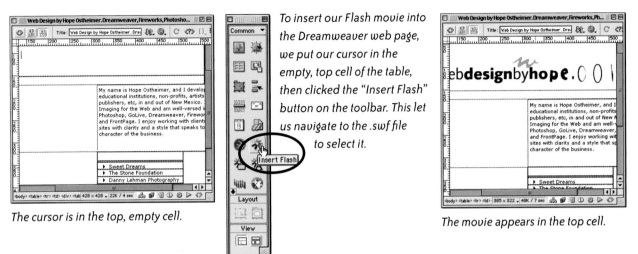

To insert our Flash movie into the Dreamweaver web page, we put our cursor in the empty, top cell of the table, then clicked the "Insert Flash" button on the toolbar. This let us navigate to the .swf file to select it.

The cursor is in the top, empty cell.

The movie appears in the top cell.

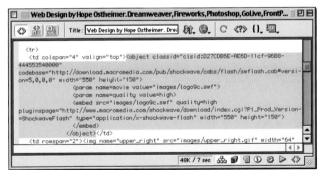

This is the code Dreamweaver generated automatically to embed the .swf file. When this HTML file is uploaded to the server, the .swf file must be uploaded also.

No plug-in?

You want to create a beautiful Flash site, but you're afraid of losing viewers who don't have the plug-in installed?

Macromedia claims that 96 percent of the web's 348 million viewers have one of the Flash plug-ins. Since Flash has become a web-standard technology with newer browsers giving full support, this figure is expected to grow.

A lack of the plug-in can make many users just leave the site because it has traditionally been a hassle to find and install a missing plug-in.

But this has changed—a visitor has several options when arriving at a page with Flash animation. For example, a Windows visitor using Internet Explorer without an installed plug-in will see something like the box shown above. Click "Yes," and it could be a short wait of a matter of seconds before the movie begins playing with the plug-in installed, and the visitor will never even leave the browser.

An old plug-in can be worse than no plug-in

A typical person viewing your site is likely to have an early Flash plug-in. If they visit your newer Flash movie, they won't necessarily get a warning, but they may not enjoy the full functionality of the site.

One way around this is to publish your movie as an earlier version of Flash. If you're not using the advanced Action-Scripting features, try publishing your movie as a Flash 3 file (at the expense of losing some of the sophisticated features found in versions 4 and 5).

To publish in a different version, go to the File menu, choose "Publish Settings…," then click the "Flash" tab.

After choosing your version, click OK and hit F12 to test your movie in a browser. If any functionality is lost, you will see it here. You can tell your viewers that they must have a specific plug-in, giving them a link to the download page on Macromedia.com: *www.macromedia.com/go/getflashplayer.* It's a small file, only 470k, with an estimated download time of one minute on a 56K modem.

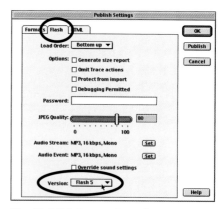

The "Publish Settings" window gives you options for saving your Flash movies.

Browser detection

Add some code

You may also want to consider enabling some kind of browser detection method for your Flash web page to make the user experience as seamless as possible.

Browser detection consists of a special script added to your HTML page. The script determines the attributes of a web browser (which plug-ins are installed) and then allows the browser to automatically redirect the user to an appropriate page. If the browser has Flash installed, it goes to a page with the Flash movie, and if Flash is not present, it redirects to a regular HTML page.

Macromedia offers a downloadable Flash Deployment Kit (URL below) that can make your Flash sites "degrade" gracefully if someone without the correct plug-in visits. The kit contains custom detection JavaScripts and other code that can be installed into your HTML page manually or from within the Dreamweaver Behaviors palette.

The low-tech approach

You can also create an introductory or gateway page on your site that precedes a Flash page. This technique allows the visitor to make a choice: to either view the Flash content, download the plug-in, or go directly to an HTML version of the page. The danger here is that someone who isn't very knowledgeable about the web may not understand those choices and leave the site in confusion. This is the reason that an automatic browser detect is often the most transparent approach.

The Flash Dispatcher Behavior is a free extension you can install into Dreamweaver. It will install the necessary Flash browser detects into your HTML code.

Flash Deployment Kit
www.macromedia.com/support/flash/player/flash_deployment_readme/

Flash or GIF animation?

Decide if your audience is ready for Flash. This Flash logo for a writers' organization generated negative feedback on behalf of several viewers who had antiquated systems with old browsers.

Flash does have an option to export movies as animated GIFs: from the File menu, choose "Export Movie" and select the "Animated GIF" format. In this example, Flash created an animated GIF that was lovely but huge—116K. By reducing the colors and selectively deleting frames, the file was reduced down to 40K, which is still large, especially compared to the 8K Flash file. The GIF animation is larger, but it works for everyone, whether they have a plug-in or not.

This movie was exported to the "Animated GIF" format to make it available to a wider audience.

Don't make them guess

It can be annoying for users to get to a site that tells them they have to have certain software to be able to utilize (or even view) the site; for instance, "You need Flash 4 or 5." Few users know exactly what versions of anything are currently installed in their system.

Rather than make them take a guess, provide something tangible before they enter the site. You might have a simple animation with a note that says something like, "If you don't see the monkey swinging from the tree, you need Flash 5," and provide a link to where the user can download it.

Or give users a choice: It's common to use an introductory page which has links to an HTML version of the site as well as to a Flash version.

You can create a page (such as the pop-up shown above) that displays a tiny Flash movie that animates if the correct plug-in is present. If visitors can't see the animation, they know they don't have the proper plug-in and can choose to view the non-Flash version of the site.

Let's hear it for sound

With all this talk about vector graphics and animation, don't forget that Flash and LiveMotion can also incorporate sound into your site. Whether it's a single sound effect prompted by clicking a button or a full-blown soundtrack played throughout, the use of audio will add another level of sophistication to the user experience.

Flash can accept audio source files in a variety of formats, including WAV, AIFF, MP3, or QuickTime. While it does a pretty decent job at compressing sounds, keep in mind that your file sizes will dramatically increase when you import an audio file. Of course the longer the clip is, the bigger the file size will be.

For this reason, if you want to have a background soundtrack playing along with your animation, you should consider making a repeating sound loop that gives the feeling of a continuous track, but downloads in a fraction of the time.

Unless you really need it to communicate your message, use Flash audio sparingly. It doesn't take much sound to be impressive, but too much can bog down the entire user experience.

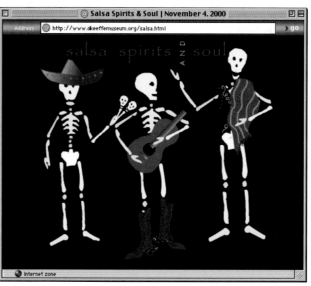

In this online Flash invitation, the mariachi skeletons don't only dance— they sing, too.

Entire sites in Flash?

It's possible to build an entire web site using Flash movies, but that's not always the best solution. Here are some questions to help you decide how Flash-intensive you want your site to be:

1. How often will your site need **updating**? If it's often, do you have the resources, skills, or personnel to handle making all the updates in Flash? You can cut down on your maintenance time and budget if most of your pages are in HTML and only parts of your site contain Flash animations.

2. Do you want **search engines** to find the inner pages of your site? If your entire site is a Flash movie, the only page the search engines will find is your home page and *only then* if you include meta tags and a title.

   When Flash generates an HTML file for you, all the text that is in the movie is repeated in a comment tag for the purpose of search engine parsing. This can be helpful, but problematic as well. Any given word will be repeated as many times in the comment tag as it appears on different frames in your movie. This can load down your HTML file significantly. Editing the comment yourself may be a good idea. If you insert a Flash movie into Dreamweaver or GoLive without using the HTML file generated by Flash, you don't get the text included in a comment tag.

   Search engines cannot follow links embedded in .swf files. If you have many HTML pages linked via the Flash movie, you may want to duplicate your links in HTML elsewhere on the pages. Also be sure to include meta tags and titles to all your pages.

   If you want maximum search engine optimization, you should be embedding your Flash files only as needed into your web pages and presenting the bulk of your information via HTML.

3. Does your site require **accessibility**? Increasingly, sites are expected to be accessible to people with visual, hearing, cognitive, and physical disabilities. Flash is not there yet—software that reads text aloud is unable to penetrate Flash movies.

   But Macromedia is planning accessibility enhancements for the Flash player and authoring environment with a goal of Flash content that is accessible to everyone. Until that's ready, you can download a free extension from Macromedia called the "Flash Accessibility Kit." When installed, it adds code to the HTML page that is published with your Flash file, copying all the text from your movie into an ALT tag that is readable by a text reader and other assistive technology (as well as search engines). The kit will also add a script to detect the presence of Flash and provide alternative GIF content if it does not exist. For more information, search the Macromedia site for "accessibility."

ActionScript

ActionScript is Flash's programming language, modeled closely on JavaScript. Flash-intensive sites rely heavily on this powerful tool, using it to control the timeline, create amazingly interactive navigation sytems, modify the properties of audio or visual content, generate content on the fly, gather data from viewers, and communicate with servers.

The Actions panel has both "Normal" mode, which allows users to select actions in a WYSIWYG format, and an "Expert" mode in which you can write your code by hand.

The Georgia O'Keeffe Museum home page contains a modular Flash movie embedded in the center of the page. This file uses ActionScript extensively, as shown in the windows to the right.

In Flash, the Movie Explorer window displays the lengthy ActionScript for this movie.

Make the right Flash decisions

As with any other web technology, use Flash wisely when constructing your site. We like Flash a lot, but tend to think it's best when used as a component of a standard page rather than as a whole-sale replacement for HTML.

Flash, at its best, should support the overall message and mission of the site, hopefully communicating information that would be hard to get across otherwise. At its worst, Flash without a clear purpose is just annoying eye candy and can actually distract a visitor from understanding the site's mission.

Frequently you will run across sites that make the user sit through an introduc-tory Flash movie before allowing them to reach the real content of the site. We're sure that the intent of the site's designer was to excite and amaze the visitors and make them want to dive into the rest of the site, but it could just as easily drive people away. The typical web user is impatient and doesn't like being forced to view information they weren't looking for in the first place.

If you do decide that a Flash introduc-tion is right for your site, be sure to make it **optional** for the visitor: place a "Skip Intro" or "Skip Flash" button on the page. If visitors really don't want to see the Flash intro, they can simply click the button and go about their business, although they miss out on your amazing visual experience. This way, visitors can make their own choices and no one gets frustrated with your site.

Your Flash introduction may be incredible, but give the visitor a choice to skip it if they wish. It will be their loss, after all.

Resources

Peachpit Press

Peachpit has a large selection of books on Flash for all user levels. Go to **peachpit.com** and search for "Flash."

www.moock.org

Free, downloadable Flash .fla files (original, layered files) and tutorials from Colin Moock, the author of *ActionScript, The Definitive Guide,* published by O'Reilly. Go to his links page at **www.moock.org/ moockmarks/** for an amazing array of Flash-built site links.

More stuff

Find chats, downloads, online tutorials, videos, tech notes, and more at these sites:

www.macromedia.com/support/flash/

www.lynda.com/products/videos

www.flashzone.com

www.flashkit.com

www.ultrashock.com

www.flasher.net

www.flashzone.com

www.flashlite.net

www.extremeflash.com

Free trial versions

Download a free thirty-day trial of Flash at the Macromedia web site: **www.macromedia.com**

For a free LiveMotion tryout version, go to: **www.adobe.com/products/ livemotion/tryreg.html**

Forms Control

If you've been surfing the web for any length of time, you've probably filled out more forms lately than you have in the entirety of your pre-web life.

Even though all of us have been bombarded our whole lives by advertisers and marketers begging us to fill out forms, we've never had any qualms about going form-less for years at a time; now it's not unusual to submit several per day. This amazing turn-around of forms attitude is due to the immediacy and simplicity that web-based forms offer.

Because your web audience is sitting in front of your web site with their fingers on an input device, you have a great opportunity to collect useful user information or take an order. So it's your responsibility to make the form both lovely and usable.

Embracing forms

One of the advantages of the web is the ability to easily collect or submit information through the use of **forms.** Not every site needs it, but if you want to get information from a visitor, forms are vastly superior to asking the viewer to send their information via email.

Beginning web designers sometimes use email forms as a substitute for real forms. Email is great for a lot of things, but it's a bad idea if you're seeking specific information from a viewer. Asking a viewer to write you a letter is asking a lot—you can expect a very low response rate using email as a response tool. On the other hand, if the viewer only has to click a few buttons and fill in a few blank spaces, you're much more likely to get a response.

The nature of forms also helps to ensure greater accuracy of input data, less ambiguity in user choices, and automatic data entry. It seems that the only reason a designer would resort to email responses over using forms is because of a lack of understanding how to make forms functional.

Popular HTML editing software makes it easy to build forms by placing input fields, radio buttons, check boxes, menu choices, and submit buttons on a page. But that alone will not make a form **functional.** The functionality of a simple form usually includes sending the submitted information to the web site's server. The information is forwarded to a small program on the server that processes the submitted

information by giving instructions to the server. The server is instructed to display a response page (a thank you page, for instance) so the viewer knows the form has been successfully submitted. The server may also be instructed to send a confirmation email to the viewer that submitted the form.

How does all this happen? And what can you do to make your forms professional looking and custom designed instead of default-ugly?

Forms need love, too

First, before we make a form functional, let's look at the aesthetics of the page and plan to make the form page as professional looking as all the other pages in our site.

We suspect that a lot of designers (or programmers) say to themselves "This is a form, and if it's ugly that's OK because forms are just naturally ugly and there's nothing you can do about it." Then they throw in some data entry fields and some radio buttons and no matter how bad it looks, it's a form.

Such a callous attitude is not very becoming of a designer, since it takes such a minimal effort to make forms look good. **But the point is not just to make the page pretty**—a clean, organized, thoughtful form is more usable, more likely to be used, a nicer experience for the visitor, and a better representation of your client.

This form is pleasant enough and readable, but it looks generic and uses more vertical space than necessary. Is there any possible reason to have three-dimensional borders on tables?

In the re-design we placed all elements into a single table, which allowed us to use colored cells for contrast and visual organization. The table also kept the form compact and prevented it from spreading down the page.

The power of alignment

The most common and glaring property of ugly form pages is **alignment,** or more specifically, the *absence* of alignment. Forms can be magically beautified using consistent alignment techniques. Almost any form looks better and is easier to read if everything in the form is flush left. Using different alignments (flush left, centered, flush right) in the same form makes the form look unorganized and scattered across the page.

To control the alignment of all elements in a form, use HTML tables. Placing each individual element of a form into a table cell enables you to keep all the elements aligned.

Use background table cell colors to visually organize various sections of a form.

Make the widths of text fields as consistent as possible to prevent visual clutter.

A visually organized and well-designed form will be completed more often simply because it *looks* easier to complete.

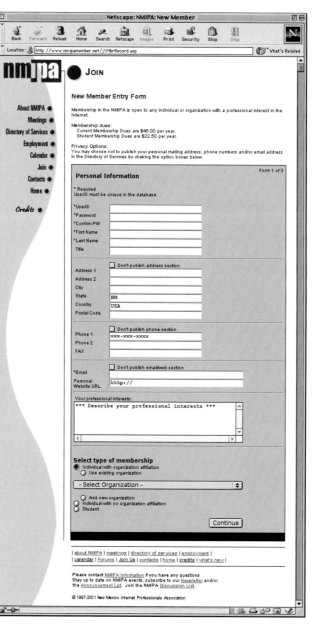

The most important feature that makes this form organized and visually pleasing is its strong flush left alignment. In this particular form, the curving edge of the page provides a lovely contrast.

When you come across a form that is a bit confusing or appears disorganized, we guarantee it is lacking alignment.

While at this shopping cart form, it's clear exactly where you are (persistent navigation), it's clear exactly what you are buying (thumbnails of the products), and the customized buttons at the bottom make it clear what your options are. It also uses clean alignments.

To prevent this form from looking too generic, we added color accents and customized the "Continue" button. The rest of the page is stark and clean to avoid adding clutter to the already busy page.

Functional forms

Once you've organized and designed a form, it's time to make it **functional.** CGI (Common Gateway Interface) scripts are used to process forms and make them functional. CGI scripts are typically written in the Perl programming language, C++, Java, JavaScript, or VBScript.

If you're working with a web team of specialists, once you've designed the form, the rest is easy: a programmer writes a script customized to accommodate your form and work with the specified server. But what happens if you're a one-person web firm without CGI skills and without a CGI budget?

Where do you get scripts?
In that case you have two choices, both of them easy to accomplish even for those of us with programming disabilities. You can use an existing free script from your web host server, if your host makes scripts available as a service.

Or you can find many good scripts (for free) on the Internet. The **CGI Resource Index (www.cgi-resources.com)** offers lots of CGI related information, including ready-made scripts.

For an introduction to CGI, visit **The Common Gateway Interface** site **(hoohoo.ncsa.uiuc.edu/cgi).** Some scripts are more versatile than others, so even if your web host offers a free script, you may want to look around for other options.

Most web hosting services' web sites have a tech support section that contains information and instructions for using CGI forms on their servers. Some hosts also offer free CGI scripts that you can customize to work with your own forms. Don't be surprised, however, if the instructions are confusing since they were probably written by a programmer who thinks this is really simple stuff.

We've often found there are better instructions and more versatile scripts available on dedicated script web sites. **Matt's Script Archive, Inc. (www.worldwidemart.com/scripts)** is a great resource for CGI scripts. You should find more than enough information if you search for "CGI scripts" or "Perl scripts" on the web.

Where does the script go?
A CGI script that provides functionality for a form resides on the server that hosts your web site. It is a page of code that sits on the server, along with all of the HTML files and folders that make up your web site. The web page with the form contains code that points to the script on the server. Servers always have a special folder in your web site space that has been designated as the location for you to put CGI scripts. The exact folder name and folder location can vary depending upon the setup of individual servers.

Sample form and script

This is a typical scenario for building a simple form like the one shown below and making it functional using a script found on the web.

First we constructed the form page using Dreamweaver's form objects from the "Forms" category of the "Objects" panel.

We dragged "Text Field" icons from the palette into the appropriate cells of the nested table, then specified the properties of each form object in the "Property Inspector" palette.

At this stage, if we look at the actual HTML code that Dreamweaver has written, the HTML FORM tag on our page looks like this:

```
<FORM name="form1" method="POST" action="">
```

The "action" value is empty at this point because we haven't yet designated a path to the CGI script on our server that will define the behavior of our form.

This is our form as it appears in a browser.

We constructed the form in Dreamweaver. We dragged Text Field icons from the "Forms" panel to the appropriate cells of the nested form table. The "Property Inspector" palette (below the form) let us specify attributes of the individual text fields.

Clicking on the overall form in Dreamweaver (the dotted red line) highlighted the entire form and changed the Property Inspector to show an "Action" option, in which we put the name of our Perl script file and the path to the file on our host server:

```
../cgi-bin/FormMail.pl
```

This path name indicates that the script is on the host server in a folder named `cgi-bin`. The "`../`" means that when the HTML form page we're building is uploaded to the server, it will need to look one level outside its own folder to find the `cgi-bin` folder. This "Action" command tells the server to implement whatever actions are specified in the Perl script named "FormMail.pl."

The actual HTML code for our form on the web page now looks like this:

```
<FORM name="form1" method="POST" action=
"../cgi-bin/FormMail.pl">
```

The path and file name for the CGI script has been added as a value to the "Actions" attribute. You don't need to know this if you're using WYSIWYG software, but it's helpful to understand what's going on behind the scenes as you enter information into palettes.

Where did we get the path information and the file name (FormMail.pl)? Our web host's tech support web site told us which folder to use for CGI scripts and where it was located. The CGI script that we downloaded from a web site was named FormMail.pl ("pl" for the Perl programming language).

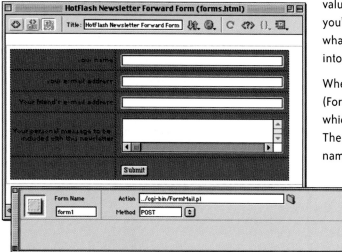

When we highlighted the entire form, the "Property Inspector" changed to the "Action" and "Method" attributes. In the "Action" field, we entered the path and file name of our CGI script.

Making the form functional

We used one of Matt's Scripts (as mentioned on page 348) called "FormMail" to make this simple form functional. When you download a good script, like from Matt's site, you'll also receive a README file that will (should) provide extensive information about the script, including descriptions of optional Form fields and instructions for setting up the script. We were instructed to add the following code to the FORM tag on our HTML page:

```
<input type=hidden name="subject" value="Forward
HotFlashes to a Friend">

<input type=hidden name="recipient"
value="forwardnews@stephaniemarston.com">

<input type=hidden name="redirect" value="http://
www.stephaniemarston.com/hotflashes/thanks_hotflashes.html">
```

This code had generic text entries for the "value" attributes, which we changed (according to the ReadMe instructions) to meet our specific needs.

Continuing to follow the script instructions, we modified two variables in the Perl script which was to be uploaded to the server. The first was a variable that defined the location of the server's sendmail program (this will allow us to receive form results via email). We plugged in the location information for our server:

```
$mailprog='/usr/sbin/sendmail';
```

The second variable was a security fix that allowed forms to be located only on servers defined in this field. We added our site address to the variable:

```
@referers=('stephaniemarston.com',
'63.136.69.49');
```

The FormMail program was now configured and we uploaded it to the server. The combination of the form code on our web page and the Perl script on the server made our form functional.

The script that we used had many options that weren't needed for our simple form. If you familiarize yourself with the features and options of a variety of scripts, you'll be able to design pages that are more powerful and versatile and ultimately more useful.

The result

The code is generic except for what we entered in the various *value* attributes:

The email's "Subject" field (first line of the code) will now show "Forward HotFlashes to a Friend" so the client can easily locate and organize her email responses from the form—she can set up an email filter that automatically organizes messages with this subject by sending them to a dedicated mailbox.

When someone submits this form, the information will be emailed to forwardnews@stephaniemarston.com, which is the value we used for "recipient" (second line of code).

After a viewer has submitted the form, they will be redirected to a specially designed thank-you page (third line of code).

The form buttons

Radio buttons vs. checkboxes

While **radio buttons** and **checkboxes** aren't considered beautiful, they're probably as pretty as they need to be. The important thing to remember about these buttons is that they perform two very different functions.

Use a **radio button** when there is only **one choice** available in the group of options. The buttons must be programmed properly (easy to do with your web authoring software) so when a user chooses any radio button, any other radio button automatically turns off. (An often-used alternative to radio buttons is the **pull-down menu** because it saves so much space.)

These are radio buttons. A visitor can only choose one.

Select One
- ○ New Member
- ○ Membership Renewal

Indicate Type of Membership
- ○ Individual Member — $35 / year
- ○ Family (Two Members) — $50 / year
- ○ Business (Up to Three Members) — $105 / year
- ○ Student / Teacher / Senior — $25 / year

Use **checkbox buttons** when a user can choose **any number** of the available options, including none.

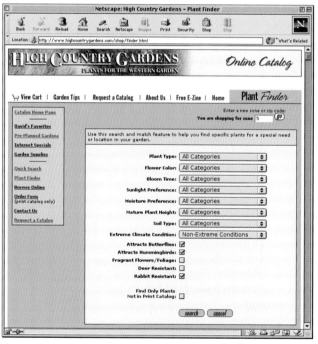

The six small boxes are checkbox buttons. A visitor can choose any number, all, or no boxes.

Customize the Submit button

The Submit button doesn't need to be pretty, but we sometimes like to customize it to fit in with the visual theme and colors of the web site.

Below is an example. We created a snazzy-looking button using Photoshop's "Styles" palette, added our own text version of "Submit," then saved the image as a JPEG.

In Dreamweaver we clicked in the desired table cell, then chose the "Image Field" icon in the "Forms" panel. That opened a window from which we selected the desired file, named *submit_btn.jpg*, and placed it in the selected table cell of the Dreamweaver document.

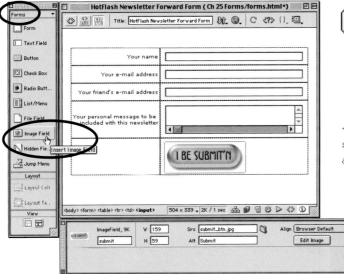

A custom-designed Submit button added a little pizazz to this simple and generic-looking form.

In the "Property Inspector" palette, we specified the ImageField name as "submit"; we also named the Alt tag "Submit" for browsers that are set to load graphics manually rather than automatically. Dreamweaver has now written the code that turns the new graphic button into a Submit button. The code is simple and if you're not using Dreamweaver, you can do the same thing by placing the following code in the appropriate table data cell of your web page.

A normal default Submit button is described in HTML code like this:

```
<input type="submit" name="Submit" value="Submit">
default submit.tif
```

 This, as you know, is the default Submit button.

The Submit button code

This is the code to use wherever you want to put a custom Submit button:

```
<input type="image" border="0" name="Submit"
src="submit_btn.jpg" width="159" height="59"
alt="Submit">
```

The input type has changed from "submit" to "image" and we've added the source (src) definition, which is the name of the graphic (*submit_btn.jpg* in this case). Width and height values have been specified for the graphic also.

This code (the same code that was automatically written by Dreamweaver) instructs the named graphic to act as a Submit button, calling on the CGI script that resides on the server.

Guidelines for good form

A thoughtful form can make certain web sites more useful and interactive. The convenience and immediacy of a form can improve a site's customer/viewer response rate and enhance the inter-active communication potential that is offered by the web.

In summary, here are a few general guidelines for designing forms:

- Don't ask for more information than absolutely necessary.

- Don't provide more directions than absolutely necessary.

- To prevent input of inaccurate data, present as many choices as possible using radio buttons and checkboxes, or menus.

- Keep forms as short as possible. The probability of receiving a submitted form is directly proportional to the form's length.

- If a long form is absolutely necessary, divide it into two or more linked pages.

- Include a verification or thank-you page so the viewer knows the submission was received.

- Use strong, consistent alignment when designing forms and use HTML tables to help control the alignment of form elements.

- Use the principles of proximity and contrast to visually organize forms and emphasize categories. The less confusing a form looks, the more likely it is to be completed and submitted.

- Include a privacy policy statement that assures viewers that their names and addresses will not be made available to third parties and that they will not receive any unsolicited email. And let's hope that's true.

Virtual Last Chapter

Our last chapter looks very short, but it's virtually an entire web site. We thought it would be useful (and fun) to create a Virtual Last Chapter to more effectively show many of the examples used throughout this book. After all, Flash, DHTML menus, animated GIFs, image swaps, and rollovers are much more interesting on a web page than on a printed page. VirtualLastChapter.com shows all this, plus provides links to the resources we've mentioned throughout *Web Design Workshop*.

As a web bonus we added a section called "For Your Clients." This section offers a basic web site education for clients who are unfamiliar with the challenges and idiosyncrasies of web design. They'll learn a little about what's involved, what to expect, and why you're so darned valuable.

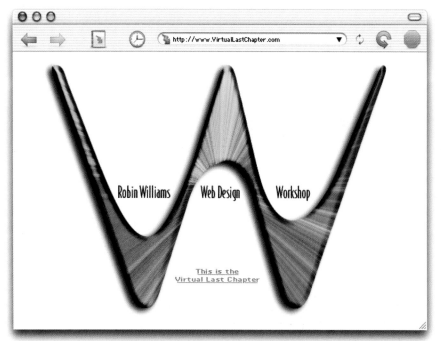

We wanted the entry page of VirtualLastChapter.com to have a strong visual connection to the book cover design. For that reason we used a simple and stark entry page approach, rather than complicating the page with navigation.

The welcome page contains navigation and an explanation of the site for those who may wander in without realizing this site is an extension of a book, rather than a stand-alone web site.

We used a sketchy, flat brush stroke to unify the luxuriously spaced navigation elements and to create contrast with the beveled, shadowed elements on the page.

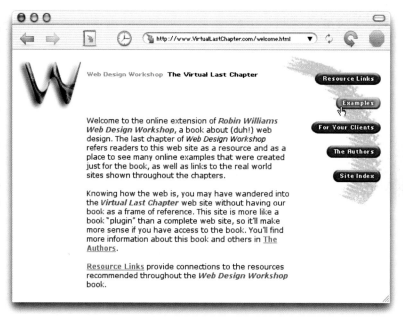

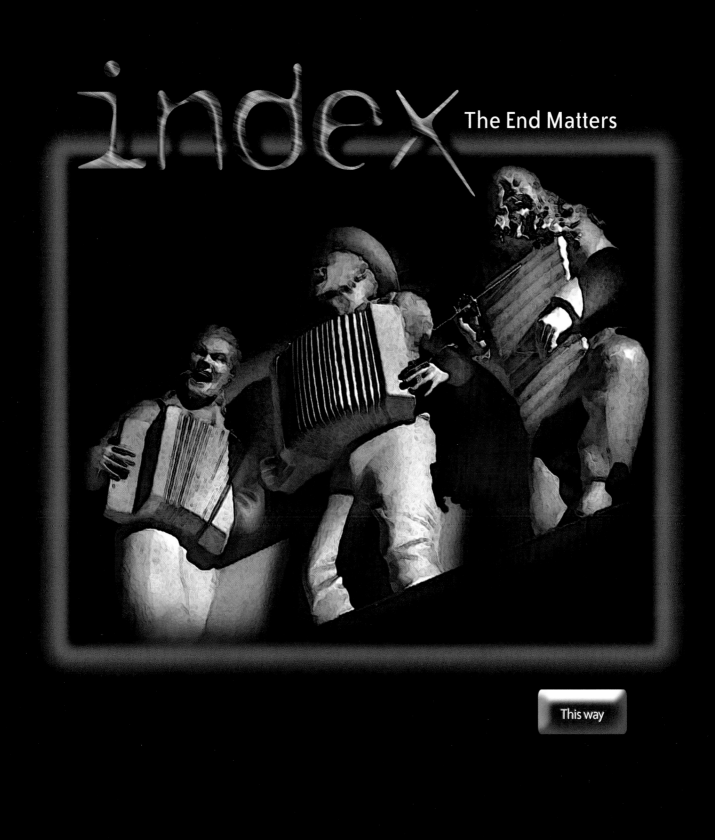

index

The End Matters

This way

No, you can't have permission to use our web site in your book because it might appear that we're endorsing your book.

—*Clueless Client*

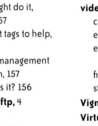

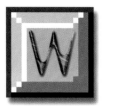

Colophon

John created the **cover** design image with a screenshot from the OmniWeb browser in Mac OS X. The large, colorful letter is in the font DropletLite (designed by Hat Nguyen, available from [T26], www.t26.com). The other font is BodegaSans (designed by Greg Thompson, available from The Font Bureau, www.fontbureau.com). John produced the cover in QuarkXPress.

Robin designed and produced this **book** in Adobe InDesign. Fabulous program. The fonts are Modern Twenty for chapter openers and major heads, and Bailey Sans for body copy and captions. The dedication and acknowledgments are in ITC Bradley Hand.

John created the **section dividers.** They are original images captured from digital video and edited in Adobe Photoshop.

The pastel and acrylic **illustrations** in this book are from Artville (www.artville.com). Thanks to Illustrators Jonathan Evans and Rob Colvin whose CD art collections ("Working Plans" and "The Big Idea") provided inspiration for editorial visuals and beautiful graphics for many web design examples. Their art is also available through EyeWire.com.

Vintage illustrations, stock photo images, textures, and skyscapes are from various collections available at EyeWire.com ("Photogear," "Circa:Art").

Other stock photo images are from PhotoDisc's Signature Series, "Emotions and Expressions" (www.photodisc.com).

A number of images are original photographs and illustrations from John.

Printed at R.R. Donnelley, Roanoke, Virginia, with computer-to-plate technology.